# Hardware Design Guide for Microsoft® Windows™ 95



## A Practical Guide for Developing Plug and Play PCs and Peripherals

Microsoft Corporation

PUBLISHED BY
Microsoft Press
A Division of Microsoft Corporation
One Microsoft Way
Redmond, Washington 98052-6399



Library of Congress Cataloging-in-Publication Data
Hardware Design Guide for Microsoft Windows 95 / Microsoft Corporation.
p. cm.
Includes index.
ISBN 1-55615-642-1
1. Electronic digital computers--Design and construction.
2. Computer software--Development. 3. Microsoft Windows (Computer file)
TK7888.3.M544 1994
004.256--dc20 94-29762
CIP

Printed and bound in the United States of America.

3 4 5 6 7 8 9 MLML 9 8 7 6 5

Distributed to the book trade in Canada by Macmillan of Canada, a division of Canada Publishing Corporation.

A CIP catalogue record for this book is available from the British Library.

Microsoft Press books are available through booksellers and distributors worldwide. For further information about international editions, contact your local Microsoft Corporation office. Or contact Microsoft Press International directly at fax (206) 936-7329.

# Contents

# Preface

The *Hardware Design Guide for Microsoft® Windows™ 95* contains information to help you design a personal computer (PC) for the Windows 95 operating system. This computer, called a PC 95, is the realization of a set of standard hardware, BIOS, and device driver designs that optimize a PC to Windows 95.

This guide defines the design target for a PC 95 by documenting the hardware features for which Windows 95 has been optimized. These features include linear-frame display buffers, advanced power management, parallel ports with IEEE P1284 support, and soft power-down. When users buy a PC 95 and see the "Designed for Windows 95"® logo, they know they'll get Plug and Play, ease of use, and enhanced hardware and software integration.

This guide emphasizes the Plug and Play concept, in which nontechnical users can add or remove hardware. Because of identification and configuration schemes in the hardware and operating system, users no longer need to manually configure such resources as IRQ signals and DMA channels. Instead, software enumerates the identities and capabilities of devices attached to the system, and then allocates the appropriate IRQ signals, DMA channels, I/O ports, and memory space to the hardware.

This guide includes many hardware, BIOS, and device driver design requirements and recommendations for the PC 95—and for Plug and Play designs, in particular. With these enhancements to standard PC designs, Windows 95 can take better advantage of the hardware, and simplify the system for the user.

---

**Note** This guide documents technical requirements and recommendations for designing and building PC systems based on the x86 microprocessor architecture and the *Plug and Play Specifications*. Such PCs are optimized for Windows 95 rather than for Microsoft® Windows NT™. Some of these implementations are x86 specific and not suitable for portable architectures or operating systems.

---

# Design Philosophy

The design philosophy for the PC 95 is that hardware changes should be as easy as possible for the user to make. Whether your design simplifies basic tasks, such as adding hardware to the system, or provides features that enhance ease of use, such as soft-eject control, the user should see the PC 95 as a tool that is easily configured and run. Any tasks that require the user to have technical skills not typically associated with an average user are targets for improvement.

# Purpose

This guide is intended for hardware, BIOS, and device driver engineers who build PCs, expansion cards, and peripherals. The guide provides technical details and guidelines for designers building PC hardware optimized for Windows 95, with additional emphasis on systems that use Plug and Play architecture. With the exception of some specialized proprietary designs, the requirements and recommendations in this guide can be used on PC systems in all countries, including Japan (PC/V). The information included in this guide is especially useful for:

- OEMs—Motherboards, systems, subsystems
- Expansion card designers—ISA bus, PCI bus, VL-bus, and so on
- Peripheral designers—Printers, plotters, monitors, and so on
- Device designers—SCSI devices, IDE controllers, and so on

Each part of the guide targets subjects of specific interest to system, expansion card, motherboard, and peripheral designers, and includes BIOS guidelines for expansion cards and motherboards. Design guidelines are divided into basic components, reflecting the interests of the hardware and BIOS developer.

Part 1 introduces the PC 95 and Plug and Play, discussing key elements of the PC 95 and describing their interaction. This part also explains improvements afforded by Plug and Play, emphasizing the impact on users.

Part 2 contains information of interest to the hardware designer, including desktop and mobile system, device, bus, and peripheral design guidelines. This part explains requirements for each device, and examines recommendations that add value to your system.

Part 3 explores the firmware design for a PC 95 system and Plug and Play, discussing both system and option BIOS functionality.

Part 4 contains appendixes with information useful to the PC 95 designer.

Although this guide divides many of the design topics into separate chapters, you can get more information by reading several chapters that pertain to your specific design. For example, for more information about designing display adapter expansion cards, including the attributes of display adapters that a system will expect to use, see Chapter 3, for desktop systems, and Chapter 4, for mobile systems. For information about specific requirements and recommendations for display adapters, see Chapter 5. For more information about the Plug and Play capabilities that are required and recommended for the expansion card, see Chapter 6. For information about what functions monitor designs will expect from the display adapter, see Chapter 7. For more information about option ROM requirements for primary input devices, see Chapter 9.

# Conventions

The following conventions are used throughout this guide:

- Signals that are active low are followed by an asterisk (*). For example, the active low I/O write signal on the ISA bus is shown as IOW*.
- If a range of signals is described, such as SA0 through SA10, the range is shown as SA[10:0], with the most-significant digit first and the least-significant digit last, separated by a colon.
- Numbers used in this guide are written as decimal, hexadecimal, or binary. Hexadecimal numbers are followed by an "h" suffix. Binary numbers are followed by a "b" suffix. For example, decimal 27 = 1Bh = 00011011b.
- Program listings are shown in `Courier` to distinguish them from surrounding text and make them easier to read.
- Words or phrases shown in *italic* are explained in the Glossary. The glossary also contains definitions of words and phrases found in various industry and Plug and Play specifications.

# How to Get More Information

Much of the material in this guide has been derived from specifications and standards available from a number of different companies and committees. For more information about these documents and how to obtain current copies of them, see Appendix D, "References." To ensure that your hardware will work properly with other existing hardware designs, always use the most up-to-date copies of the specifications and documents pertaining to your designs.

For current updates and additional hardware documents and Plug and Play specifications pertaining to this guide, check the Microsoft Internet FTP server ftp.microsoft.com in the /developr/pc95 directory.

# Acknowledgments

The authors wish to thank everyone who supplied information and support for this guide. Special thanks for their many contributions, patience, and long hours go to Dennis Adler, Talal Batrouny, Avi Belinsky, Eric Bidstrup, Martin Borve, Heidi Breslauer, Marshall Brumer, Jeff Camp, Julie Carter, David Cole, Tom Davis, Joe Decuir, Peter Delaney, Mark Enstrom, Mike Flora, Pat Fox, Mike Gallop, Brian Gluth, John Gray, Brad Hastings, Doug Hogarth, Blake Irving, Naveen Jain, Keith Kegley, Douglas Klopfenstein, Jim Kott, Keith Laepple, Thomas Lennon, Moshe Lichtman, Ralph Lipe, Jim Nellis, Bill Parry, Ray Pedrizetti, Victor Raisys, Pierre-Yves Santerre, Brad Silverberg, Andrew Silverman, Matthew Squires, Carl Stork, Steve Timm, Ed Tremblay, Eric Tucker, Bill Veghte, Rogers Weed, and Christian Wildfeuer.

PART 1

# Design Overview

Part 1 contains general information about the Personal Computer for Microsoft® Windows™ 95 (a PC 95 computer) and the Plug and Play aspects of a PC 95 system, and discusses the reasons for designing a PC 95.

Chapter 1 defines the basis for the PC 95 and examines baseline PC systems from a historical perspective. This chapter also explains hardware and software improvements for a standard PC 95 from the viewpoint of user expectations.

Chapter 2 introduces the Plug and Play concept and discusses historical reasons for improving customer confidence in hardware changes. This chapter also describes how easy Plug and Play is to use, compared to older designs, and outlines each step of the Plug and Play process, as well as needed changes to hardware, BIOS, and device drivers.

CHAPTER 1

# The PC 95

---

**Note** PC 95 refers to a platform designed to be the minimum standard PC for Microsoft® Windows™ 95 during 1995. By early 1995, almost all new PCs are expected to meet these criteria.

---

The *PC 95* is a new platform consisting of three key elements—a minimum set of hardware features, *Plug and Play* components, and Windows 95. This platform provides the user with a PC that is easy to use and configure. In a sense, it offers the power of a PC without the hassles commonly associated with complex devices. With the PC 95, complexities are handled internally; the user sees only a device that is as easy to use as any other appliance in the home.

This chapter introduces the PC 95, discusses its costs and benefits, and describes the relationships between the hardware, Plug and Play, and Windows 95.

The PC 95 requirements define the basic hardware platform necessary to qualify for the Microsoft® Windows™ 95 Logo. The logo also indicates that Windows 95 is preinstalled and has passed the Microsoft Windows 95 *Hardware Compatibility Tests* (HCT), so users will not have to worry about hardware and software compatibility. For more information about meeting the requirements for the Windows 95 Logo program, contact the Microsoft Compatibility Labs (MCL) at 206-635-4949.

# What Is a PC 95?

The PC 95 is the physical realization of the concept that the power of computers should extend to the ordinary user. Combining the advantages of the Plug and Play hardware and software architecture, the standardized features of the PC hardware design, and the easy-to-use, attractive interface of Windows 95, the PC 95 establishes a new standard. It is simple, versatile, and usable.

The PC 95 also specifies as standard certain features that have only been options, in the past. Users and software developers can count on the availability of these standard features, making product design and purchase decisions easier.

Baseline PC systems have evolved incrementally over the years. The basic PC was defined in 1981 with the shipment of the IBM® PC. Many advances since then have become standard, including the 16-bit AT® bus, VGA display technology, and the 386 (80386) CPU architecture. A number of optional features have also increased in popularity, notably, audio, CD-ROM, *small computer system interface* (SCSI), modems, mice, and alternate expansion buses such as the *Peripheral Component Interconnect* (PCI) bus and the Personal Computer Memory Card International Association *(PCMCIA)* bus. The arrival of Windows 95 is an opportunity to raise the standard for what users and manufacturers expect in a basic PC.

The PC 95 represents the current standard for a Windows 95–based PC, the next logical step in this evolution. The PC 95 provides hardware specifically designed and optimized for both Plug and Play and Windows 95.

## Plug and Play

The Plug and Play initiative is a set of hardware and software specifications that define a minimum Plug and Play system. Implementations of these specifications are found throughout the PC 95, including a Plug and Play BIOS, Plug and Play methods of identifying and configuring hardware resource requirements for expansion cards and peripherals, and operating system software that recognizes and uses the Plug and Play features of the system.

A Plug and Play system contains a Plug and Play BIOS that identifies and configures the integrated resources on the PC system. For example, the system BIOS identifies *motherboard* devices such as parallel ports and display adapters, and allocates their *resources*.

Expansion cards and peripheral hardware must also be designed to implement the Plug and Play specifications. This guide includes the design criteria for Plug and Play expansion *devices* and peripheral hardware in addition to the descriptions of hardware requirements and recommendations for the PC 95.

Plug and Play software, such as Windows 95, uses the features of Plug and Play hardware to identify the resources of all devices in the system, including attached peripherals such as Plug and Play printers. When the software "knows" the system resources, it can use the unique features of each device, optimizing system performance.

# The Windows 95 Operating System

Windows 95 is one of the most significant updates yet to the core Windows product line. Windows 95 offers compatibility with existing applications while introducing many easy-to-use features that increase productivity.

Plug and Play is one of the key ways in which Windows 95 enhances ease of use. Windows 95 fully supports all of the configuration management, resource arbitration, and device *enumeration* functions defined in the Plug and Play specifications. Windows 95 enumerates the PC system devices (by retrieving identification from the devices), places the information in a system data structure called the *hardware tree*, and determines the resources available on each of the devices. Windows 95 also examines the resources for all of the devices, configures the devices so they don't conflict with one another, and loads the appropriate device drivers.

In essence, Windows 95 performs a dynamic configuration of the system using only the resources and device drivers requested by the system devices. If the configuration of the system changes—for example, if a portable PC is plugged into a *docking station* with a SCSI host adapter—Windows 95 reenumerates the system, reconstructs the hardware tree and device resource information with the new capabilities of the SCSI host adapter, and loads the appropriate device driver for the new device. Hardware designs that allow flexible allocation of all of the resources on the PC enhance the dynamic nature of Windows 95.

Windows 95 maintains backward compatibility in a number of ways with older, non–Plug and Play systems. Windows 95 can be used on an older PC that is not Plug and Play enabled, and will attempt to identify the devices and resources that are available. If a device driver is available for the older hardware, Windows 95 identifies the driver and loads it.

Windows 95 supports the changing hardware resources of docking mobile systems by examining the system hardware and, often, automatically choosing the correct configuration. For example, a multiconfiguration portable PC might have two states called "docked" and "undocked." Undocked might mean, for example, no network adapter or audio adapter. The Windows 95 detection routine calls the system BIOS, determines the system configuration state, then selects the proper hardware profile and loads the appropriate device drivers for the current system configuration. The docking station can also change this state by generating dynamic docking and undocking events.

Windows 95 also enables more cooperative behavior between applications. Each time Windows 95 identifies a change in the system, it notifies applications—for example, switch on battery power, establish fast network connection, or switch to low-resolution display. With this capability, applications can make smart decisions based on the new information, such as stop background reformatting, download all new mail messages, use smaller fonts, or determine network identifier based on the user's location and the available hardware.

Windows 95 also supplies an increased amount of useful information about the PC system configuration, for example, the identities and allocated resources of the devices attached to the system.

The availability in Windows 95 of dynamic configuration, PCMCIA support, *warm docking* or *hot docking*, and other new capabilities creates many opportunities for new business products, better hardware, and new applications for the PC 95.

The PC 95 concept means increased ease of use and more flexible hardware configuration for users. But Windows 95 is also designed to run well on almost any PC-compatible system that runs Microsoft® Windows™ 3.1 in enhanced mode and has a 386 or later microprocessor, at least 4 MB RAM, and a VGA display. In fact, although this configuration represents the minimum PC capable of running Windows 95, it will typically run the user's existing applications better than Windows 3.1, and will be a good fit for users who are upgrading their existing operating system. These systems will not, however, offer all the benefits available with a Plug and Play–enabled system.

This guide defines an improved baseline PC, or reference system, for running Windows 95. With a common baseline system, users can count on a minimum set of features with any PC purchase, applications can begin to rely on these features, and the industry as a whole will benefit.

# The New Hardware Standards

The PC 95 concept sets a baseline minimum hardware standard for the next generation of PCs. This standard includes hardware requirements for a variety of different PC systems and peripherals. The resulting base system meets the requirements of Plug and Play and is easy to use and configure.

This list is an overview of some of the requirements for a desktop PC 95. (It is not a complete list.)

- A Plug and Play system BIOS (version 1.0a or later)
- A 386 or compatible architecture, minimum (for example, 386, 486, Pentium™, and so on)
- 4 MB RAM, minimum
- Flat-frame buffer display, with at least 640 × 480 × 8 bits per pixel (bpp)
- A dedicated mouse port or integrated pointing device
- One serial and one parallel port, minimum

For more information about the requirements and recommendations for a desktop PC 95, see Chapter 3, "The Desktop PC 95."

Most often, mobile systems must follow the same requirements and recommendations that apply for desktop systems, but there are a few exceptions. For example, although the display on a mobile PC 95 must support 640 × 480 × 8 bpp, it can be displayed as 64 shades of gray. Some features that are required for a mobile system are strongly recommended but not required for a desktop system. These include features such as a 16550A-compatible serial port universal asynchronous receiver-transmitter (UART), which enables higher-speed remote computing while allowing smoother multitasking. For more information about these and other exceptions for mobile systems, see Chapter 4, "Mobile Hardware Designs."

Internal and external peripherals included with the PC 95 must also follow all of the applicable Plug and Play specifications. Essentially, a peripheral must be able to identify itself to the system, and must be able to either automatically or through software control set up its hardware to run on the system whenever the user plugs the peripheral into the system. For new peripheral designs, only minor changes to the firmware on the peripheral may sometimes be required. For more information about peripherals and their hardware requirements and recommendations for a PC 95, see Chapter 7, "Designing Peripherals."

# Costs and Benefits

As with any engineering project, there are advantages to weigh and obstacles to overcome in implementing the PC 95. The benefits of the PC 95 will be readily apparent to reviewers, dealers, and customers. Compared with earlier PCs, it is more appealing to use, it creates more user satisfaction and fewer support costs, and it provides more hardware features. To achieve these benefits, however, hardware manufacturers will have to make some investments, primarily one-time engineering costs. Some designs may increase hardware costs slightly, but these costs should be offset by savings in customer support costs and by market growth.

Windows 95 on the PC 95 increases flexibility in hardware design by providing standard software interfaces. With these standard interfaces, you can differentiate your PC with a greater variety of hardware designs, in such areas as graphics, networks, and audio.

The PC 95 also offers improved integration of all parts of the system, which allows applications to run faster and more efficiently. These improvements will increase the demand for smarter applications and better and faster hardware. Better integration also means that the system can run without being configured by the user, which will mean substantial savings in customer support costs.

Those users who don't have the time or inclination to learn the details of PC hardware will want to buy an easy-to-use PC such as the PC 95. The buyer will know that the PC 95 system contains high minimum standards at minimal cost, while other systems will remain unknowns. Users will recognize that the PC 95 is as easy to use as other home appliances, and will want to take advantage of its features.

A PC 95 will also fit well into many of the systems management schemes being developed today, such as the Desktop Management Task Force's (DMTF) Desktop Management Interface (DMI) initiative. Corporate customers find that initiatives such as these are critical in helping them control their vast PC investments. They will undoubtedly favor machines that provide rich support for this capability.

CHAPTER 2

# The Plug and Play Initiative

The Plug and Play initiative is a set of specifications describing hardware and software changes to the PC and its peripherals that free the PC user from manually configuring the hardware. Instead, the software itself arbitrates *conflicts* between devices, and makes changes automatically to resolve those conflicts. A user can simply attach a new device (plug it in) and begin working (playing).

This chapter describes the types of problems commonly associated with non–Plug and Play PC systems, and offers Plug and Play as the solution. This chapter also looks at the advantages and consequences of implementing Plug and Play for the device manufacturer and the user.

# Current PC Problems

For a user who is not a trained technician, installing or configuring a device on a PC can be a daunting task. Most users have neither the time nor the inclination to learn about such arcane subjects as *interrupt request* (IRQ) signals, *direct memory access* (DMA) channels, SCSI termination, or monitor timings. However, if users want to add devices to their PCs or take advantage of the features of a new device, they often must address these subjects, because most existing PC systems offer no alternative. Potential PC users hear about problems that current users encounter in these areas, which reinforce their viewpoint that PCs are complex, intimidating, and difficult to use.

Problems experienced by PC users have even become a part of our culture. The perception that computers must be difficult to use seems to have become ingrained in our society. It is against this backdrop—of cultural and social beliefs that PCs are hard to install, configure, and use—that you must convince users to purchase your products.

The root of the problem goes back to the original PC design. No architecture was defined for installing, identifying, and configuring hardware devices because the PC was designed primarily for engineers. The market for PCs has changed over the years, however; many people who now buy PCs do not have technical backgrounds.

Although the availability of add-on devices is an advantage of the PC, the fact that the typical PC contains devices made by many different vendors tends to compound the hardware and software configuration problem. The hardware, operating system, and applications don't know what is in the PC system, and the hardware can't tell when conflicts exist between different devices trying to share the same system resource.

Today's PCs based on the *Industry Standard Architecture* (ISA) bus architecture —the most popular *expansion bus* in the PC industry—lack any mechanisms for configuration management. The ISA bus architecture requires resources such as memory and I/O address spaces, DMA channels, and interrupts to be allocated among several ISA cards. But the ISA specification has no standard hardware or software interface for allocating these resources. As a result, configuration of ISA cards is typically done with "jumpers," manual changes to the card that reroute the decode maps for memory and I/O address space, and steer the DMA and interrupt signals to different pins on the bus. ISA cards can also be configured by software, but this process uses a proprietary protocol that doesn't have the common, system-wide resource management available with a nonproprietary method.

PCs using the ISA bus architecture also have limited system resources, particularly IRQ signals and DMA channels, and many ISA cards are not able to use all the possible choices. Under these conditions, someone has to determine a combination that meets all the requirements and that doesn't create conflicts. Unfortunately, this task often falls to the user. The user is also typically required to edit system configuration files. Even with a card that can be configured by software, the user must generally determine the correct settings and enter them into an installation program to set the card.

As CD-ROM drives and *expansion cards* such as fax cards and audio cards become more popular, users continue to put more and more complicated options into their PCs, creating more conflicts over system resources.

Alternative bus architectures such as the *Micro Channel®* and *Extended Industry Standard Architecture* (EISA) buses have hardware and software mechanisms to identify the resources requested by a card and resolve conflicts. These configuration mechanisms could be improved, however, if they were integrated with the operating system. When adding or removing devices on existing systems, users must first configure the hardware using a character-mode configuration utility that requires a set of floppy disks for the configuration program and for each card. These disks are often lost or separated from the PC. So each operating system driver must be set up separately. The setup mechanisms require users to restart their PCs to make any type of configuration change—a definite inconvenience.

The trend toward providing PCs with preconfigured hardware and preinstalled software has helped the user's dilemma somewhat. But this approach doesn't accommodate customers who want to upgrade their PCs after purchase, nor does it address the technical requirements of new form factors and system designs. Mobile systems, in particular, must have greater hardware and software integration to make possible such features as dynamic addition and removal of devices, warm docking, and instant-on. The configuration solution must be general and flexible to accommodate the mix of device architectures used in existing system designs, from *local bus* to ISA to cards meeting the standards of the PCMCIA.

# The Plug and Play Solution

Plug and Play is an architecture jointly developed by Microsoft® and PC product vendors that dramatically improves the integration of PC hardware and software. Plug and Play architecture is designed to greatly simplify installation and configuration of new devices. Plug and Play devices must be able to identify themselves to the system and declare their services and resource requirements. With this information, the operating system determines and establishes a working configuration for all devices on the PC system and automatically loads the appropriate device drivers.

The three major benefits of Plug and Play architecture are:

- Add-on devices can be installed and configured without user intervention. A user can turn a standard desktop system into a multimedia computer, for example, by plugging in a Plug and Play sound card and CD-ROM, turning on the PC, and "playing" a video clip.
- PC systems can be designed with new features. A businessperson, for example, with a docking station featuring hot-docking capabilities, could remove the portable system while it was running, to go to a meeting. The portable PC would automatically adjust for the absence of the net card, large disk drive, and other devices left at the docking station.
- The product manufacturer saves on support and development costs. For example, as many as half of all support calls currently received by operating system and device manufacturers are related to installation and configuration of devices. Device driver development is also simplified, because device manufacturers can write one driver that works for many bus types. Currently, device manufacturers must include bus-specific code in each of their drivers. With Plug and Play, specific bus configuration code is contained in "bus drivers." Operating system preinstallation and configuration is also simplified for original equipment manufacturers (OEMs), because Plug and Play devices automatically install and configure during setup.

Plug and Play requires close cooperation between PC hardware, add-on hardware, operating systems, and drivers, as shown in Figure 2.1. Plug and Play is defined in a series of specifications that address each of these component pieces. In brief, each hardware device must be uniquely identified, must state the services it provides and the resources it requires, must identify the driver that supports it, and must allow software to configure it. To be effective for users, Plug and Play must be applied to the broad range of existing hardware, as well as to hardware of the future. Table 2.1 lists the titles of the Plug and Play specifications, and Table 2.2 lists some of the documents related to Plug and Play. Be sure to obtain current copies of these specifications for up-to-date information about Plug and Play designs. For information about where to obtain current copies of these and other specifications and documents, see Appendix D, "References."

**Table 2.1 Plug and Play Specifications**

| Specification title |
|---|
| Plug and Play BIOS Specification |
| Plug and Play ISA Specification |
| Plug and Play SCSI Specification |
| Plug and Play Parallel Port Devices |
| Plug and Play External COM Device Specification |

**Table 2.2 Plug and Play–Related Documents**

| Document title |
|---|
| Microsoft® Windows™ 95 Docking System Design Guide |
| SCSI Configured AutoMatically (SCAM) |
| Advanced Power Management (APM) BIOS Interface Specification, Revision 1.1 |

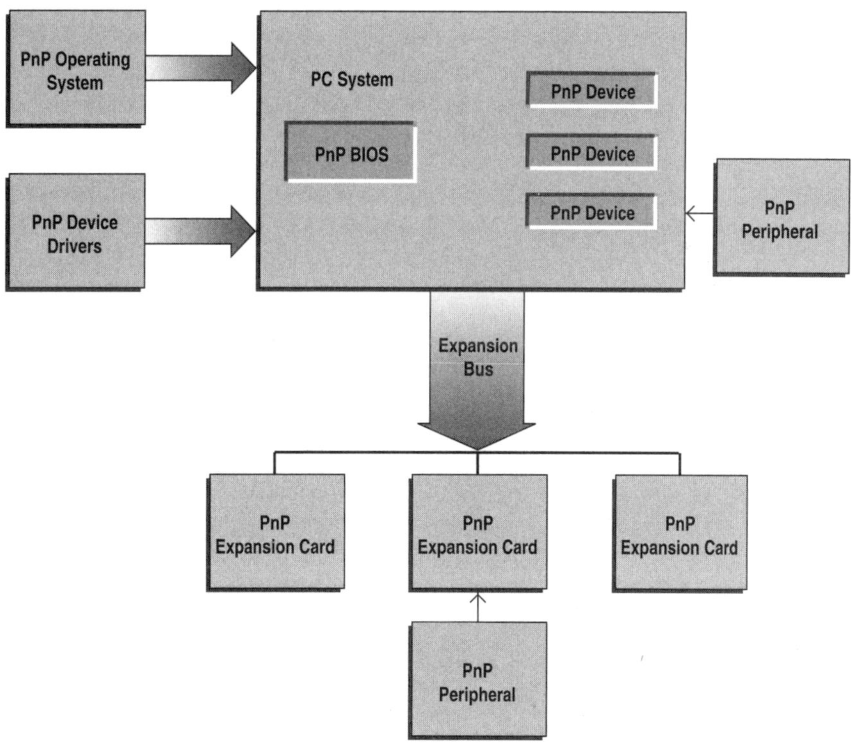


**Figure 2.1 Plug and Play PC System Block Diagram**

The Plug and Play architecture is an open, flexible, and economic framework for designing Plug and Play products. Plug and Play was developed by a group of leading vendors who obtained reviews for their design proposals from hundreds of companies in the industry. Plug and Play offers a framework that works on many types of bus architectures—ISA, EISA, and PCMCIA buses, *Video Electronics Standards Association* (VESA) local bus (*VL-bus*), the PCI local bus, and so on—and I/O port connections, and can be extended to future designs. Vendors who implement Plug and Play in their products will incur few additional costs.

# How Plug and Play Works

The Plug and Play architecture defines several base components that can be implemented in any operating system. Buses, devices, and resources are abstracted from the base components through hardware-specific *enumerators* (which identify and list the hardware), *arbitrators* (which juggle the configuration options), and device drivers. This ensures that Plug and Play can be expanded to future bus designs and device architectures.

The basic functions that must be performed are:

- Devices are uniquely and positively identified, their resource requirements are read, and their drivers are loaded.
- Resources are allocated and reallocated when devices request identical resources.
- If any change is made to the system configuration, the process described in the two previous bulleted items is repeated.
- The configuration process is managed centrally, which ensures complete coordination.
- Configuration information is shared through system-wide communication between the hardware, BIOS, and operating system.

Existing PCs are made up of many bus and device architectures. Such PCs can be viewed using a *tree model* to describe the relationships between the buses and devices. In the PC system tree model shown in Figure 2.2, buses and devices may appear at different levels of the system hierarchy in multiple "parent-child" relationships, may require system resources, and may provide resources that are understood, or not understood, by their parents. The relationships are complicated by the fact that some of the buses (SCSI, PCMCIA) are hidden from their parents until they are initialized.

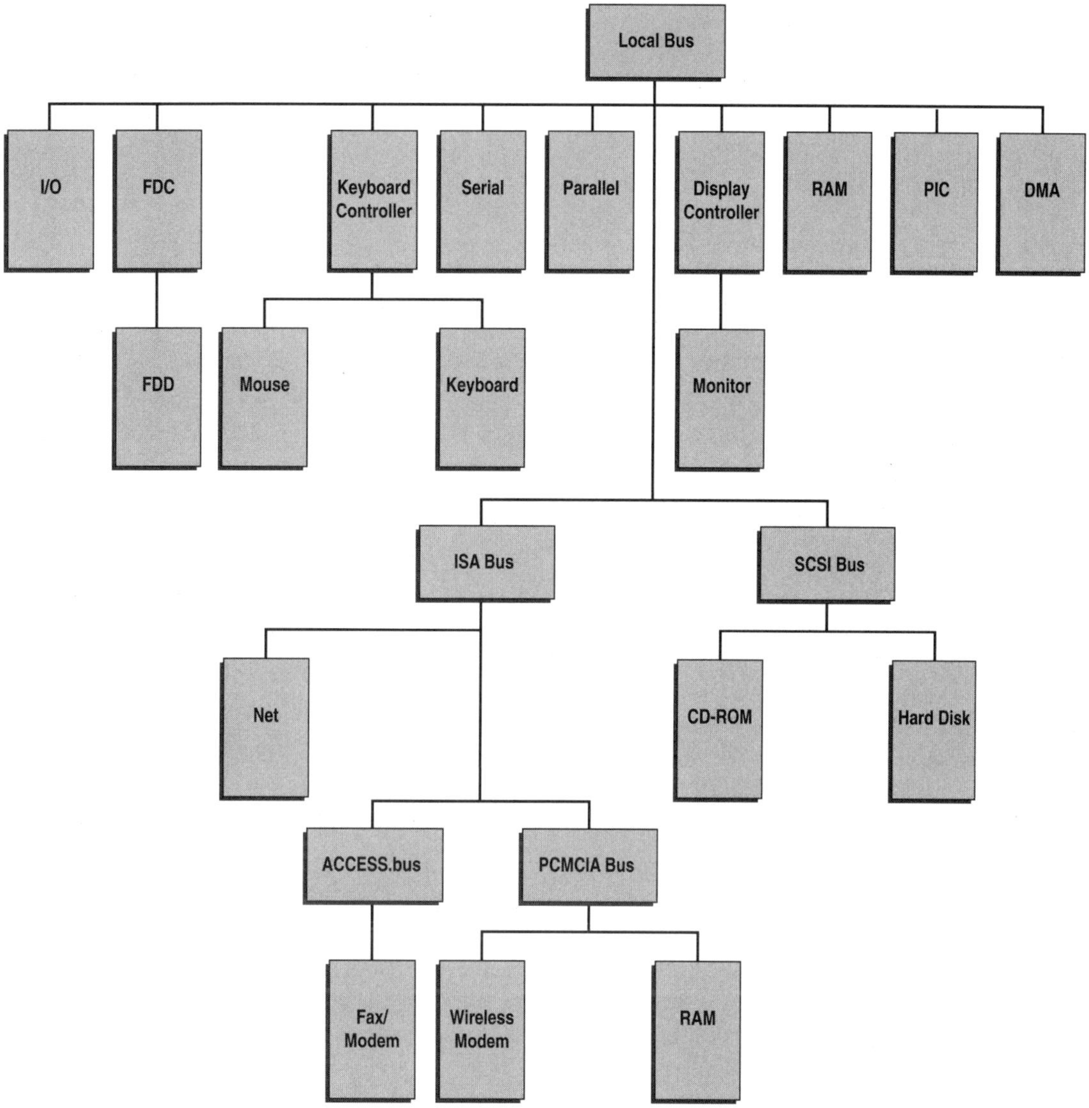


**Figure 2.2 Logical Enumerated Tree Model of an Arbitrary PC System**

Each branch in the tree defines an object, called a *device node*, that must be addressed by the Plug and Play framework. Configuring the device node requires the following information:

- A unique identification code
- The device node resource requirements
- The resources allocated to the device node
- Whether the device node is a bus (because a bus has *children*, that is, "child" device nodes)

The identification code is simply a string, called a *device identifier*, that uniquely describes each logical device on the system, including buses, on-board CPU and devices, expansion card devices, and peripherals. Each of these logical devices is represented as a separate node in the tree model and requires a unique device identifier. The device identifier is made up of information derived from the identification methods documented in bus specifications and Plug and Play specifications, or from the system BIOS.

Each resource requirement must identify both the resource type (such as IRQ or memory range) and constraints associated with the specific resource. Some devices may require specific IRQs, for example, and some constraints may involve interdependencies. A COM port, for example, may require either IRQ3 and I/O port 02F8h, or IRQ4 and I/O port 03F8h.

If the device is a bus, the PC system must identify the additional device nodes associated with that bus and keep track of the device node's resources. This is important even if these are nonshared resources (such as SCSI identifiers) because the PC system can maintain a central database with all configuration information, which device drivers can access to learn about their assigned resources.

The tree model defines the device node as the fundamental data structure that can be manipulated by components of the PC system to manage installation and configuration of devices. The next step toward building a framework for a Plug and Play architecture is to define the configuration process that manipulates the device nodes to establish a working system configuration. This process, in turn, defines the system components required to deliver Plug and Play functionality.

The system BIOS must perform a certain amount of configuration during the power-up phase. For the PC system to boot, the BIOS must configure, at a minimum, a display device, an input device, and an *initial program load* (IPL) device, passing the information about each of these device nodes to the operating system for additional configuration of the PC. (Nonboot devices can remain unconfigured until the operating system loads.)

The operating system must continue the configuration process by identifying every device node on the PC system and its resource requirements. Each nonboot device should be inactive on power-up so the operating system can identify any conflicts between the resource requirements of the devices before configuring them. The operating system must store information about each device node in a central database and then load the device drivers for each device node.

In the event that different devices require the same resources, the devices must be able to inform the operating system about alternative resource requirements, which the operating system then uses to identify a working PC system configuration. The operating system resolves the resource conflict and assigns new resources to the conflicting devices. After the resource conflict has been resolved, the operating system must store the new configuration information in the central database and notify the device drivers about the new resource assignments.

If the PC system configuration changes during operation (for example, if a docking event occurs or a PCMCIA card is inserted), the relevant *bus enumerator* (BIOS or PCMCIA) must notify the operating system about the event so the operating system can configure the new device and load the appropriate drivers. Applications must be able to respond to configuration changes to accommodate new devices, and respond appropriately when devices are removed.

# Plug and Play Components

To fully implement a Plug and Play PC system, you must make changes to the BIOS, the hardware, the device drivers, and the operating system.

## Plug and Play BIOS

To meet the requirements of Plug and Play, the system BIOS must be enhanced to provide boot device configuration and dynamic event notification services. These capabilities must also be closely integrated with the operating system.

A Plug and Play BIOS must conform to the *Plug and Play Association (PPA) Plug and Play BIOS 1.0a Specification* (or later), and implement all relevant functions. A system BIOS that only contains extensions to configure ISA Plug and Play expansion cards is not considered a Plug and Play BIOS because it does not report motherboard device nodes or implement the other functions defined in the BIOS specification.

A Plug and Play BIOS must be able to configure the PC motherboard devices (at a minimum) before passing control of the configuration process to the operating system. This process involves isolating and initializing the motherboard devices, such as the programmable interrupt controller (PIC), DMA controller, system display controller, floppy disk drive controller, and so on. In the Plug and Play framework, each of these devices is associated with a unique identification code recognized by the operating system. The BIOS also maintains a list of system board device configuration information, and communicates this information to the operating system after the *power-on self test* (POST) process is complete.

To provide complete Plug and Play functionality, the BIOS must be able to notify the operating system about dynamic configuration events, such as the insertion of a notebook system into a docking station. A Plug and Play BIOS provides a mechanism for a Plug and Play operating system to reconfigure motherboard devices in response to a dynamic event. With this mechanism, the operating system can reconfigure the PC without requiring the user to turn it off, and can also notify applications and drivers about the new PC system configuration. In addition, for software-controlled devices (such as VCR-style docking systems), the BIOS can give the operating system early warning and prevent errors and data loss when the device is removed.

# Plug and Play Hardware

To implement Plug and Play, some changes must be made to the hardware in the PC. These design changes relate to the basic functions of the motherboard, the expansion cards, and the peripherals.

## Motherboards

Only a small number of changes must be made for motherboards to support Plug and Play. On a motherboard that contains the standard "AT" motherboard devices, only a Plug and Play BIOS need be added to provide the benefits of the Plug and Play architecture. Although this change gives basic Plug and Play functionality, other changes to the motherboard—such as implementing software control of functions typically associated with jumpers and switches on the motherboard—add value to the motherboard design.

If you place other devices associated with expansion cards on the motherboard, such as parallel and serial ports, display adapters, and so on, these devices require extra circuitry to meet Plug and Play standards. Individual motherboard devices should be as flexible as possible with regard to configuring IRQ signals, DMA channels, memory locations, and I/O ports. A basic device should be capable of relocating these resources to a number of different locations, reducing the risk of conflict with other devices on the motherboard or any other devices that may be added to the expansion bus.

When motherboard devices are attached to the CPU bus, the BIOS identifies and configures the devices, and no extra Plug and Play hardware is required. If these devices are attached to an expansion bus, such as a VL-bus, ISA bus, or PCI bus, they may either be identified and configured using the standard methods for the bus they're connected to, or the BIOS can identify and configure the devices. For the ISA bus and VL-bus, BIOS configuration is probably less expensive. For the PCI bus, the PCI configuration technique will usually be required.

### Expansion Cards

Depending on your bus architecture, you may need to make hardware changes to expansion cards to implement Plug and Play. ISA expansion cards, for example, require additional hardware to isolate, identify, and configure the devices on the card. This hardware can consist of an integrated circuit (IC) placed between existing devices and the bus interface, or of new functions programmed into an existing application-specific integrated circuit (ASIC). Other bus architectures, such as the PCMCIA or PCI bus, generally do not require any hardware changes.

Devices on expansion cards should be as flexible as those found on motherboards. The expansion card should be designed such that each device can relocate IRQ signals, DMA channels, memory locations, and I/O ports to as many locations as possible, so the bus can reduce the risk of conflict with other devices.

### Peripherals

A peripheral device—a SCSI disk drive, a modem, a printer—can connect to a PC either internally or externally. Each peripheral must be able to identify itself to the system. The system, in turn, determines which device driver is appropriate for the peripheral, and automatically loads that driver. Some peripherals already have the ability to identify themselves, but others will need new hardware or software to perform this function.

## Plug and Play Device Drivers

The Plug and Play architecture builds on existing device driver models to provide additional application programming interfaces (APIs) required for Plug and Play device configuration. Device drivers must be capable of dynamically loading and unloading, both to enable reconfiguration and to make the most efficient use of PC system memory. Device drivers must communicate with other components of the PC system in a number of ways. They must register with the *configuration manager* when they are first loaded, remain inactive until they are given their resource assignments, and be able to communicate with applications to respond to dynamic configuration events. For example, a word-processing application may need to save files before removal of a SCSI hard disk, or block the removal altogether. A PCMCIA socket enumerator that recognizes the insertion of a new card will want to notify the configuration manager about the insertion of the card so the appropriate device drivers can be found and loaded, and will want to have resources assigned to the card.

# Windows 95: A Plug and Play Operating System

Windows 95 incorporates several new capabilities to provide complete Plug and Play functionality. These include:

- Software to control the configuration process and communicate with all components involved in that process (the configuration manager)
- A database of information used to configure the PC system (the hardware tree)
- Drivers to identify all the devices on a particular bus and their resource requirements (the bus enumerators)
- Software to allocate resources among all devices (the *resource arbitrators*)

## Configuration Manager

The configuration manager plays the central role during all phases of the configuration process, orchestrating the flow of operations performed by all the components involved in configuration.

The configuration manager takes control of the configuration process when it receives the motherboard device configuration list from the BIOS, and when the BIOS sends notification of a dynamic configuration event. The configuration manager then coordinates communication between the bus enumerators, hardware tree, device drivers, and resource arbitrators to establish a working configuration for the PC system. The configuration manager also notifies device drivers and applications about any pending or current changes in the PC system layout (for example, new or removed devices).

To perform this role, the configuration manager calls on the bus enumerators to identify all the devices on their specific buses and their respective resource requirements, then stores this information in the hardware tree as a hierarchical arrangement of device nodes. For each device, a driver is loaded, and is instructed by the configuration manager to await assignment of specific resources. The configuration manager calls on the resource arbitrators to allocate resources for each device and, in the event of a conflict, performs an interactive process of reconfiguration until it determines a working configuration. It then informs the device drivers about the device configuration, which completes the process. This process is reinitiated when the BIOS or one of the other bus enumerators informs the configuration manager about an event, such as the removal or insertion of a PCMCIA card, that necessitates a change to the PC system configuration.

## Hardware Tree

The hardware tree is a record in RAM of the current PC system configuration. The tree information is drawn from a central database of configuration information for all devices, whether or not they are currently installed. This record is created every time the PC system boots or a run-time change occurs to the system configuration. The format for the hardware tree defines a standard scheme for identifying each device, its resource requirements, and resource constraints (if any). There may also be interdependencies between specific resources, such as COM ports and IRQs. Applications and drivers can access the central database to get information about alternative configurations, software required to operate the devices, and user-defined settings.

## Bus Enumerators

Bus enumerators—required for each specific bus type—are responsible for building (enumerating) the hardware tree on a Plug and Play PC system. Each enumerator is designed to understand the implementation details of a specific bus architecture so it can identify the devices on that bus, read their resource requirements, and configure them as instructed by the configuration manager.

These enumerators may use part or all of existing drivers or BIOS services to access hardware. The SCSI driver, for example, performs the SCSI bus enumeration, and the Card Services and Socket Services drivers perform the PCMCIA enumeration. These enumerators can also be implemented at the BIOS level for specific buses such as those on the motherboard.

The bus enumerator assigns a unique identification code to each device on its bus. Bus enumerators also retrieve the device configuration information either directly from the device (for example, PCMCIA card configuration tuples) or from the central database (for existing ISA cards). The identification code must be unique and consistent, so that each time the PC boots, the identifier for a particular device is the same. The Plug and Play framework uses existing identification codes for most buses. For example, the EISA device identifier scheme identifies Plug and Play ISA devices, and a fixed set of identification tuples on the card identify PCMCIA cards.

## Resource Arbitrator

The resource arbitrator allocates specific types of resources to devices and resolves conflicts between devices that request identical resource assignments. To this end, the resource arbitrator contains all the information about how a resource is structured, and algorithms for determining a feasible resource configuration given a set of device requirements and constraints. This functional separation of the resource arbitrator and the configuration manager makes it possible for the operating system to address new types of resources.

The resource arbitrator interacts extensively with the configuration manager to iteratively assign resources, both at power-up and in response to dynamic configuration events. In the event of a run-time reconfiguration of the PC system, the configuration manager may require the resource arbitrator to release resources and reassign them to meet the needs of a new device.

### Initial Setup of Existing Legacy Devices

The central configuration database is created when the PC system setup program runs. During initial setup, Windows 95 calls a number of detection and enumeration modules to perform an inventory of all devices on the PC and record information about those devices in the configuration database.

## Costs of the Plug and Play Initiative

Cost is an obvious consideration in evaluating whether to implement Plug and Play, and for this reason, the Plug and Play specifications have been designed to minimize the per-unit cost of PCs and devices. The cost depends on the type of device or PC system being developed.

From the engineering point of view, Plug and Play will have an impact on current designs and add minimal cost. For example, if you have an ISA card design that uses jumpers and switches to set the IRQ signals, I/O port addresses, memory addresses, or DMA channels, implementing Plug and Play will add approximately 4000 gates to your current design. For most other bus architectures, no additional hardware is needed for Plug and Play functions. Existing identification and configuration registers in most standard buses are sufficient to provide a Plug and Play PC with the information needed to perform all Plug and Play functions.

The degree to which you must become familiar with new techniques required by Plug and Play depends on the type of component or PC system you are developing. Some cards (PCMCIA, PCI, Micro Channel, and so on) require no hardware changes to add Plug and Play, but minor changes to system BIOS, *option ROMs*, and device drivers may be required. Other cards, such as ISA or SCSI cards, require hardware changes that support standard identification and configuration schemes to implement Plug and Play. The creators of the Plug and Play specifications made a conscious effort to minimize the cost of these changes.

The Plug and Play architecture is documented in a set of specifications with the information needed to design a variety of Plug and Play devices. The specifications are open and independent of specific operating systems and hardware implementations, and were designed to minimize the new skills required to design Plug and Play PC systems.

Plug and Play maintains software compatibility with existing PCs and peripherals, and Plug and Play PC systems can often accommodate the lack of device-reporting mechanisms for non–Plug and Play devices. These devices are given first priority, which prevents the more flexible Plug and Play devices from using the resources needed by the older, inflexible devices. To help prevent conflicts with these older devices, Plug and Play devices should be designed so they can be configured as many different ways as possible (such as the capability to use eight possible IRQs).

Designing device drivers for Plug and Play PC systems can be much simpler than designing device drivers for non–Plug and Play systems. Much of the code used in previous iterations of a driver can be reused. If, for example, you are designing a new Plug and Play ISA card, the default I/O ports, IRQs, DMA channels, and so on can remain the same as in previous designs, providing backward compatibility with older PCs. You still must add new capability and make device driver configurations as flexible as possible. The major benefit of writing device drivers for new Plug and Play devices is that you can use common device drivers for multiple bus architectures. You can use a single *Network Driver Interface Specification* (NDIS) driver, for example, for a PCMCIA network card, an ISA network card, and a network chip on the motherboard, which reduces the cost of writing drivers.

Plug and Play offers an economically feasible way to identify and configure devices, while reducing hardware complexity and increasing hardware flexibility for the user. Clear design guidelines and standardized interfaces between PC system components provide an economically attractive solution for PC system and component vendors.

# Benefits of Plug and Play

Plug and Play updates the PC architecture in such a way that it improves system performance for users working with existing PCs and provides new ways to work with PCs. These improvements will benefit OEMs and independent hardware vendors (IHVs), as well as users.

## Benefits to Users

Plug and Play will benefit the user enormously. No longer will the user be required to set jumpers and switches manually to redirect IRQs, DMA channels, or I/O port addresses. This will save the user's time and will also save OEMs and IHVs the expense of supporting large numbers of user service calls related to these configurations.

Plug and Play is designed so that adding a device, whether permanently or dynamically, requires nothing more than taking it out of the box and plugging it in. The PC seamlessly adjusts to the new configuration. For example, if a user has a portable PC and a docking station, and the PC has additional resources, such as a color monitor and a network card in the docking station, the system software automatically adjusts to the changes and invisibly changes its configuration to comply with the new hardware.

Users need not concern themselves with the inner workings of Plug and Play. The Plug and Play specifications define how the various hardware pieces, software drivers, and operating systems interact. At the level at which the user interacts with the PC, the PC simply works. Plug and Play reduces the time users spend on technical problems and increases their productivity and satisfaction with PCs.

The Plug and Play functionality built into Windows 95 provides a means of detecting dynamic events. For example, when a portable PC is plugged into a docking station, Windows 95 detects the event, reenumerates the system, reconstructs the hardware tree with the devices in the docking station, and offers immediate access to these devices. If a PCMCIA card is added to the system, Windows 95 offers immediate access to the card. If the portable PC is undocked, or if the PCMCIA card is removed, Windows 95 is aware of its absence, and acts appropriately.

Plug and Play also benefits users who install Plug and Play devices into older, non–Plug and Play PC systems. Components using the Plug and Play architecture are able to accommodate the lack of device-reporting mechanisms in non–Plug and Play devices. Information about these devices is stored in the system, and devices that cannot be configured by the software receive first priority when resources are allocated.

## Benefits to OEMs and IHVs

The benefits of Plug and Play for manufacturers of PC components and systems relate directly to the benefits experienced by the user.

PCs and PC components are currently most often purchased by users with some computer experience, who generally know what to do when a problem arises in the system. A person with fewer computer skills, however, may be reluctant to invest in a system because of the perception that PC hardware is hard to set up, and especially hard to modify. Small businesses that can't afford to make the infrastructure investment for supporting PC systems can be financially discouraged from purchasing new systems or upgrading older systems. Plug and Play helps alleviate these problems and makes hardware easier for everyone to use.

Plug and Play will change the way people view PCs. Easy-to-use PCs will make it unnecessary for users to learn technical information about the configuration of the PC system, which will encourage those who haven't yet bought a computer to rethink their reasons for hesitating. These new customers, and users who want to upgrade their PCs with the new hardware, will increase the demand for Plug and Play–compatible systems and components.

Plug and Play will also reduce support costs, because many procedures that were once done manually, such as setting IRQ lines, figuring out what the right jumpers are, or installing the correct device drivers, are now performed by the Plug and Play PC system. Problems encountered by users with non–Plug and Play PC systems generate a tremendous support burden. Customer frustration with the configuration process depresses demand for add-on and upgrade products. For businesses, the high cost of supporting PCs inhibits increased use of PCs in the workplace and diverts information systems personnel from focusing on using computer technology to solve business problems. Customer histories have shown that device-bus systems that can be configured by software, such as the Micro Channel bus, reduce the need for hardware support by 30 percent and the need for software support by as much as 50 percent.

Plug and Play meets the goal of simplifying initialization and use by integrating the hardware and software configuration into one operation. Because the system automatically configures itself, a user simply plugs in the PC, or adds new components, and begins "playing." Plug and Play systems create more customer satisfaction, reduced support costs, more capable PCs—as users add new functions—and new sales, as the market for new PCs and add-on devices expands.

Another benefit of Plug and Play will be reduced OEM manufacturing costs. With Plug and Play, an OEM need not keep multiple "master" installations just because one system may contain a modem and another may not, or because the systems contain different display cards. The installation process is simplified because the hardware and its resources can be identified by the Plug and Play process, allowing installation configurations to be changed automatically by the setup routines. In this way, Plug and Play can greatly reduce the number of different OEM master configurations required, and reduce manufacturing times.

PART 2

# Hardware Design

Part 2 explains the importance of implementing Plug and Play and other easy-to-use features in the PC 95, and outlines hardware design criteria for systems, devices, buses, and peripherals. This part also supplies information about external components (such as cables) that should be standardized.

Chapter 3 contains requirements and recommendations for assembling a desktop PC 95. This chapter examines motherboard, expansion card, and Plug and Play features, with emphasis on new technologies to enhance the interaction between the system hardware and Microsoft® Windows™ 95.

Chapter 4 describes requirements and recommendations for the mobile PC 95 and discusses different types of Plug and Play enhancements.

Chapter 5 discusses design features and Plug and Play aspects of devices for the PC 95, examining requirements and recommendations for each type of device.

Chapter 6 describes Plug and Play designs for buses and cards on the PC 95. It also discusses the changes required to give ISA bus expansion cards Plug and Play functionality. This chapter also explains the process of identifying, configuring, and accessing Plug and Play expansion cards, and gives implementation examples. It also discusses special cases, such as Plug and Play boot devices and designing Plug and Play cards to be used in non – Plug and Play environments, and describes hardware changes to other types of expansion bus cards.

Chapter 7 examines the design of both internal and external peripheral devices, exploring ease of use and Plug and Play designs for storage devices, display monitors, common input devices (such as the keyboard and mouse), and devices attached to serial and parallel ports.

CHAPTER 3

Chapter 3

# The Desktop PC 95

This chapter summarizes the fundamental design features of a PC 95, including component changes for all new hardware and specific requirements for a desktop PC 95. Implementing these component changes is a first step in designing Plug and Play motherboards and expansion cards. This chapter also discusses optimization of a desktop PC 95 to accommodate Microsoft® Windows™ 95.

To increase the performance and value of the system in the eyes of the user, read and implement the recommendations for advanced features. Windows 95 takes advantage of these features (when present)—in some cases, through architectural designs, such as the graphics device-independent bitmap (*DIB*) *engine*; in other cases, with drivers designed to take advantage of advanced hardware functionality, such as *Extended Capabilities Port* (ECP) printer ports, 16550A-compatible serial ports, and drives that can eject media under software control.

The final section discusses the certification process for the PC 95 and includes an overview of the tests conducted to obtain certification.

# System Component Changes

Some changes must be made to the basic motherboard to provide Plug and Play functionality and ensure ease of use and optimization with Windows 95. Hardware changes are also necessary for a few types of expansion cards (depending on the bus to which they connect). These changes enable Windows 95 to identify and relocate various resources, and to automate a number of interactions on the system. For example, for each device you should add sufficient resources to allow for relocation in the event of conflicts. (A device is any circuit that performs a specific function, such as a parallel port.)

## Motherboards

The types of motherboard buses, components, and devices you use determine the speed and cost of the basic system. Devices traditionally placed on an expansion card, such as parallel ports or display adapters, are now often designed on the motherboard.

Motherboards optimized for Windows 95 should be able to be configured by software so the user does not need to open the PC case and set jumpers or switches to change the motherboard configuration.

## Determining Motherboard Components

The motherboard is made up of the core, local bus, expansion bus, and devices. The core usually consists of the CPU, memory, and support ICs. The local bus connects directly to the CPU. An expansion bus can be an extension of the local bus or completely separate.

The number of expansion cards that can be connected to the system depends on the type of expansion bus designed on the motherboard. The number of slots on the PCI bus and VL-bus is typically limited. The PCI bus supports up to 10 device loads, although each expansion card uses a minimum of two loads. The VL-bus supports up to three slots, depending on the speed of the system clock. Because of these device limitations, and requirements to provide PC register–compatible DMA and interrupts, the PCI bus and VL-bus are generally combined with some other type of expansion bus (usually an ISA bus) to allow a wider range of expansion cards. Bridges can also be added to the PCI bus or VL-bus to add extra loads. Expansion buses such as the ISA, EISA, and Micro Channel buses allow for a higher number of cards to attach directly to the bus.

Many motherboard designs include high-performance *integrated devices* such as display adapters, mass storage devices, and network adapters, among others. You can enhance the performance of Windows 95 by directly connecting these devices to a high-speed expansion bus such as a PCI bus, VL-bus, Micro Channel bus, or EISA bus. These integrated devices attach to the CPU through the expansion bus interface logic. This increases their performance, and in some cases, gives the CPU more time to take on other tasks.

Integrated devices attached to expansion buses must follow the appropriate bus specifications. For the PCI and Micro Channel buses, this means incorporating the standard resource enumeration and configuration procedures for those buses. For the ISA bus and VL-bus, you can use the Plug and Play system BIOS to enumerate and configure these devices directly, rather than using the ISA Plug and Play procedures. For the EISA bus, you can choose to use either the EISA configuration procedures, the Plug and Play ISA configuration procedure, or direct configuration through the Plug and Play system BIOS.

Placing devices on the motherboard allows them to run at speeds higher than most expansion cards can run, and decreases cost by reducing parts count. Devices placed on the motherboard can take advantage of the local bus for their interface to the CPU or can be connected to a motherboard expansion bus. Devices that require fast access, such as display adapters in multimedia systems, should be connected to a high-speed expansion bus. If a device uses slow memory accesses or is inactive for long periods of time, it can be connected to a slower expansion bus and still operate effectively.

A display adapter is one type of device that benefits from a motherboard location. By placing the adapter directly on a high-speed bus on the motherboard, you significantly increase the data transfer rate to the display. With the addition of a linear frame buffer, Windows 95 can draw optimally onto the display frame buffer. Using an on-board display adapter also frees up a slot on the motherboard for other expansion cards. On-board display adapters are becoming more common because of the lower cost (no slot connectors) and because the design can be revised more easily.

Figure 3.1 shows a sample block diagram of one possible motherboard configuration of static and Plug and Play devices. Connected to the CPU core are the BIOS ROM, static devices such as the interrupt and DMA controllers, BIOS-configured Plug and Play devices such as the parallel and serial ports, and the expansion bus.

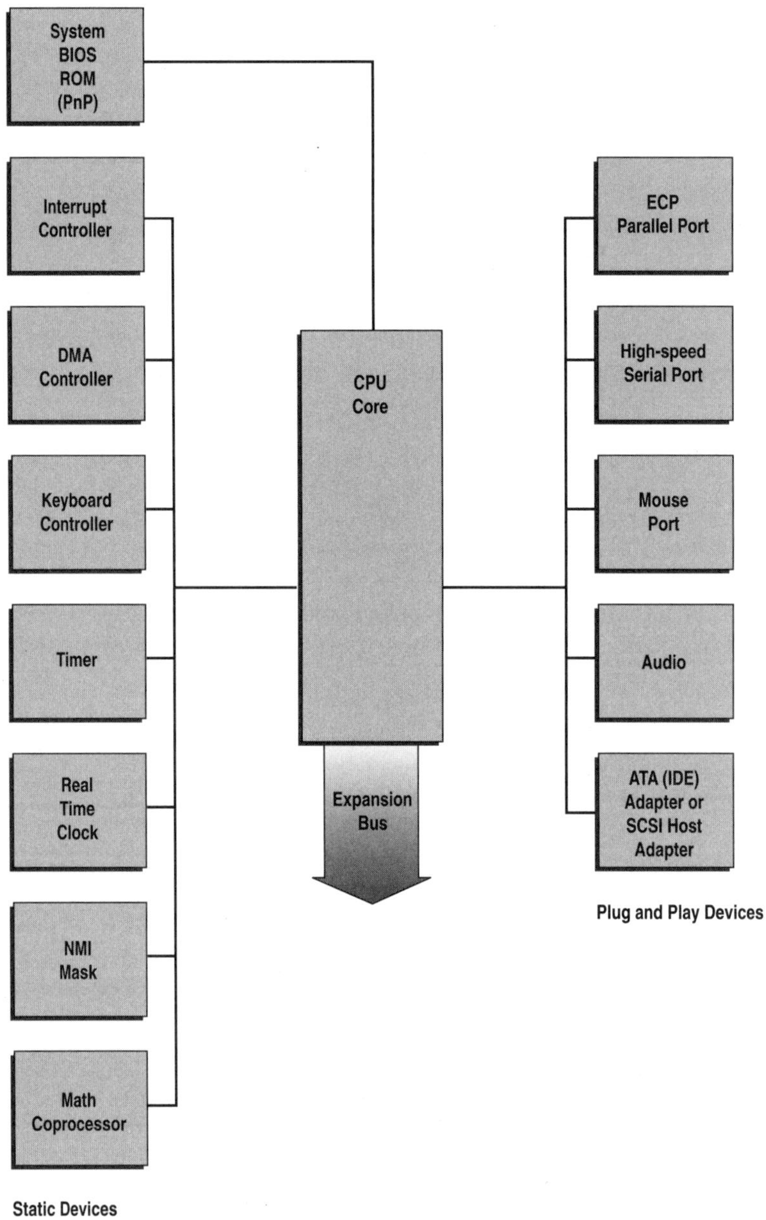


**Figure 3.1 Motherboard Components**

**Important** All motherboard devices that are directly connected to the CPU, the ISA bus interface logic, or to VL-bus interface logic can be enumerated and configured using the system BIOS rather than the ISA Plug and Play enumeration logic. Motherboard devices that attach through the PCI bus or Micro Channel bus should conform to the resource configuration requirements of that bus. EISA bus devices can use either technique.

## Designing Plug and Play Motherboards

A motherboard should be as flexible as possible, and configuring it should not require the user to open the PC to alter jumpers or switches. A Plug and Play motherboard that is configurable by software makes manual configuration unnecessary.

The components for a Plug and Play motherboard are a new system BIOS, programmable logic to replace configuration jumpers and switches, and, in some cases, new device drivers. Determine how flexible and configurable the motherboard is, balancing the functionality of the Plug and Play environment against the design and building of the circuitry needed to implement Plug and Play.

The key specifications for designing a motherboard are the *Plug and Play BIOS Specification* and the specifications for the buses on the motherboard. These specifications define the resource structures needed for the subsystems you are designing. For information about the design requirements for a Plug and Play system BIOS, see Chapter 8, "System BIOS Design."

The basic motherboard chip set (that is, the IRQ controller, DMA controller, and so on) can be set to use *static resources* available in the system BIOS, because these are located in the reserved I/O address space (00h through 0FFh). For these subsystems, no new hardware need be added to implement Plug and Play.

Other devices on the motherboard, such as parallel or serial ports, should contain multiple resources that can be configured by software, such as I/O port addresses, IRQ signals, and DMA channels, to ensure maximum flexibility. For more information about resource requirements and recommendations for these devices, see Chapter 5, "System Devices." The system BIOS should configure these resources. You may need to add new hardware to the motherboard or chip set to allow the resources to be configured.

One of the limitations of the original PC design was the incomplete I/O address decoding of 10 bits, rather than 16 bits. This limited the number of usable I/O addresses to 1024 unique values. By contrast, one of the benefits of Plug and Play is the ability to map a Plug and Play ISA expansion card into different address locations in the full 16-bit I/O address space. Motherboard and chip set designers can facilitate this by implementing a full 16-bit decoding of the resources of the basic motherboard chip set and of any integrated devices, such as Super I/O chips. Full 16-bit decoding of these devices should limit their active address space to below 3FFh.This can be implemented simply and inexpensively by using a logical AND gate to combine address lines A15:A10 with *AEN, *IOR, and *IOW to create new signals *AEN10, *IOR10, and *IOW10. These signals could then be used for all standard integrated devices.

### Eliminating Jumpers and Switches on the Motherboard

A PC 95 motherboard should contain few, if any, jumpers and switches. Typically, the user benefits if the functionality and resources sometimes selected by these jumpers and switches can instead be programmed using software. A PC 95 motherboard should incorporate as much automatic and software-controlled configuration of common motherboard functions as possible.

Jumpers and switches on a motherboard are usually associated with either component configuration functions, such as CPU type, or device resource allocation, such as selecting the proper on-board, parallel port, interrupt request resources. When eliminating jumpers and switches from the motherboard, you should design all device resources with programmable logic circuits. The settings can then be selected by the system BIOS.

Although jumpers and switches for many general functions on the motherboard can be replaced by programmable logic, there are some exceptions. For example, the following general functions need not be replaced with programmable logic: component configuration functions such as CPU type, jumpers for factory test, advanced manufacturing diagnostics, and model variation.

## Expansion Cards

Expansion cards allow you to add more devices to the PC. They connect to the system motherboard through a number of different types of buses. Each of these buses connect logical devices located on the expansion card to the core logic on the motherboard. One or more logical devices are commonly designed on an expansion card.

In general, expansion card designs require many of the same changes as motherboards when you are incorporating Plug and Play functionality. In all cases, you should design Plug and Play functionality into the hardware. As on the motherboard, jumpers and switches on expansion cards should be replaced by logic that can be configured by software.

## Plug and Play Expansion Cards

The changes you are required to make to add Plug and Play to an expansion card vary, depending on the type of system bus to which the card is connected. Plug and Play identifies the devices on the expansion card and, if possible, configures the devices so they don't conflict with other devices on the system. The process by which devices are identified is called enumeration.

You may occasionally need to design new hardware on the expansion card so the system can successfully enumerate the card's devices. For example, the ISA bus has no means to identify which devices are connected to the bus. To enable an expansion card connected to the ISA bus to identify its devices, you must add new hardware to the card. This hardware gives the ISA bus Plug and Play functionality and the ability to configure the devices. For information about changes required for an expansion card on the ISA bus, see the *Plug and Play ISA Specification* and Chapter 6, "Plug and Play Cards and Buses."

Plug and Play specifications for other buses usually require implementing specific software registers on the expansion card. The PCMCIA bus, for example, contains a set of *tuples* identifying the resources of a particular card; the bus also allows the system to configure the device on the card. In the past, PCMCIA cards sometimes included a subset of configuration tuples to implement; however, it's possible that such cards won't contain enough information for Plug and Play system identification. To alleviate this problem, Plug and Play requires that you implement a minimum set of tuples for PCMCIA cards. For more information about the PCMCIA tuple requirements, see Chapter 6, "Plug and Play Cards and Buses."

Some expansion cards are Plug and Play compatible without any changes. You needn't make changes, for example, to expansion cards that connect to the EISA bus, Micro Channel bus, or PCI bus. The specifications for these buses ensure that sufficient identification and configuration hardware is available for the system to identify, configure, and resolve conflicts between devices.

## Eliminating Jumpers and Switches on Expansion Cards

One of the goals of Plug and Play is to eliminate manual configuration in favor of software configuration, which is more convenient. In almost all cases, functions rendered by jumpers and switches can be replaced by hardware that allows software control of these functions.

Device resources such as IRQ signals, DMA channels, and I/O port addresses should all be able to be configured by software, which will eliminate the need for switches on the expansion card. Resources that can be configured by software allow the operating system to change the values of these resources in the event of conflict with other devices. When there are irreconcilable differences, the software must be able to disable each logical device on the expansion card individually.

It may not be possible to eliminate jumpers and switches from an expansion card completely. If an expansion card contains a boot device such as a hard disk controller, for example, it may be necessary to load an initial value for the I/O port at power-up if the card is connected to a system motherboard that does not contain a Plug and Play system BIOS. To provide this backward compatibility, switches may be required to initialize this value. After the system has booted, however, this initial value must still be able to be changed by software to comply with Plug and Play.

# Device Resource Recommendations

The motherboard components shown in Figure 3.1 illustrate the differences between static devices and integrated devices that require new Plug and Play functionality. Static devices are common to all AT-style motherboards, and their resources, such as I/O port addresses, are well established. However, integrated Plug and Play devices must be able to relocate their resources to prevent conflicts with other devices that may demand one or more of the same resources.

---

**Note** Occasionally, devices you design may not need, for example, any DMA channels or IRQ signals. For such devices, ignore the DMA and IRQ requirements listed in this chapter. If the requirements are not needed for a given device to function, you need not implement them to meet the requirements for a PC 95.

---

To decrease the chance of conflict between device resources, you should make the number of resources available to each integrated device as flexible as possible. Eight configurations per resource are recommended for the PC 95. In addition, each device as a whole must be able to be disabled. This can be implemented as seven configurations plus disable for IRQ signals, I/O addresses, and starting memory space for resources that are optional to a device's functionality. (This applies primarily to ISA, EISA, and VL-bus components. Buses that have fewer resources should implement the maximum flexibility possible for those resources.) To provide this level of Plug and Play flexibility, integrated devices should meet the following minimum configuration requirements, if they use a resource:

- Support of at least eight IRQ signals, or seven IRQ signals plus disabled (eight configurations).
- Support of at least three DMA channels plus disable (four configurations).
- Mapping of the base I/O address to at least eight locations, or seven plus disable. This disabled I/O address configuration in many devices can be used as the device disabled configuration.
- Mapping of the base memory address to at least eight locations, or seven plus disable. This applies to option ROMs, and to direct memory buffers, on most devices.

The parallel port example later in this chapter demonstrates how to design a mapping circuit that meets these recommendations by using a single IC to decode the logic into seven configurations plus resource disable for the IRQ and DMA resources. The I/O port is configurable to seven locations, or is used to disable the entire device.

It may sometimes be possible to easily implement eight working configurations plus disable. This is done by using a linear select method composed of an 8-bit latch. To select an IRQ signal, the latch enables one of its eight outputs. If no IRQ signal is selected, interrupt requests are disabled. In this case, the software must not select more than one bit at a time in the latch; this prevents illegal interrupt configurations.

If you use DMA channels, you should implement a minimum of three DMA channel configurations for devices in the PC 95. You can use either 8-bit or 16-bit DMA channels, depending on the requirements of the device. DMA controllers should be able to support Type B or Type F transfers for better DMA performance (to ensure smoother multitasking, and so on) and increased DMA flexibility in future products.

In some cases, you may not be able to supply the minimum number of resource configurations listed here, such as IRQ signals. If you cannot supply the minimum selection of resources because of the configuration of the bus architecture, you needn't supply the resources listed in this section in order to meet the requirements for the PC 95. It's in the best interest of Plug and Play, however, to supply as many different resources as possible to avoid conflicts with other devices.

For PCI bus motherboard logic, each of the PCI bus interrupts should follow the preceding rules. In other words, each of the four PCI bus interrupts should be programmable to use at least 7 of the standard 15 available 8259 interrupts. The most flexible solution would be to allow each one to be mappable into any of the 8259 interrupts.

# Plug and Play vs. Static Resources

Plug and Play promotes ease of use with a specific set of software configuration rules and designs. But not every device on a motherboard must be able to be configured by software. It may sometimes still be necessary to use jumpers and dual inline package (DIP) switches to configure hardware devices, depending on cost and component availability.

- Some devices will always be purely static (resources cannot be relocated). One example is the 8259A PIC at address 20h.
- Some devices will continue to use switch or jumper settings to set resource configurations. In these cases, the Plug and Play BIOS must read and report the resource requirements as fixed—that is, as if they were static devices. Because switch and jumper settings should only be changed while the power is off, the system BIOS reads them when it reboots, and reconfigures using the new settings.
- Some devices have the ability to read and report resources and disable them with software. In this case, the motherboard device resources are hardware mapped but can be disabled with software if a card (such as an advanced audio card) is plugged into the expansion bus.
- Some devices will support full software configuration, where applicable, such as for serial ports, parallel ports, and so on.

---

**Note** The PC 95 motherboard should be fully programmable, where applicable. Initially, systems will qualify for a Windows 95 Logo if they merely report all system resource requirements accurately, even those set with jumpers and switches, but this will be phased out, and eventually such systems will no longer qualify for a Windows Logo.

---

# Plug and Play Device Example

The sample Plug and Play ECP parallel port shown in Figure 3.2 should give you an idea of the differences between a standard motherboard circuit and a Plug and Play circuit. (The ECP is an enhanced protocol of the existing parallel port hardware that supports complete backward compatibility and allows higher performance and additional functionality.) This example shows an ISA bus implementation that demonstrates the Plug and Play interface between standard components.

---

**Note** Although schematic examples are shown using discrete logic for clarity, most practical implementations would use programmable logic or gate arrays to implement these functions. These examples illustrate concepts and are not necessarily recommended design implementations.

---

Figure 3.2 contains a block diagram of a Plug and Play version of an ECP parallel port. This example shows one possible hardware configuration for a Plug and Play parallel port circuit.

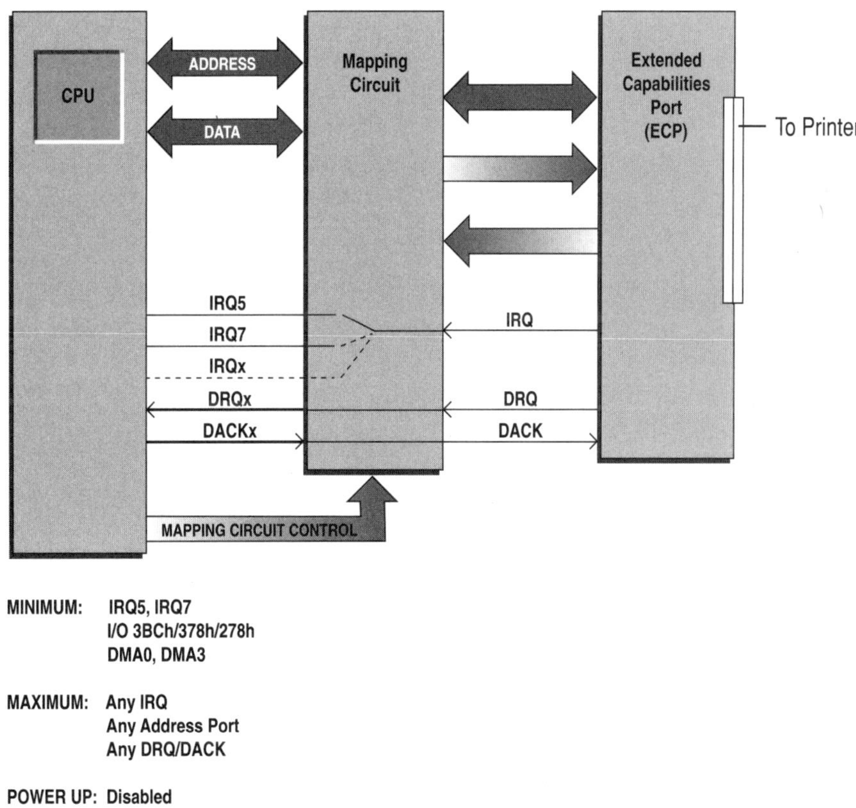


**Figure 3.2 Plug and Play ECP Parallel Port**

Placed between the ECP parallel port circuits and the expansion bus is a mapping circuit. This circuit manipulates selected address, data, and control lines from the expansion bus to establish communication between the bus and the parallel port. The large lines between the two circuits indicate any bidirectional, input, or output lines to the port circuit. The IRQ signals and DRQ channels from the parallel port circuit enter the mapping circuit, where they can be redirected by software to a selected IRQ or DRQ line on the expansion bus. The mapping circuit also passes through the corresponding DACK line from the core that acknowledges that the DMA request was received. The port address for the parallel port can also be set using the mapping circuit.

Figure 3.3 shows a design for the mapping circuit control for a minimally programmable parallel port. This figure is shown only as an example of one method of selecting the parallel port.

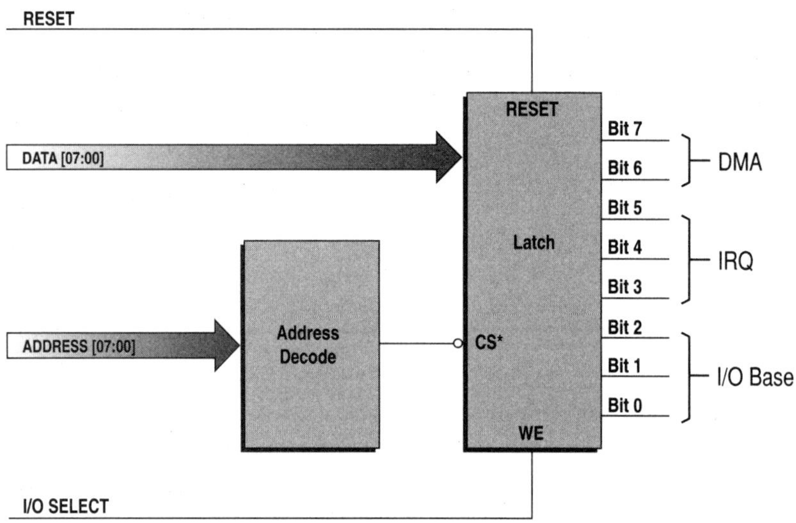


**Figure 3.3 Mapping Circuit Control**

The control circuit consists of an I/O latch that has a fixed address somewhere between 00h and 0FFh, in the reserved space for static devices. The I/O latch address is known by the BIOS, which uses this one static address space to select the I/O base address, the interrupt number, and the DMA channel. These selections are made from the limited number available with this circuit. The system software writes specific data to the I/O latch address to select how the signals to and from the parallel port are gated.

In this example, the first three lines select the I/O base address. Bits 0, 1, and 2 of the data bus are multiplexed by the mapping circuit to select from the addresses shown in Table 3.1.

**Table 3.1 Selecting the I/O Base Address**

| Bit 2 | Bit 1 | Bit 0 | I/O base address |
|---|---|---|---|
| 0 | 0 | 0 | Disable parallel port |
| 0 | 0 | 1 | 3BCh — LPT1 |
| 0 | 1 | 0 | 378h — LPT2 |
| 0 | 1 | 1 | 278h — LPT3 |
| 1 | 0 | 0 | Vendor-selected address 1 |
| 1 | 0 | 1 | Vendor-selected address 2 |
| 1 | 1 | 0 | Vendor-selected address 3 |
| 1 | 1 | 1 | Vendor-selected address 4 |

The next three lines select the interrupt number. Bits 3, 4, and 5 are multiplexed by the mapping circuit to select from the interrupt numbers listed in Table 3.2.

**Table 3.2 Selecting the Interrupt Number**

| Bit 5 | Bit 4 | Bit 3 | Interrupt number |
|---|---|---|---|
| 0 | 0 | 0 | Disable IRQs (IRQ not used) |
| 0 | 0 | 1 | IRQ7 |
| 0 | 1 | 0 | IRQ5 |
| 0 | 1 | 1 | IRQ12 |
| 1 | 0 | 0 | Vendor-selected interrupt 1 |
| 1 | 0 | 1 | Vendor-selected interrupt 2 |
| 1 | 1 | 0 | Vendor-selected interrupt 3 |
| 1 | 1 | 1 | Vendor-selected interrupt 4 |

The next two lines select the DMA channel. Bits 6 and 7 are multiplexed by the mapping circuit to select from the DMA channels listed in Table 3.3.

**Table 3.3 Selecting the DMA Channel**

| Bit 7 | Bit 6 | DMA channel |
|---|---|---|
| 0 | 0 | Disable DMA |
| 0 | 1 | DRQ1, DACK1 |
| 1 | 0 | DRQ2, DACK2 |
| 1 | 1 | DRQ3, DACK3 |

Using the example demonstrated here, the system could configure the ECP circuit many different ways. For example, the following combinations of configurations could be selected by the system:

- LPT1, IRQ7, DMA1 (a standard configuration)
- LPT2, IRQ5, DMA3 (a standard configuration)
- LPT3, IRQ12, Disable DMA (a nonstandard configuration)
- Vendor-selected address 1, IRQ12, Disable DMA (a nonstandard configuration)

If you add extra latches to the data bus, you can use additional lines to select more configurations for the parallel port.

Windows 95 will typically configure all devices into their standard configurations whenever possible. If another device is already using the standard configurations, however, Windows 95 can also use an alternate configuration. For instance, if a system had all of the four ECP ports discussed previously, Windows 95–based drivers would be able to access each ECP port. Older programs might be limited to using only the first two ports.

This design requires that there be at least one fixed address that latches configuration data, usually from the reserved range 00h through 0FFh. Thus, by using one address from the list, the BIOS can configure the rest of the system. The small number of programmable IRQ numbers, DMA channels, and I/O base addresses is also a limitation.

As a shortcut, the system BIOS could report only the address of the parallel port circuit. The BIOS would assign this fixed address to the parallel port circuit and assign other devices around the address. To minimize the chances of conflict between the fixed address and other parts of the system, you would need to design into the circuit some means of allowing the BIOS to disable the parallel port.

Plug and Play does not require that all circuits on the motherboard be completely configurable. For example, the mapping circuit in Figure 3.3 could be constructed to provide for a limited number of IRQ addresses, such as IRQ5 and IRQ7 only, and require that the I/O address be situated at specific locations, such as 3BCh, 378h, and 278h. This minimum capability would allow for enumeration of static definitions for the device to be located in the system BIOS. Other enumerated devices that contain more flexible resources could be mapped around the static requirements for this minimally compliant device.

# System Requirements for Windows 95

Windows 95 is designed as an upgrade for a wide variety of existing PCs. The basic PC required to run Windows 95 has the following characteristics:

- A 386 or compatible microprocessor, minimum
- 4 MB RAM, minimum
- VGA display
- Runs Microsoft® Windows™ 3.1 in enhanced mode

This set of features allows Windows 95 to perform well but does not add all possible Plug and Play and ease-of-use features to the system. This type of system might not contain any Plug and Play expansion cards, motherboard devices, BIOS routines, or peripherals. Although Windows 95 can resolve many conflicts in systems with this minimum set of features, it cannot, for example, relocate hardware resources. Therefore, irreconcilable conflicts can still occur.

This type of system may not be able to use the built-in ease-of-use facilities of Windows 95 optimally. It may not, for example, contain a linear frame display buffer, which may limit its capabilities as a multimedia-ready machine.

This basic system is considered the typical PC on which Windows 95 upgrades will take place. Users will expect new PCs to have better performance and extended capabilities, however. Hardware enhancements on these new PCs will enable Plug and Play features and ease-of-use capabilities, allowing optimum performance of Windows 95.

# The PC 95

More than just a basic computer to run Windows 95, the PC 95 contains hardware and software features that conform to Plug and Play standards, and hardware enhancements optimized for Windows 95. With these improvements as basic features, the user knows that the system can be modified without changing jumpers or switches.

# Required vs. Recommended Features

Although many different devices can be designed in the PC 95, the hardware designs in this guide represent the minimum requirements for Plug and Play configurations and the minimum features required for ease of use in the PC 95. The guide defines two levels of implementation for these features:

- Required. These features are required for the PC 95.
- Recommended. These recommended features take advantage of the native capabilities of hardware drivers included with Windows 95, generally without imposing major cost increases.

You must implement the required features in your PC design to be eligible to use the Windows 95 Logo. You are not required to implement the recommended features, but you can use them in your PC 95 design to add value to the system. In the future, some of the features that are currently recommended will be required. To qualify for a Windows logo in the future, for example, a system will have to meet requirements beyond those for a PC 95.

The recommendations in this chapter are a minimum step up from the required features. Still far more advanced recommendations could have been made, but they would have been costlier and might have gone beyond the needs of the typical user. Also, recommended features for specialized, high-performance systems are constantly changing as technology changes.

For example, a 386-class CPU is required for a PC 95 desktop system. A 486/33 is recommended but is only a single step up from the 386. Even this processor is becoming a low-end system in today's DX4 and Pentium-class marketplace. Obviously, Windows 95 will perform better on a Pentium 100 than on a 386/20. The OEM should decide what type of CPU to use and how many enhancements to add to the system. This guide does not intend to limit the types of technology that can be added to a PC 95.

This chapter documents the required and recommended features for the desktop PC 95. For information about the differing requirements and recommendations for a mobile PC 95, see Chapter 4, "Mobile Hardware Designs."

# Required Desktop System Features

For a PC to be considered a PC 95 and qualify for a Windows 95 Logo, it must meet a minimum set of requirements. These requirements guarantee that the PC contains a basic set of features that enable Plug and Play and make the PC easy to use. The logo makes this easily identifiable to the user.

The following list contains the minimum set of features required for the PC 95:

- A Plug and Play system BIOS (version 1.0a or later).
- 386 (or compatible) architecture, minimum.
- 4 MB RAM, minimum.
- Internal floppy disk drive. Not required, but, if included, must be compatible with 3.5-inch, 1.44-MB disks.
- System display adapter must use a *packed-pixel frame buffer* with at least $640 \times 480 \times 8$ bpp.
- Dedicated mouse port or integral pointing device built in.
- At least one parallel port. The parallel port must support IEEE-P1284-I mode protocols for *compatibility mode* and *nibble mode*. The system must be capable of receiving the parallel device's identifier in nibble mode.
- One serial port built in, minimum. If a serial port is intended to be used for the mouse port, there must be at least two serial ports.
- Molded-in or permanently printed icon labels on the computer case for built-in ports. (If similar icons appear on the cable connectors, icon matching will be easier.)

## Desktop Motherboard Requirements

Although desktop motherboards can be designed with many different characteristics, buses, and on-board devices, each with their own unique requirements on a PC 95, some motherboard changes are common to all designs. The changes described in the following list are required for a PC 95.

- A Plug and Play system BIOS, as described in the *Plug and Play BIOS Specification* (version 1.0a or later). At a minimum, the system BIOS must be capable of reading back and reporting all resources on the motherboard.

- A 386 or compatible architecture, minimum. This includes all 32-bit microprocessors beginning with the 386.
- 4 MB RAM, minimum, to ensure that Windows 95 works well with the system.
- Standard motherboard devices whose I/O port addresses are located within the reserved range 0h through 0FFh should use their AT-compatible addresses. Some bus architectures may require other reserved I/O port addresses, such as 100h through 107h on Micro Channel systems. The Plug and Play system BIOS can reserve the resources as static resources. Some examples of devices that claim static resources are:
  - DMA controller 1
  - Interrupt controller 1
  - Timer (8254-2)
  - Keyboard controller (8042)
  - Real-time clock
  - NMI mask
  - DMA page registers
  - Interrupt controller 2
  - DMA controller 2
  - Math coprocessor (if included)

## Required Motherboard Devices

Integrated motherboard devices can be connected either directly to the microprocessor chip bus (possibly buffered) or through expansion bus interface logic (such as the ISA bus) as if they were located on an expansion card. If the devices are connected through PCI or Micro Channel logic, they must use the resource configuration logic of the appropriate bus.

The following integrated motherboard devices are required on the PC 95:

- Mouse port or *integrated pointing device*
- Keyboard port
- Serial port
- Parallel port

For information about the design of these ports, including configurability requirements, see Chapter 5, "System Devices."

# System Components

Other features of PC 95 desktop systems include such components as hard disk and floppy disk drives, display adapters, parallel and serial ports, and icons. Most of these components are required; some are just strongly recommended.

## Hard Drives

A hard disk drive is not required for a PC 95 but is strongly recommended. The minimum hard disk size is a variable controlled more by users' needs and desired price range than by the needs of the operating system. For a Windows 95 installation, the system will require somewhere between 20 MB and 40 MB of hard disk space, depending on the installed features. The remaining hard disk space is used by applications and application data; the amount depends on the user's needs. A user running primarily Microsoft® Works™ or some other type of integrated productivity software package may not need a large hard disk; 80-MB to 100-MB may be adequate for that user. But a user with a full suite of modern business applications or a large database can easily use up 500 MB of hard disk space.

You should use either the *ATA* (Integrated Device Electronics [IDE]) or SCSI interface for the hard drive interface on the PC 95 system. For information about these interfaces, see Chapter 5, "System Devices," for ATA (IDE) and SCSI host adapters. For more information about the drivers themselves, see Chapter 7, "Designing Peripherals."

## Floppy Disk Drives

An internal floppy disk drive is not a requirement for a diskless workstation PC 95, but all other systems should have a floppy disk drive. The floppy disk drive must be able to read 3.5-inch, 1.44-MB–formatted-capacity floppy disks.

## Display Adapters

The PC 95 system must contain a display adapter capable of a minimum VGA resolution of 640 × 480 × 8 bpp. The display adapter must also contain a packed-pixel frame buffer to enhance graphics performance. For more information about the display adapter requirements for the PC 95, see Chapter 5, "System Devices."

## Parallel Ports

At least one parallel port must be included with the PC 95. This port must support the compatibility mode and nibble mode protocols of the IEEE P1284 specification, *Standard Signaling Method for a Bidirectional Parallel Peripheral Interface for Personal Computers*. Compatibility mode is used with parallel peripherals that comply with the standard Centronics® protocols. Nibble mode is used with parallel peripherals that are capable of sending device identifier strings to the PC. The system must be capable of receiving the device identifier in nibble mode.

For more information about the requirements for a PC 95 parallel port, see Chapter 5, "System Devices." For more information about requirements for peripherals that attach to the parallel port, see Chapter 7, "Designing Peripherals."

## Serial Ports

The system must contain at least one serial port, which should be capable of communicating with serial devices at 115.2K baud, minimum. For information about baud rates and other serial port requirements, see Chapter 5, "System Devices." If the requirement for an integrated mouse port is met with a serial port, the system must contain at least two serial ports.

## Icons

A set of icons must be added to any external connector on the PC 95. Although not required, the same icons should also be added to any cable connectors that plug into the PC 95. (Icons are not required for peripherals or the peripheral end of the cable.) You can base the icons either on existing vendor designs or on the icons shown in Table 3.4. No specific types of icons are required, but some icons in Table 3.4 will be reflected in the Windows 95 user interface design. For PC cases and cable plug housings, the icon can either be molded into the plastic or can be a permanently printed image (printed icons on labels that can be permanently affixed are acceptable).

**Table 3.4 Connector Icons**

| Icon | Description |
|---|---|
|  | Monitor |
| 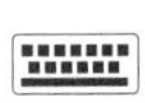 | Keyboard |
|  | Mouse |

**Table 3.4 Connector Icons (*continued*)**

| Icon | Description |
|---|---|
|  | SCSI |
|  | Parallel/Printer |
|  | Gameport/Joystick |
| 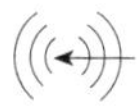 | Monaural/Stereo In |
| 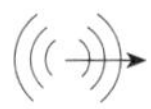 | Monaural/Stereo Out |
|  | Microphone |
|  | Serial Port |
| 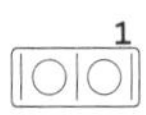  | Serial Port 1 |
| 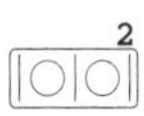  | Serial Port 2 |
| 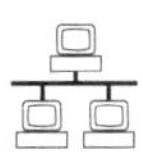 | Network/Thicknet+Twisted |
|  | Headphone |
|  | Expansion Bus/Docking Station |
|  | Telephone Line |
| 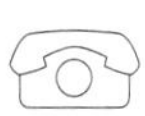 | Telephone Set |

A serial port that is being used as a serial mouse port can optionally contain both the serial port icon and the mouse icon, separated by a slash ( / ).

### Motherboard Device Drivers

All devices shipped on the motherboard must ship with Windows 95–certifiable, 32-bit device drivers that enable the system to pass the Hardware Compatibility Tests (HCT) for Windows 95. For more information about HCT, see the section "Hardware Compatibility Tests" later in this chapter.

## Recommended Desktop System Features

The requirements in the previous sections define a PC that is able to use the built-in functionality in Windows 95 to increase the capabilities of the system when compared with standard PCs. If all designers implemented only the requirements, however, every PC would have the same features, and would function similarly. You can increase the value of a PC 95 by adding features that enhance the computer's abilities and take advantage of more of the options that Windows 95 offers. Adding Plug and Play features and other easy-to-use options also makes the PC "friendlier" for the user.

You can choose to design recommended features into the system to improve the basic PC 95 capabilities. A PC 95 system should provide the following:

- Complete support of Plug and Play in all subsystems (for example, motherboard, BIOS, expansion cards, and peripherals).
- A 486/33 (or compatible) microprocessor, minimum.
- 8 MB RAM, minimum.
- If a floppy disk drive is present on the system, it should report "write protect" when no floppy disk is present in the floppy drive. This allows Windows 95 to automatically detect a floppy disk being inserted.
- The system display adapter should use a linear frame buffer with at least 1024 × 768 × 8 bpp (minimum of 256 colors). Display adapters should support the DDC1 requirements (at a minimum) documented in the VESA *Display Data Channel* standard.
- The monitor should support the DDC1/2B requirements (at a minimum) described in the VESA *Display Data Channel* standard. It should also support the VESA *display power management signaling* (DPMS) and ergonomic monitor timings.

- Dedicated mouse ports should be able to withstand *hot-plugging* of a mouse without system damage. (Dynamic reenumeration will not occur, however.)
- The parallel port should support the protocols of the ECP mode documented in the IEEE P1284 specification. Most super-I/O chips currently support this protocol.
- The serial port should use a 16550A (or equivalent) chip to take advantage of the support in Windows 95 of higher data-rate communications. Most super-I/O chips currently support this capability.
- Support of 22kHz, 8-bit, mono, output-only sound capability and a speaker (as an absolute minimum).
- Interfaces for *advanced power management*, as described in the *Advanced Power Management (APM) BIOS Interface Specification*, Revision 1.1. As the Environmental Protection Agency (EPA) *Energy Star* program proceeds, this will be an important design feature of desktop systems. The PC 95 should also contain a software-controlled power supply for *soft power-down*.
- A high-speed expansion bus (such as a PCI or VL-bus) for high-data-rate devices such as the display, mass storage, and networking.
- Devices or media that can be dynamically removed from the system, such as docking portables, or removable media drives, such as tape or CD-ROM drives, should be capable of *soft ejection* or software unlatch of the device or media.
- Built-in SCSI port. An integral SCSI port makes plugging in hardware much easier.
- Built-in CD-ROM drive. Strongly recommended, but not required. An IDE CD-ROM is a lower-cost choice than a SCSI system.
- Cabling between PCs and peripherals should be designed to prevent users from plugging in cables incorrectly.
- Jumpers or switches on the motherboard or expansion cards should be labeled.
- Although a PC 95 can receive a Windows 95 Logo if it ships with non–Plug and Play expansion cards, these systems should ship with new Windows 95–based device drivers installed and operating for those expansion card devices.

## Desktop Motherboard Recommendations

These general modifications to the motherboard, though not required, are recommended:

- The system BIOS should be able to configure all resources on the motherboard using software.
- The system should provide a 486/33 (or compatible) microprocessor, minimum. The 486/33 is a standard part that is widely available and relatively inexpensive. Low-voltage versions are also available.
- The system should provide 8 MB RAM, minimum. This additional RAM will speed up some applications, improving support for modern and future business and home applications.
- All motherboard devices (static and integrated) should use 16-bit decoding for their I/O port addresses, which makes the I/O address range of the motherboard more flexible. (16-bit decoding is required for expansion card devices.) 16-bit decoding lessens the chances that motherboard devices will conflict with the fixed 10-bit aliases claimed by a non–Plug and Play expansion card. (If an ISA device on the motherboard uses anything less than 16-bit I/O decoding, such as 10-bit or 12-bit decoding, it must claim 10-bit decoding in the I/O port descriptor.)
- Where non–AT-standard I/O ports are used, motherboard devices should claim one, two, or four contiguous 10-bit addresses and map additional I/O ports using 16-bit address aliases.
- DMA controllers should support Type B or Type F transfers for better DMA performance (to ensure smoother multitasking, and so on) and increased DMA flexibility in future products. The DMA controller should also support scatter-gather DMA transfers, to transfer noncontiguous blocks of data without interrupting the microprocessor.
- Any unused addresses in the range 0h through 0FFh that are not used for static devices should be reported by the system BIOS as available resources. Addresses are considered unavailable if they are either actively used by a device or decoded by the device as part of a contiguous block. For example, in one typical configuration, Interrupt Controller 1 uses I/O port addresses 20h and 21h, but the Chip Select of the controller is enabled whenever any address in the range 20h through 2Fh is selected. Therefore, none of these addresses can be reported as available; they are all considered used.

## Recommended Motherboard Devices

The following integrated motherboard devices are recommended for the PC 95:

- IEEE P1284-I–compliant parallel port
- 16550A-compatible serial port

For information about the design of these recommended devices, see Chapter 5, "System Devices."

## General Expansion Card Recommendations

To enhance the capabilities of expansion cards, you can implement the following recommendations as added features for the PC 95:

- Each logical device on an expansion card should support at least seven base I/O addresses plus disable, at least seven starting memory addresses plus disable (if needed), seven IRQ signals plus disable, and (if supported) at least three DMA channels (either 8 bit or 16 bit). For information about these requirements and any exceptions to them, see "Device Resource Recommendations" in this chapter.
- Device designs should be as independent of the bus as possible. For example, device designs placed on expansion cards for different buses should be able to access common I/O addresses that will allow one device driver to control any of the cards on whatever bus is used.
- All expansion card devices should claim one, two, or four contiguous 10-bit addresses (as convenient) and map all I/O port addresses using 16-bit decoding into the base address aliases.
- Each logical device on an expansion card should be able to be individually disabled to prevent conflicts, but should still allow use of the other logical devices on the card.
- Each logical device on an expansion card should have its own bus-specific identifier.

## Floppy Disk Drives

The floppy disk drive included with a desktop PC 95 should be capable of reporting "write protect" to the floppy disk drive controller (FDC) whenever a floppy disk is not in the floppy drive. This allows Windows 95 to automatically detect a floppy disk being inserted.

## Display Adapters

Display adapters should use a linear frame buffer that supports monitor resolutions of at least 1024 × 768 × 8 bpp. This resolution takes better advantage of the DIB engine high-speed graphics code supplied with Windows 95. Higher color depths, such as 16 bpp, can also be implemented.

Display adapters should also support the DDC1 requirements for identifying monitors and their capabilities that are documented in the VESA *Display Data Channel* standard.

For more information about these and other recommendations, see Chapter 5, "System Devices."

## Monitor Support

Monitors that connect to the PC 95 should support the DDC1/2B requirements for identifying monitors and their capabilities, at a minimum. This will require the addition of new hardware to the monitor to store the monitor identification and transmit the information to the display adapter.

Monitors that attach to the PC 95 system should support VESA display power management standards and ergonomic monitor timings. The *Display Power Management Signaling (DPMS)* standard describes methods for sending signals to the monitor that initiate various power management states. The *Monitor Timing Standards for 640 x 480, 800 x 600, 1024 x 768 and 1280 x 1024 at 75Hz* standard describes timing requirements for monitors that increase ergonomic performance. (The monitor should support 75Hz or higher VESA standard timings.)

Monitors should also be able to withstand being plugged into a fully powered PC display adapter without resultant damage to the monitor or the display adapter. Neither the overcurrent circuit in the monitor nor the one in the display adapter should require the user to open the case and replace parts if an overcurrent condition occurs.

For more information about these and other requirements and recommendations for PC 95 monitors, see Chapter 7, "Designing Peripherals."

## Mouse Ports

The mouse port should also be able to withstand having a mouse plugged in while power is on without resultant damage to the mouse or PC. Neither the overcurrent circuit in the mouse nor the one in the mouse port should require the user to open the case and replace parts if an overcurrent condition occurs.

For more information about these and other recommendations for a PC 95 mouse port, see Chapter 5, "System Devices."

## Parallel Ports

The parallel port on the PC 95 should be designed as an IEEE P1284 Level 1–compliant device, as described in the IEEE P1284 specification. Level 1 compliance requires the parallel port hardware and software to conform to the standards defined in the specifications.

The parallel port should also support the ECP mode described in IEEE P1284. ECP mode defines a method of high-speed, bidirectional transfer of information to and from the PC parallel port and an attached peripheral.

For more information about these and other recommendations for a PC 95 parallel port, see Chapter 5, "System Devices."

## Serial Ports

A 16550A or equivalent chip should be used on the PC 95 serial port to support high-speed communications. The 16550A can support the serial port baud rates required for the PC 95. For more information about the design of a 16550A serial port and other recommendations, see Chapter 5, "System Devices."

## Basic Audio

Basic audio on the PC 95 should be capable of more than the single tone generated by the audio circuit designed in the original IBM PC. The PC 95 system should have an audio circuit capable of 22kHz, 8-bit, monaural, output-only sound, and a speaker, minimum. Windows 95 directly supports this audio capability.

To enhance the features of the audio portion of the PC 95, you can add the following recommended features:

- If the desktop system contains a microphone jack for audio input, ship an electret condenser microphone with the system.
- Place headphone and microphone jacks on the front of the system case to make these connections easier to reach.
- Place speaker jacks on the back of the case, or integrate speakers into the case.
- If the audio capabilities of the desktop PC include stereo sound, ship a set of stereo headphones with the system.

For more information about these and other recommendations for built-in audio capabilities in the PC 95, see Chapter 5, "System Devices."

## Power Management

Power management is an enhanced feature of the PC 95 design. Reduced PC power consumption is rapidly becoming a mainstream competitive advantage. Because of the EPA Energy Star program, power management is no longer confined to the mobile computing domain; it has bridged the gap to desktop computers. Although power management is not a required feature for the PC 95, it is strongly recommended.

Power management on both desktops and portable systems, if implemented, must support advanced power management, as described in the *Advanced Power Management (APM) BIOS Interface Specification*, version 1.1. This document defines the various states of the system and its devices, and describes power management control through system BIOS routines. Windows 95 fully supports APM 1.1.

Hardware changes to support power management on a standard motherboard include:

- Detection of recent access of individual devices on the motherboard. This information allows power management control of infrequently used devices.
- Ability to place individual devices into various stages of power management. The APM 1.1 specification describes these stages.
- Ability to continually refresh dynamic RAM during a suspended state or to use a "hibernation" mode, in which the system stores its state to disk.

The system BIOS must be able to regulate power management hardware on the motherboard, while relegating some control of peripheral power management to device drivers. For information about system BIOS control of power management features and its interaction with Windows 95, see Chapter 8, "System BIOS Design." For information about device driver control of peripheral power management, see the *Microsoft® Windows™ 95 Device Driver Reference*, supplied with the Microsoft Windows 95 Device Driver Development Kit (DDK).

## Soft Power-Down

Soft power-down is an extension of the power management capabilities of the PC 95. It allows the user to turn off power to the entire PC without having to use the power switch.

With soft power-down, the user can select a command in the operating system that shuts power off in an orderly fashion. After receiving the shutdown command, the operating system informs the applications and hardware that a power-down is imminent and that they should complete all tasks. After the applications respond that all applications and hardware have finished their tasks, power to the system is turned off.

The system BIOS should be able to supply the interface between the system and a software-controlled power supply. Sending a Set Power State (Off) function to an APM 1.1–compliant system BIOS powers down the system. For more information about APM 1.1 extensions, see Chapter 8, "System BIOS Design."

## High-Speed Expansion Bus

To support devices that require the rapid transfer of large amounts of data, a high-speed expansion bus (such as a PCI or VL-bus) on the system motherboard is recommended. A high-speed expansion bus provides sufficient throughput for devices such as display adapters, mass storage devices, and network adapters.

## Software-Activated Ejection or Latch

Devices or media on a desktop system should be capable of software ejection or latch. On a docking station, use a software-activated ejection or latch to prevent the user from removing the portable PC if, for example, the user initiated a suspend but network files were still open. The software would not eject the portable PC, and would display a warning that the files were open, giving the user the opportunity to close them.

Peripherals that contain removable media should also be designed to eject the media when prompted by the user or the operating system. For example, tape or CD-ROM drives should provide either ejection mechanisms or mechanical latches that can be activated by the software. Future initiatives are expected to address PCMCIA cards and floppy disk drives. The built-in support in Windows 95 for ejectable and lockable media can easily be extended to support these new devices.

## SCSI Ports

An integrated SCSI port will simplify plugging in hardware—the goal of Plug and Play. Including this port on the system makes a wide variety of SCSI devices available. Wide acceptance of SCSI as an expansion standard will help lower the implementation cost of this option.

## CD-ROM Support

CD-ROM support is recommended because a large portion of future software will be delivered on CD-ROM. Already the media of choice for multimedia applications, CD-ROMs are becoming more common, especially in the home. CD-ROMs are also becoming more common in business, especially for databases.

CD-ROM drives for the PC 95 can take advantage of either the ATA (IDE) or SCSI interfaces. If the CD-ROM drive uses the SCSI interface, it must meet the Plug and Play SCSI peripheral requirements. If the CD-ROM drive uses the ATA (IDE) interface, it must support the *AT Attachment Packet Interface* (ATAPI) protocols. For more information about both SCSI and ATA (IDE) peripheral requirements, see Chapter 7, "Designing Peripherals."

If the system contains an ATA (IDE) hard drive, ship the system with an ATA (IDE) adapter that provides support for four drives (in other words, contains primary and secondary channels). The CD-ROM should not be connected to the same channel as the hard drive. Because of the interface characteristics of the ATA (IDE) interface, adding a relatively slow CD-ROM to the same channel as the fast hard drive (in a master-slave configuration) may not provide adequate concurrent I/O processing, and will provide less than optimal support for Windows 95. By placing fast and slow devices on their own channels, you can maximize concurrent I/O processing.

## Standardized Cabling

One of the most perplexing problems for users has been computer cabling. Internal and external cabling has been confusing because there has not been a standard for identifying and guaranteeing that cables and connectors are correctly attached.

Cables for PC 95 systems should meet the following recommendations:

- Cables should either be keyed or shaped so they cannot be plugged in incorrectly.
- IEEE P1284–compliant cables should be labeled.

### Cable Connector Shapes

Cables and the connectors to which they attach should be constructed in such a way that the user cannot plug in the cable incorrectly. For most external cables, connector and cable plug are shaped so the cable will not plug in unless it is attached properly. Internal cables should either be shaped asymmetrically (like a DB-25 connector, for example) or should be slotted or keyed in such a way that the user cannot plug the connector in upside down or off center.

### IEEE P1284 Labels

According to the IEEE P1284 specification, cables that meet the requirements of a P1284 cable must contain a clear and permanent label that reads "IEEE Std 1284-19XX compliant." This label distinguishes the cable from other cables that use the same connectors but have different electrical characteristics.

### Circuit Board Labeling

It is not always possible to completely eliminate jumpers and switches from the motherboard or expansion cards. For example, some expansion cards containing boot devices may require switches to set the default I/O address when the card is plugged into a non–Plug and Play PC. If jumpers or switches are located on the card, their function should be clearly labeled, by silk-screening, for example.

## Multimedia Hardware Design for the PC 95

As multimedia support becomes more of a driving force behind the design of PC systems, a minimum set of design features will be expected for multimedia-capable computers. PC 95 multimedia hardware designs should include all of the requirements and recommendations discussed earlier in this chapter.

Windows 95 will provide multimedia support for a standard PC 95 that includes a CD-ROM player and an audio card. Although the standard PC 95 will be able to play back multimedia audio and video at an adequate rate, additional features are recommended to enhance the capabilities of this system. To take advantage of the large amounts of data that must be transferred in a multimedia system, more advanced hardware should be designed into a multimedia PC 95. This hardware will provide very high quality audio and video output for consumer systems. Multimedia PC 95 systems can also be designed to support commercial multimedia development systems for companies that produce multimedia titles.

PC 95 multimedia computer systems can generally be categorized into at least three varieties:

- Consumer systems. Geared for individuals who want to purchase and play back multimedia titles. Consumers want good sound and video quality, and a system that does not halt when it plays multimedia titles.
- Development systems. For people who create PC-oriented multimedia titles. These systems include the same playback capabilities that consumer systems do, as well as editing capabilities. Multimedia developers want fast read-write capabilities, substantial amounts of storage, and support for data capture and compression.
- Studio-quality development systems. For people who create video or audio products used in a TV or sound studio, or for broadcast. High-end multimedia systems are the fastest and most powerful of the three types of systems. They have more connectivity capabilities for a variety of input and output options, and a huge amount of storage for data capture.

The recommended consumer and developer systems will support playback and development of current and future multimedia titles.

Table 3.5 lists the minimum hardware recommendations for each category of multimedia PC 95. The first column lists the system components needed in the multimedia-capable machine.

The second column describes the recommended consumer system. This system has the power to run not only the standard multimedia titles, but newer titles that include better resolution, animation, and so on, and that require more power to run well.

The third and fourth columns describe development systems for PC-quality multimedia development and studio-quality development. Developers need to do everything consumers need to do; that is, they need to be able to run the titles they create. Developers also need ample power to capture data, author sequences, and compress data, preferably while doing other tasks at the same time. Developers of studio-quality development also require much more data than PC-quality development: Video frames are generally larger and audio samples more complex.

---

**Note** The multimedia hardware recommendations in this table should not be taken to imply that this guide endorses any particular design for a multimedia PC.

---

**Table 3.5 Multimedia Recommendations**

| Component | Consumer system | CD-ROM–quality developer system | Broadcast-quality developer system |
|---|---|---|---|
| **CPU** | 486DX2 66MHz | Pentium 60MHz | Pentium 100MHz |
| **RAM** | 8 MB | 16 MB | 32 MB |
| **Bus** | VL-bus or PCI bus | PCI bus | PCI bus |
| **I/O** | | | |
| Hard drive | N/A (see text) | 1 GB; 3Mps sustained transfer rate | 6 GB; 6Mps sustained transfer rate |
| CD-ROM | 300Kps (double speed); 400ms access time; Mode 2; Redbook audio playback support | 600Kps (quad speed); 250ms access time; Mode 2; Redbook audio playback support | 600Kps (quad speed); 250ms access time; Mode 2; Redbook audio playback support |
| Joystick port | Digital | Digital | Digital |
| Additional ports | Not required | SCSI, 2 PCMCIA slots | SCSI, 2 PCMCIA slots |

**Table 3.5 Multimedia Recommendations (*continued*)**

| Component | Consumer system | CD-ROM–quality developer system | Broadcast-quality developer system |
|---|---|---|---|
| **Video** | | | |
| Resolution | 800 × 600, 16 bpp | 1024 × 768 × 24 bpp | 1024 × 768 × 24 bpp |
| Acceleration hardware | Stretching, YUV to RGB converter, double buffering | Stretching, YUV to RGB converter, double buffering | Stretching, YUV to RGB converter, double buffering |
| Other video | Socketed for MPEG decompression | Socketed for MPEG decompression | Socketed for MPEG decompression |
| **Audio** | | | |
| Waveform | 16-bit digital-to-analog converter; 8, 11.025, 22.05, 44.1kHz; stereo channels; 16-bit analog-to-digital converter at 8, 11.025, 22.05, 44.1kHz | 16-bit digital-to-analog converter; 8, 11.025, 22.05, 44.1, 48kHz; stereo channels; full duplex; 16-bit analog-to-digital converter at 8, 11.025, 22.05, 44.1, 48kHz | 16-bit digital-to-analog converter; 8, 11.025, 22.05, 44.1, 48kHz; stereo channels; full duplex; 16-bit analog-to-digital converter at 8, 11.025, 22.05, 44.1, 48kHz |
| MIDI | 16-voice polyphony; polymessage (recommended); General MIDI; sample sound (recommended); standard MIDI port | 20-voice polyphony; polymessage; (General MIDI; sample sound [recommended] ); standard MIDI port | 20-voice polyphony; polymessage; (General MIDI; sample sound [recommended] ); standard MIDI port |
| Audio I/O | Microphone port, Line-In, Line-Out | Microphone port, Line-In, Line-Out | Microphone port, Line-In, Line-Out |
| Mixing capabilities | See "Mixing Capabilities" section. | See "Mixing Capabilities" section. | See "Mixing Capabilities" section. |
| Signal-to-noise ratio | Not required | 90dB (optional) | 90dB (optional) |
| **Multimedia other** | MPEG playback (optional) | Video capture and compression (optional) MPEG encode (optional) and decode. | MPEG encode and decode. Video capture and compression using MPEG, JPEG, or other high image–quality codec. DAC for PAL and NTSC output. |

# Balanced Multimedia Systems

In general, multimedia systems should be designed to balance the capabilities of the hardware. If the system has a very fast CPU but a slow video bus, the net result will not be as satisfactory as a system with more balanced components would be. Use the following recommendations to provide a more balanced approach to your multimedia design:

- Consumer systems. A balanced system is better than one that only has a lot of horsepower. Build a system that has a local bus (such as a PCI bus or VL-bus), rather than the 8-bit ISA bus, to transfer more data at a time. Use a 800 × 600 Super VGA system, minimum, with at least 16 bpp color. Use a double-speed CD-ROM drive, minimum.
- Developer systems. Include all of the features of a consumer system plus a high write rate to the hard drive (that is, a sustainable 3Mps for PC quality, or 6Mps for studio quality). Also, for development systems, the bigger and faster the computer, the better (a Pentium 60 for PC-quality development and a Pentium 100 for studio-quality development). Also select a good, well-shielded audio system.

Digital video involves enormous amounts of data. For example, suppose you have a full-color video with 640 × 480 resolution. Because full color requires 3 bpp, only one frame of full-color video in this resolution equals nearly 1 MB of digital data. A developer could easily use up 1 GB of hard disk space by storing less than one minute of uncompressed digital video information.

When this much data is involved, it is important to ensure that no system component will impede playback of multimedia titles. Make sure that the system has enough space on the CD-ROM or hard disk and that the driver for the CD-ROM or hard disk is able to retrieve data fast enough to play back well. Ensure that the CPU has enough power to handle video decompression. The bus on the display adapter must be fast enough to move all of the data to the screen. A balanced system considers all of these elements and provides sufficient power in each.

# Recommendations for Multimedia Systems

The following paragraphs provide recommended configurations (by system component) for consumer, PC-quality development, and studio-quality development multimedia systems. For a summary of these recommendations, see Table 3.5.

## CPU

A 486 DX2-66 computer, minimum, provides consistently good playback results. Increasingly, future multimedia titles will be written to this minimum. With this extra CPU power and speed, multimedia sequences can run more smoothly and with less noticeable interruption for processing. Current multimedia titles commonly process a 320 × 240 image at 15 frames per second using standard Indeo™ or Cinepak image compression. Many multimedia titles in the planning stages will require playback speeds faster than 15 frames per second. A 486 DX2-66 computer system should be used so the CPU does not become a gating factor.

Because the process of compressing raw multimedia data is CPU intensive, use a Pentium 60MHz system for developer systems. For commercial broadcast–quality editing, the situation becomes even more critical because, rather than compressing PC-sized 320 × 240 frames, developers compress full TV-quality video. For this type of editing, use a Pentium 100MHz. TV-quality video needs as much CPU and operating system power as possible.

## RAM

Multimedia systems that include additional RAM offer a substantial performance advantage over those with less memory. A minimum of 8 MB RAM is recommended for consumer systems to play back multimedia titles well. Less RAM tends to result in "jerky" playback.

For developer systems, a minimum of 16 MB RAM allows you to multitask between data compression and other tasks. For professional-quality development systems, you should use at least 32 MB RAM. Professional-quality development systems use copious amounts of memory, especially for multitasking.

## Bus

In a multimedia system, the bus affects how quickly data transfers from the CD-ROM to the CPU, to the video display, and to other places on the system.

Although the ISA bus is common in many systems today, it is based on an old standard that is increasingly outmoded for high-volume, high-velocity data streams.

For both consumer and developer systems, you should use one of the newer style buses, called local buses, which transfer larger data increments at faster rates. The PCI bus and VL-bus, both local buses, are commonly designed onto new motherboards, and are readily available. The VL-bus runs at 40MHz with 32-bit or 64-bit data increments (although the number of expansion slots at this speed is limited). The PCI bus runs at 33MHz with 32-bit or 64-bit data increments.

For developer systems, the PCI bus is recommended. The speed and flexibility this bus affords is necessary to support the I/O rates needed on development systems. It is also well suited to work with a Pentium-class processor.

## Hard Drive I/O

Because consumers tend to play back CD multimedia titles and not write the information to the hard drive, this category does not apply to consumer systems.

On development systems, developers write video data to the hard drive. Developers need a 1-GB hard drive and, more importantly, 3Mps of sustained transfer rate. (Note that many hard drives can perform at this rate, but they cannot all sustain this rate. A sustainable rate is very important.) The 3Mps data rate provides sufficient speed for a real-time compression technology called Joint Photographic Experts Group (JPEG), which is increasingly popular among multimedia developers.

If you are capturing full-color (3 bytes) 640 × 480–resolution video at a rate of 30 frames per second, the resulting data stream is 27Mps. A Motion JPEG data-capture card provides real-time compression of data at a ratio of about 10 to 1, meaning that instead of 27 MB of data per second, the system generates 2.7 MB of compressed data per second. Therefore, if the hard disk I/O can sustain a transfer rate of 3Mps, it can easily accommodate data at the rate it is compressed by a Motion JPEG data-capture card.

A developer using a commercial broadcast–quality system processes at resolutions higher than 640 × 480, and needs faster transfer rates than does the PC-quality multimedia developer. These systems also need huge amounts of storage, especially if developers use offline compress, a method of capturing full frames of completely uncompressed data to disk and then compressing them using software online. Capturing this way will take a *long* time without a very fast hard drive.

Developers of broadcast-quality data will look for the fastest sustained hard drive write rate they can find and for lots of disk space (in many cases, this will require SCSI drives that are chained together). For these types of systems, a hard disk with 6 GB of storage and 6Mps per second as the transfer rate is recommended. (The data compression process is another reason to use a 100MHz CPU.)

---

**Note** A sustained transfer rate of 6Mps has been achieved on workstation platforms. Hardware developers creating multimedia systems for TV-quality editing will be competing with systems such as these.

---

## CD-ROM

CD-ROM drives vary in speed, access speed, and CPU use. Speed refers to how quickly data is read from a CD in the CD-ROM drive. A single-speed CD-ROM runs at 150Kps. Double-speed CD-ROM drives are much faster and have led to a development boom in excellent multimedia titles.

A consumer system should use at least a double-speed CD-ROM drive, which reads data from a CD at a rate of about 300Kps. This is the rate needed to play a high-resolution, $320 \times 240$ digital video clip at a reasonable frame rate with no undue screen compression. (Screen compression changes resolution, causing the image to be somewhat grainier. At extreme compression, an image of a person might look like a bunch of blocks, for example.)

Access time refers to how long it takes for the CD-ROM drive to find and read a piece of information on the CD. The CD-ROM drive should have a 400ms access time, minimum. Title developers will create transition effects to cover seek times of this length. If the hardware is slower than the seek rate the title was designed for, playback will be choppy and awkward.

The CD-ROM drive should support Mode 2. Mode 2 is a set of standards for encoding data on a CD. A CD-ROM with Mode 2 capabilities can read photo CDs and movie CDs.

A developer's system should have quadruple speed (reads data from the CD at 600Kps), a 250ms access time, and Mode 2 support. Quadruple speed is important for reading in high-quality source material from a CD at a reasonable rate.

For both consumer and developer systems, playback support for Redbook audio should be included. Redbook is a standard for uncompressed CD-quality digital audio, and most audio CDs are written to the Redbook standard.

## Serial and Parallel Ports

A PC 95 designed for multimedia support must meet the serial and parallel port requirements of the standard PC 95. Because consumers may want to use a serial port to connect two systems to play two-person computer games, you should also include a null modem cable with your system.

## Keyboard, Mouse, Joystick, and Other Ports

A keyboard and mouse are required for the standard PC 95. A digital, rather than analog, joystick port is recommended because a digital joystick port is easier to manage from a system resources point of view. A digital joystick also feels more responsive than an analog joystick.

Developer systems should include at least two PCMCIA slots and at least one SCSI slot. PCMCIA slots provide for connectivity with many peripherals coming out on the market, including scanners and sound components. A SCSI slot allows the user to add more hard disk drives.

Developer systems should also be able to accept input from sources such as video tape recorders and laser discs. Design developer systems to be as versatile as possible.

## Display Resolution

A consumer system should provide at least a Super VGA display with a minimum resolution of 800 × 600. A display with 64K colors (16 bpp) is also recommended to handle the richness of multimedia video. To comprehend this richness, suppose you are playing a video segment with a shaded maroon background that includes one underwater scene, followed by a skydiving scene, followed by a city-street scene. Each of these scenes and the background will have very different color qualities. At least one of these scenes or the background (or both) will look odd if you translate the full-color clip to a 256-color display.

Developers need even more colors on their systems than do consumers because, for example, they may want to edit down videos or have several video windows open simultaneously. Because of these specialized needs, developers want to create video with as high a quality as possible, then make compromises as needed at the end of the development cycle.

Although a high-powered display adapter requires a substantial amount of memory for a 1024 × 768 resolution and millions of colors (24 bpp), the resulting resolution and intensity of colors are needed for development systems.

## Display Acceleration Hardware

Microsoft® and Intel® have jointly developed a new device driver technology called *Display Control Interface* (DCI). With DCI, display adapters can include hardware features used by Windows 95 that enhance the adapter's capabilities when playing back video or Windows 95–based games.

Three display adapter features are of particular importance to improve video playback:

- Stretching hardware. With this feature included on the display adapter, the video image is enlarged without requiring the CPU to do more work. The CPU passes the same number of pixels to the display adapter and the video hardware adjusts the size of the image. Note that the card manufacturer must supply a level 2 DCI driver with the card to take advantage of stretching.

- Color space conversion, or YUV-to-RGB conversion. This is a method of color management that provides better video playback.

  Computer monitors display colors in combinations of red, green, and blue (RGB), but the human eye comprehends (or perceives) colors differently. For example, red is often perceived as a warm, assertive color, whereas blue is perceived as cool and receding. The eye also perceives a difference in brightness more readily than it does a difference in hue. The YUV color standard is based on this understanding of color perception. In the compression process, RGB color is translated to YUV and then compressed. During decompression at playback, the reverse happens. If the display adapter contains an IC with this conversion information, considerable CPU time can be saved. The system can then play much bigger and more colorful videos at a faster frame rate.

- Double buffering. Including more memory on the display adapter allows for video techniques such as page-flipping. This means that instead of one memory space on the video hardware to draw a frame or an image, there would be two. The first might be the one currently used for display on the screen. Meanwhile, the second would be used to draw the next frame in a sequence before it was displayed. This advanced processing makes videos and game animation play back very smoothly.

For more information about obtaining the *DCI Level 2 Specification*, see Appendix D, "References."

## Other Display Components

Consumer and developer systems should include an expansion slot for Motion Picture Experts Group (MPEG) IC, at a minimum. Alternately, consider using a motherboard that includes the IC as an integrated component.

MPEG is a computationally intensive and thorough way of compressing data. It allows for TV-quality (640 × 480, 30 frames per second) digital video playback at very low data rates. That is, a double-speed CD-ROM would suffice for playback of video of this quality.

---

**Note** If you include MPEG or an expansion slot for MPEG on your system, be sure that your CD-ROM driver supports Mode 2. Much of the MPEG content on the market today is encoded using Mode 2; specifically, using a format called XA.

---

## Audio Waveform

Although the standard PC 95 with a minimum recommended audio adapter will run multimedia, an 8-bit sound card will produce only adequate audio. A sound card with a 16-bit digital-to-analog converter for playback and (for developers) a 16-bit analog-to-digital converter for recording is recommended for consumer and development multimedia systems.

The hardware should support 8, 11, 22, and 44kHz waveforms. A frequency of 44kHz is used for CD-quality sound. Fractions of 44, such as 11 and 22, are often used for compressed waveforms meant to save CPU processing.

Support for an 8kHz frequency should be included because of a new capability in Windows 95 called TrueSpeech™ compression. TrueSpeech is optimized for compression and playback of human speech. With TrueSpeech, users can record notes in documents or spreadsheets, store voice mail on their computer, and so on.

Developer systems should also include support for 48kHz for higher-quality sound.

Both consumer and developer systems should include stereo support for a perceived sound-source-location effect. For example, when playing a video game, the user might hear someone coming from the right or the left before seeing the figure on the screen.

Developer systems should also support full-duplex. With this support, sounds can be recorded and played at the same time. This could be helpful, for example, if the user has an alert system that plays while recording sound from a CD.

## MIDI

MIDI is an electronic, or digital, equivalent of sheet music. Sound cards that support MIDI sound synthesis are able to take a MIDI data stream and produce sound according to the digital sheet music instructions that they receive.

Increasingly, games and multimedia titles are being written with MIDI. Many of today's sound cards support MIDI. Using MIDI, you can create background musical effects with a low investment in data storage and system use.

Sound cards for both consumer and developer systems should support the following:

- Polyphony, or the ability to play several sounds at the same time. Consumer systems should include 16-voice polyphony; developer systems should include at least 20-voice polyphony. Support for more concurrent sounds means a fuller-sounding playback.

- Polymessage MIDI, an efficient new capability included in Windows 95 that allows a sound card to receive and batch-process multiple MIDI messages (such as Note On and Note Off). This is useful because many things happen simultaneously in music. By building polymessaging sound support into your sound subsystem, you free your CPU from managing those messages individually. This results in nearly flawless playback, even when the CPU is being heavily taxed by large-frame video playback.
- General MIDI refers to a system of assigning numbers to each type of instrument, so that instrument 12 on one computer is the same as instrument 12 on all others.
- Sampled sound rather than waveform synthesis. Waveform synthesis uses a mathematical approximation of a sound, such as a piano. Sampled sound is an actual recording of the piano, and sounds much better. (MIDI reveals the difference in quality between sound cards.)
- A standard MIDI port to enable consumers and developers to plug in MIDI devices such as piano-style keyboards.

## Audio I/O

All systems should have a microphone port, a Line-In, and a Line-Out.

Optionally, consider including an extra internal connector for the CD-ROM (for example, from the sound card), a Speaker-Out port (for unpowered speakers), and a Headphone-Out port.

## Mixing Capabilities

Both user and developer systems should have mixing capabilities. The mixer should mix input from 4 (Wav, MIDI, Redbook, Aux) and present the output as a stereo, line-level audio signal at the back panel of the computer. Each input should have, at minimum, a 3-bit volume control (8 steps) with logarithmic taper.

All sources should be sourced with –10dB (consumer line level: 1 milliwatt into 600 ohms = 0dB) and without attenuation. This will ensure that the mixer will not clip, meaning that if a sound peaks, the audio clicks rather than playing the sound. It also ensures that the mixer will output between 0dB and +3dB.

Individual audio source, master digital volume control registers, and extra line-level audio sources.

### Signal-to-Noise Ratio

Developer platforms, especially high-end platforms, should target a 90dB level, minimum. Noise is a common but difficult problem in PC audio systems. An otherwise exceptional sound card may perform poorly because it receives interference from the rest of the PC. Consider adding magnetic shielding to the sound card and cables for protection. Also, place the card in the PC chassis to minimize interference with the signal.

### Other Multimedia Components

The following recommendations can also be added to enhance the performance of the multimedia PC 95:

- For developer systems, include video capture and compression support. Technology is rapidly advancing in this area. Two types of capture and compression technology are real-time and offline. Offline compression requires a lot of storage space and produces TV-quality output (best for studio-quality results). Real-time compression requires less storage but results in somewhat lower quality (usually fine for PC-quality development).
- To create a finely tuned development system, consider balancing the capability of the system's capture card with the capabilities of the hard disk drive. (For an example, see the "Hard Drive I/O" section for information on why 3Mps is good for supporting Motion JPEG.)
- For studio-quality development, a digital-to-audio conversion capability for Phase Alternating Line (PAL), in Europe, and for the National Television System Committee (NTSC), in the United States, is recommended.

## Certification for the Windows 95 Logo

The Microsoft Windows 95 Logo on eligible systems and expansion cards helps users recognize Plug and Play PCs and ensure hardware and software compatibility. Microsoft, for its part, has defined the set of features a PC must contain to qualify for the Windows 95 Logo.

To be eligible for the logo, the PC hardware must implement Plug and Play and pass the Hardware Compatibility Tests (HCT). For more information about specific requirements for the logo, contact Microsoft Compatibility Labs (see Appendix D).

---

**Note** This section outlines the basic hardware requirements a system must meet to be eligible for the Windows 95 Logo. For a complete list of the current logo requirements, and to determine system eligibility, contact Microsoft Compatibility Labs. Microsoft reserves the right to change these requirements and the logo program in response to market needs and without notice.

---

# PC 95 Feature Set

For a basic desktop PC system to qualify for the Windows 95 Logo, it must include a minimum set of features. These features are described in three tables: Table 3.6 shows the basic system configuration, Table 3.7 shows Plug and Play capabilities, and Table 3.8 shows overall system features.

In addition to including the required features, you can add a variety of more advanced hardware to the PC. The recommended additional features and functionality make full use of the hardware features supported by Windows 95.

For a more complete explanation of each of these features, see the appropriate sections in this chapter.

**Table 3.6 Basic PC System Configuration**

| Feature | Logo requirement | Recommendation |
|---|---|---|
| CPU | 386 architecture | 486/33, minimum |
| RAM | 4 MB | 8 MB |
| Floppy disk drive, if present | 3.5", 1.44 MB | 3.5", 1.44 MB |
| Write-protect detection | No | Yes |
| High-speed expansion bus (PCI or VL-bus) | No | Yes |
| Soft power-down | No | Yes |
| Connector icons | Yes | Yes |

**Table 3.7 PC System Plug and Play Capabilities**

| Feature | Logo requirement | Recommendation |
|---|---|---|
| Plug and Play BIOS 1.0a | Yes | Yes |
| Read back all resources | Yes | Yes |
| Soft-set all resources | No | Yes |
| All expansion cards individually Windows 95 certified | No | Yes |
| 16-bit I/O decode for all integrated motherboard devices (ISA bus) | No | Yes |

**Table 3.8 PC System Features**

| Feature | Logo requirement | Recommendation |
|---|---|---|
| Display adapter | VGA 640 × 480 × 8 bpp | VGA 1024 × 768 × 8 bpp |
| Display monitor | Color | VESA DDC1/2B (PnP) |
| Parallel port | Standard (nibble mode) | ECP (P1284-I) |
| Serial ports | One required | 16550A compatible |
| Pointing device | Yes | PS/2®-style port |
| Integrated or separate port | Yes | Yes |
| Include barrel button on devices | No | Yes |
| APM 1.1 | No | Yes |
| Option ROMs use PnP header format | Yes | Yes |
| SCSI-2 host adapter | No | Yes |
| CD-ROM (ATA or SCSI) | No | Yes |
| Soft ejection | No | Yes |
| Audio | No | 22kHz, mono, output |
| Serial infrared devices | No | Follow IrDA specification |
| Network adapter | No | Optional |
| All devices/cards MCL certified | No | Yes |
| Motherboard device drivers | Windows 95 certifiable | Yes. |

**Note** All integrated motherboard components must comply with the requirements listed in the tables at the end of Chapter 5 in order for the system to qualify for a Windows 95 Logo.

# Hardware Compatibility Tests

The Hardware Compatibility Tests (HCT) verify hardware and device driver operation under a specific operating system environment. A device, a software driver, and an operating system are tested together under controlled conditions to verify that all three components are operating correctly.

For OEM systems, OEMs run tests that exercise all key PC subsystems, such as memory, display, keyboard controller, PIC, DMA controller, mouse, serial port, parallel port, and so on. For individual hardware devices, such as network adapters, display adapters, printers, IDE/SCSI hard disks, CD-ROMs, floppy disk drives, and other peripherals, individual device-specific HCTs test the device and driver much more exhaustively.

The Hardware Compatibility Tests for Windows 95 are expanded versions of the tests for Windows 3.1 and Windows NT™, adapted for Windows 95. They test Plug and Play compliance as well as software and driver compatibility with Windows 95. The Plug and Play Hardware Compatibility Tests exercise the Plug and Play features of a device and monitor the response to the various Plug and Play specifications, including the reporting of resource requests, the reconfigurability of specific resources, and the operation of a device in different configurations. A device or system must pass the Hardware Compatibility Tests under the supervision and policies of an individual certification lab, such as Microsoft Compatibility Labs.

## Plug and Play Device Drivers

A device driver for a PC 95 must support Windows 95 Plug and Play as follows:

- Must be able to retrieve configuration information from the configuration manager.
- Must be dynamically loadable and reconfigurable.
- Must react to system messages about the insertion or removal of new devices.

An ideal Plug and Play driver has the following capabilities:

- Requires minimal user interaction to select the proper driver.
- May need to "understand" state information; that is, the settings for the device may need to change based on which user is logged in, whether the computer is docked or undocked, and so on.

CHAPTER 4

# Mobile Hardware Designs

Telecommunications technologies and the issue of connectivity are becoming more important hardware considerations for mobile systems. Demand for high-speed communications, power management, warm and hot docking capabilities, and other advanced features now drives new mobile system designs.

This chapter discusses the hardware requirements and recommendations for mobile systems, including support for docking stations, telephony, networks, and advanced power management. Although many of the mobile design features in this chapter are similar to the design features for desktop systems, there are many significant differences.

# Mobile Features of Microsoft® Windows™ 95

Microsoft Windows 95 contains a large number of new features under the umbrella of mobile services. In contrast with the features in some other areas of the product, most of these features have hardware implications. The major mobile features of Windows 95 include:

- Support for hot and warm docking of notebook systems, including messages that are passed to applications running in the system before and after these events occur.
- Support for hot insertion and removal of devices such as PCMCIA cards, including support for dynamic loading and unloading of device drivers, on-the-fly hosting of network services over a newly inserted adapter, and other system support for dynamic events.
- Better support for dialup communications by modem, including a new 32-bit, high-performance communications driver; remote node access to networks (including the Internet) using IPX, TPC, or NetBEUI via the PPP protocol; telephony API (TAPI) support for device-independent access to modems; TAPI arbitration of incoming and outgoing calls allowing multiple communications applications to use the modem simultaneously; Remote Mail support via the Windows 95 messaging API (MAPI); Microsoft at Work™ fax technology for transmitting and receiving faxes and even binary files by using a fax modem on your computer or somewhere on the network; an improved Terminal application that automatically negotiates communications settings for parity and stop bits and includes predefined settings for the most popular online services; support for direct connection of two Windows 95 systems using a null modem cable and the serial or parallel ports.
- Built-in support for advanced power management, version 1.1, including information exposed in the Windows 95 user interface when running on an APM 1.1 computer.
- Flexible video-resolution support that allows a notebook computer running Windows 95 to dynamically change video resolution when it is docked or undocked.

- Support for automatic synchronization of files between a notebook computer and the network when the notebook is reconnected.
- Built-in and improved support for pen-based input.
- An extensible communications architecture designed to accommodate drivers for wireless devices such as infrared (IR) and radio frequency (RF) devices.

By following the hardware design suggestions in this chapter and in Chapter 6, "Plug and Play Cards and Buses," you can create a system that takes maximum advantage of these new mobile features. If your system follows these guidelines, passes the Microsoft Windows 95 Hardware Compatibility Tests, and preinstalls Windows 95, it will deliver a more compelling mobile computing solution than anything available on the market today.

# Requirements vs. Recommendations

For each feature discussed in this chapter, there are two sections: feature requirements and feature recommendations. You must implement the required features in your PC design to qualify to use the Windows 95 Logo. You are not required to implement the recommended features, but you can use them in your PC 95 design to add value to the system.

The recommendations in this chapter are a minimum "step up" from the required features. Far more advanced recommendations could have been made, but they would have been more expensive to implement, and might have gone far beyond the needs of the typical user.

The designer should decide how many enhancements to add to a mobile system. This guide does not intend to limit the types of technology that can be added to a PC 95.

# Required Mobile Features

A mobile system must implement a minimum set of required features to receive the Windows 95 Logo. However, not all of the requirements for this logo are unique for mobile systems. Many of the features required by a mobile system are exactly the same as those for a desktop system.

The following list reflects the required features common to a desktop PC 95 and a mobile PC 95:

- Both systems must contain a Plug and Play system BIOS (version 1.0a or later).
- The motherboard must contain a 386 microprocessor or compatible architecture, minimum.
- Both systems must contain 4 MB of RAM, minimum.
- A mobile system does not require a floppy disk drive. If one is installed, however, it must be compatible, at a minimum, with 3.5-inch, 1.44-MB disks.
- The system display adapter must use a packed-pixel frame buffer with 640 × 480 × 8 bpp, minimum.
- Both systems must have an integrated pointing device or a separate port for connecting a pointing device (such as a mouse).
- Both systems must have at least one parallel port. The parallel port must support IEEE P1284-I mode protocols for compatibility mode and nibble mode. The system must be able to receive the parallel device's identifier in nibble mode.
- Molded-in or permanently printed icon labels must be located on the computer case for built-in ports. If the same icons appear on the cable connectors, icon matching will be easier.
- Any option ROMs must use the Plug and Play header format in the *Plug and Play BIOS Specification.*
- Windows 95–certifiable device drivers for all integrated motherboard devices.

For information about designing these requirements into the mobile system, see the related features for desktop systems in Chapter 3, "The Desktop PC 95."

Some features required for the mobile PC 95 are different from those required for the desktop PC 95. The following list describes these differences:

- Like a desktop system, a mobile system must have at least one serial port built in. The serial port for a mobile system must be 16550A compatible. (On a desktop system, a 16550A-compatible port is not required.)
- On a mobile system, APM 1.1 is required. (APM 1.1 is recommended for a desktop system.)
- Although the built-in display panel on the portable system must be capable of at least VGA-compatible 640 × 480 × 8 bpp, this resolution can be displayed as 64 shades of gray.

# Serial Ports

The communication capabilities of Windows 95 were designed with the 16550A buffered UART in mind. Advanced communications support is critical for a mobile system. Connectivity will be the most important Windows 95 feature for the mobile user. Because a mobile system must connect seamlessly to phone lines (land based and wireless), LANs, and directly attached computers (the user's desktop computer, for example), the serial port is a more important component in a mobile system than it is in a desktop system.

A 16550A or compatible high-speed UART in conjunction with the sophisticated communication capabilities of Windows 95 will cover these needs. Your mobile system must contain a 16550A or compatible UART to receive the Windows 95 Logo. For information about one possible technical design for a 16550A serial port using a super I/O chip, see Chapter 5, "System Devices."

# Power Management

Hardware on a mobile PC 95 must be designed to take advantage of the power management capabilities provided by a system BIOS that contains APM 1.1. For information about the APM 1.1 interface commands, see the *Advanced Power Management (APM) BIOS Interface Specification*, Revision 1.1.

APM 1.1 extends the life of system batteries to increase system availability. The APM 1.1 specification defines a layered software interface for cooperation among applications, operating systems, device drivers, and the APM 1.1 BIOS to jointly reduce power consumption.

APM 1.1 defines five power states for the system:

- Full On.
- APM Enabled. The system power is managed and the CPU clock is allowed to slow or stop as needed. Device power is managed as needed.
- APM Standby. No one appears to be using the system, so its power state and the power state of the devices are lowered. The clock may be stopped. Returning to Full On is quick.
- APM Suspend. No one is using the system, so the power state is lowered for maximum power savings. It takes a bit longer to return to Full On from this state.
- Off.

Likewise, the APM 1.1 specification defines four power states for peripheral devices. In addition to On and Off, APM 1.1 defines device states analogous to Standby and Suspend (called Device Power Managed and Device Low Power). APM 1.1–aware device drivers can manage the power consumption of their corresponding peripherals. They can learn from the system's APM driver when the system will be suspended, for example, and can save device information to be restored when the system resumes.

APM 1.1–aware applications assist in power management by registering with the system when they are not being used. They can respond to APM driver information about impending changes in the system's power state (such as when the system is about to go to standby). They can also modify actions that may con-sume more power when the system is running on the battery. For example, a mail application could download only message headers instead of whole messages, or another application might wait to carrry out a hard disk–intensive activity until AC power is available or until another application must spin the disk to access it..

The APM interface is particularly important for docking systems. APM 1.1 is used to warn the operating system about suspend and resume events on docking stations. When a portable system comes out of a suspend, Windows 95 uses the APM 1.1 notification to reexamine the available hardware, note what has been added or taken away, and reenumerate the hardware tree, identifying and configuring resources to avoid conflicts. Without the APM 1.1 interface, Windows 95 would not know that the system had come out of suspend.

With an APM 1.1 interface, applications may also reject a suspend request to ensure that information stored in buffers is not lost. For example, if an application has an open file, the application may reject the suspend request until the user has decided whether to close the file or not.

In addition to controlling the suspend and resume power management procedures afforded by APM 1.1, the power management hardware must be able to determine the status of the battery and report the status to Windows 95 through the APM 1.1 interface.

For information about designing a system BIOS with APM 1.1 features, and their interaction with Windows 95, see Chapter 8, "System BIOS Design."

# Display Panels

Design requirements for an internal display panel for a mobile system are similar to those for monitors found in a desktop system. The internal display panel must meet the requirements for display monitors described in Chapter 7, "Designing Peripherals." The display adapter in the mobile PC 95 must meet the requirements for display adapters as described in Chapter 5, "System Devices."

One exception to the rules for desktop monitors is that a mobile display panel is required to support only 64 shades of gray. Although many new mobile systems are turning to flat-panel color technologies, less-expensive models are still using black-and-white display panels to lower the overall cost of the PC.

A dockable mobile system should be able to resolve conflicts that may occur between its integrated display components and adapters installed in the docking station. For example, the integrated display adapter should be disabled automatically if one is present and enabled in the docking station.

To enhance support for the mobile system display panel, ensure that integrated display adapters connect to a high-speed local bus, provide hardware acceleration of basic graphics functions, and support high-resolution output to an external monitor port.

# Recommended Mobile Features

Including the requirements covered in the previous sections yields a mobile PC that qualifies for a Windows 95 Logo. If only required features were added, however, all mobile PCs would contain the same features and function as equals. Although some features recommended for a mobile PC 95 are the same as those recommended for a desktop PC 95, others specifically add user-requested capabilities to a mobile system.

The recommended features common to a desktop PC 95 and a mobile PC 95 are:

- Both systems should contain a 486/33 (or compatible) microprocessor, minimum.
- Both systems should contain 8 MB of RAM, minimum.
- If the system has a floppy disk drive, it should be able to detect the insertion of a disk using the write-protect scheme.
- Both systems should use a standard high-speed expansion bus (such as a PCI bus or VL-bus) for high-data-rate devices such as the display, mass storage, and networking.
- The system should contain a software-controlled power supply for soft power-down.
- The hardware should be capable of having its resources reconfigured by the Plug and Play BIOS (as opposed to just being able to report static resources).
- All motherboard devices should use 16-bit decoding for their I/O port addresses. Both static and integrated devices should use 16-bit decoding to make the I/O address range of the motherboard more flexible.
- To enable high-speed, bidirectional communication, the parallel port should support the protocols of the ECP mode documented in the IEEE P1284 specification. Most current super-I/O chips support this.
- A PS/2-style port should be used for external pointing devices, such as an external mouse.
- A SCSI-2 host adapter can be included on the mobile system to gain access to a variety of external storage devices.
- The mobile system should support 22 kHz, 8-bit, mono, output-only sound capability and a speaker (as an absolute minimum), so the baseline operating system can take advantage of the built-in hardware.
- One or more PCMCIA ports can be built in to provide expansion capability.
- Although network adapters are not required, they are highly recommended for the mobile system.

Although many recommended features of the mobile system are the same as those for the desktop system, others are specifically adapted for the mobile system. The following list indicates the order of importance of these features, which progressively add value to the most functional Windows 95 mobile systems. These features include:

- A 14,400 bps modem, minimum, built in or PCMCIA, with error correction and data compression.
- A mobile system associated with a docking station or port replicator should be capable of warm docking and undocking capability, at a minimum. Optionally, it can also be capable of hot docking and undocking.
- A docking station, *port replicator*, or *advanced port replicator* should contain either a VCR-style docking and undocking mechanism, or at least contain a locking mechanism for a docked mobile system, at a minimum.
- An external peripheral should be identifiable and configurable. If the external peripheral overrides an internal device, the internal device should be disabled.
- An expansion card's identity and resources should be made available to the system.
- The portable system's internal display panel should be capable of supporting at least 64 colors.
- A serial IR device should follow the standards in the Infrared Data Association (IrDA) specification.
- Pen pointing devices should be untethered and include a barrel button.

## Modem

A 14,400 bps modem is a key component for communicating with the home office. Most analog phone lines allow data throughput of 1200 to 14,400 bps. A 14,400 bps modem (minimum) included on a mobile system provides an efficient, workable communications solution. A modem with 14,400 bps fax capability is also highly recommended. It allows users to communicate with fax users all over the world; it also allows enhanced point-to-point communication using Microsoft at Work messaging with other Windows 95 users and with Microsoft at Work devices.

In addition to an improved edition of the Terminal application, Windows 95 contains a number of new communications features that take advantage of a good modem. Windows 95 includes the capability to remotely dial into networks using a modem connection, enabling a remote computer to be a node on the network. Windows 95 also contains the ability to send and receive faxes directly from the PC. Windows 95 includes remote mail capabilities so that remote MAPI service providers will enable you to remotely access mail through a dialup connection, rather than requiring a direct network connection.

## Warm or Hot Docking

Warm or hot docking is recommended for the mobile PC 95. One of the major constraints of current cold-docking stations is that whenever the portable PC is docked or undocked, the system must be rebooted, which takes time. With warm- or hot-docking capabilities, the portable system need not be rebooted each time it is docked or undocked, which gives the user instant access to the system.

A docking system as a whole can be rated as capable of cold, warm, or hot docking. *Cold docking* means that the computer must be rebooted before it can dock or undock. Warm docking means that the computer can be docked or undocked while in a reduced power state, such as suspend. Hot docking means that the user can dock or undock with the computer running at full power. The type of docking the system is capable of is determined by the computer hardware, the operating system, and the add-on hardware and its accompanying drivers. Although Windows 95 will support cold docking, the extended docking and undocking features of Windows 95 can be utilized only by a system that supports either warm or hot docking.

To support the added functionality of warm or hot docking, the following components will need to be added to the system:

- Plug and Play BIOS. Windows 95 cannot support warm or hot docking on a PC without a Plug and Play BIOS.
- Advanced power management (APM) 1.1.
- The system must be electrically able to switch between AC power and battery power on the fly. This should not be difficult to accomplish, because most portable systems currently have this capability.
- The system must be capable of recognizing when a docking or undocking event has occurred so it can redirect its input and output signals to adjust to the new docking state.

For more information about Plug and Play system BIOS design for warm and hot docking and APM 1.1, see Chapter 8, “System BIOS Design.”

# VCR-Style or Locking Mechanism

A mobile system that connects to a docking station can be ejected using two different methods. One method will not allow the operating system or the system BIOS to override the ejection. The other will allow the operating system or the system BIOS to override the ejection.

A *surprise-style ejection mechanism* is a simple mechanical button that physically disconnects the portable system from the dock without any previous warning to the operating system or BIOS. This mechanism does not allow the operating system or system BIOS to override the operation, even if files will be lost or if devices will be arbitrarily disconnected. A surprise-style ejection mechanism is not recommended for any new docking systems.

A *VCR-style ejection mechanism* and a *locking-style ejection mechanism* provide a fail-safe (locking) system for docking and undocking. The eject button signals the user's intent to the BIOS, which consults Windows 95, which in turn consults various hardware and software components of the system. Programs have a chance to save and close files they had open over the network, and potentially even to veto the undocking event. Only when everyone approves the undocking event is the computer actually ejected.

A VCR-style or locking-style mechanism is also useful during docking because the docking station may reject a portable system that the user has attempted to insert while it was in the wrong power state.

The only difference between a VCR-style mechanism and a locking-style mechanism is the mechanical design. A VCR-style system consists of a fully motorized locking and unlocking mechanism in which the portable system is automatically ejected or inserted by the mechanism itself. A locking-style system consists of a locking mechanism similar to the VCR-style system, but the portable system must be manually removed and inserted into the docking station.

Providing a VCR-style or locking-style interface:

- Prevents the user from docking or undocking in the wrong power state.
- Gives applications, device drivers, and Windows 95 the opportunity to warn the user when resources currently in use are in danger of being lost.
- Allows the user to initiate the ejection process in software, through the Eject Computer system menu item in Windows 95.
- Allows the BIOS to reject actions such as warm undocking without a battery pack.

The Plug and Play system BIOS provides a method of two-way communication with the ejection mechanism of a VCR-style or locking-style system using the system BIOS Function 5, Get Docking Station Information. The operating system first confirms button-initiated ejections, and the Plug and Play BIOS provides an interface for software-initiated ejections.

To implement a VCR-style or locking-style docking and undocking mechanism, consider the following system design changes:

- When a user inserts a portable system into a VCR-style docking station, there should be a mechanism that grabs the portable system, pulls it all the way into the docking station, and locks it in, or rejects the docking action and ejects the portable system. (Although a motorized VCR mechanism is probably the most desirable for user experience, cost limitations may prevent this design. In this case, you should implement a locking-style mechanism. The key is a locking mechanism that prevents "surprise" undocking and docking.)
- The docking system must have a Plug and Play BIOS. If the docking system does not have a Plug and Play BIOS, the operating system cannot be warned about an impending undocking event, nor can it initiate undocking events at the user's request.
- When the user pushes the eject button on the docking station, the Plug and Play BIOS must broadcast the ABOUT_TO_CHANGE_CONFIG message and wait for approval before suspending and ejecting the portable system. If the portable system was suspended when the button was pressed, it must be resumed so the operating system can be warned.
- If the Plug and Play BIOS gets an UNDOCK message, it should behave exactly as if the user had pressed the eject button on the docking station.
- If a fully powered system is inserted into a docking station, it needs to be suspended before docking. If the suspend fails, the portable system should be ejected.
- The system should never send an ABOUT_TO_CHANGE_CONFIG message when the portable system is about to dock. Windows 95 relies on the APM 1.1 suspend notification interface to cancel an unsafe docking event. The system should not send the message because any application receiving it could display a dialog box to wait for user interaction, but at this point in the docking process nothing on the display may be visible.

For more information about Plug and Play system BIOS design for VCR-style mechanisms, see Chapter 8, "System BIOS Design."

# External Peripherals

Flexible peripheral resources allow the Windows 95 configuration manager to reassign resources. This ensures that peripherals and devices do not conflict. External peripherals that attach through a standard port (such as a serial or parallel port) should be able to identify themselves using the methods described for that particular port. For example, if a printer is connected to the mobile system's parallel port, the printer should be able to identify itself using the techniques described for nibble mode in the IEEE P1284 specification (as described in Chapter 7, "Designing Peripherals").

Peripherals that connect to the mobile PC 95 should also be capable of power management. For information about power management recommendations for peripherals, see Chapter 7, "Designing Peripherals."

When external peripherals are connected to the mobile system, the system should be capable of disabling any internal peripherals that may conflict with the external peripherals (or at least allow them to operate simultaneously without conflict). Flexible peripheral resources give the configuration manager in Windows 95 the maximum ability to reassign resources and ensure that peripherals and devices do not conflict. Freeing these resources by disabling the internal peripheral will give Windows 95 the maximum flexibility to ensure that all devices on the system continue to work correctly. If the internal peripheral cannot be disabled and conflicts irreconcilably with the new peripheral, you may not be able to operate the new peripheral.

The ability to identify the capabilities of the internal display panel and the external monitor allows the operating system to run applications at the maximum resolution of the display. In the case of a portable system that allows a higher-resolution external monitor to take over the display, the identity of the monitor gives the operating system and drivers the ability to configure the display adapter to display the highest resolution possible for that monitor or display panel.

# Expansion Cards

Expansion cards that connect to a mobile PC 95 through a standard bus should incorporate the same recommendations for these devices that are documented in Chapter 3, "The Desktop PC 95." These recommendations primarily give the configuration manager in Windows 95 flexible resource allocation options. These options ensure a working configuration for all devices and peripherals on the system when new expansion cards are inserted into the system.

If a mobile system uses a proprietary interface to add devices to the system, the system BIOS must identify the device, report its resources to the operating system, and configure those resources.

# Display Panel

The internal display panel for a portable system should be capable of displaying 64 colors (with an 8-bpp palette). Although the required resolution for the internal monitor is 640 × 480 × 8 bpp, higher resolutions and color depths are recommended (as they become available). No particular style of display panel is recommended over another (active matrix, passive matrix, or other future developments). There is a tradeoff between brightness, higher resolutions, and battery life. However, the higher the resolution and color depth the display panel will support, the more flexible Windows 95 will be, and the better it will look to users.

# Infrared Ports

Hassle-free point-and-shoot connectivity could be a very attractive feature for the mobile user. Infrared (IR) is a promising direct-connection mechanism between a mobile system and other systems or printers. IR ports can allow file and data synchronization between desktop and mobile computers.

The Windows 95 retail package will not include specific IR drivers because no IR hardware exists in end users' systems at the time that Windows 95 is being developed. However, the Windows 95 VCOMM driver architecture and serial network access technology and protocols are designed with IR-style links in mind. It should not be difficult to create and preinstall IR drivers on new systems with this capability.

For more general information about IR technology, contact the Infrared Data Association (IrDA), an organization that defines infrared standards. For more information about how to contact the IrDA, see Appendix D, "References."

# Pen

For mobile users, a pen is often more convenient to use than is a mouse or similar pointing device. A pen is especially useful with handheld computers. Windows 95 contains support for pen input in the form of an improved release of the Pen Extensions for Windows.

The pen is used for pointing, drawing, and inputting. A pen can also issue commands when it is pointed or tapped on visual controls or used to draw gestures.

## Pen Hardware Designs for Mobile PCs

To design hardware systems that provide full-featured pen support, consider including the following components:

- An etched-surface display monitor, to give the feeling of writing on paper (not glass) when the user draws the pen across the surface.
- A pen that is weighted and shaped similarly to a regular ink pen. The pen should include a tappable tip (the equivalent of the left mouse-button click) and a barrel button (the equivalent of the right mouse-button click).
- The total weight of the system should be minimal. By nature, notebook systems will be used most often in the field and ideally should be no larger in size and weight than a pad of paper.
- Since most notebook systems will be used away from AC power, the battery must be long-lived. For more information about this issue, see the power management section earlier in this chapter.

### Barrel Button

Pen- or tablet-based computers should contain a pen equipped with a barrel button equivalent of the right mouse button. The right mouse button in Windows 95 is designed to be a very helpful shortcut for power users.

Position the button on the pen in such a way that it will not be used accidentally. Usability testing has shown that accidental activation is confusing for the average or novice user, and is annoying for the power user who wants deliberate access to this functionality. Note that the pen button is the only functional counterpart of the right mouse button on a Windows 95–based pen-only system. If the pen is not equipped with a button, the user will not have this functionality.

# Certification for the Windows 95 Logo

Mobile systems that qualify for the Windows 95 Logo are designed to help users recognize Plug and Play PCs and ensure compatibility between their hardware and software. Microsoft will help OEMs communicate this message through the Windows 95 Logo by defining a minimum feature set for a mobile PC that reflects these user needs. For more information about this logo, see Chapter 3, "The Desktop PC 95."

# Mobile PC 95 Feature Set

A basic mobile PC must include a minimum set of features to qualify for the Windows 95 Logo. These system features are described in Table 4.1, for the basic mobile PC system configuration, Table 4.2, for Plug and Play capabilities, and Table 4.3, for overall system features.

In addition to the required features, a variety of more advanced hardware can be included in the PC to improve the user's experience with the PC. These recommended additional features and functionality tie together the hardware features supported by Windows 95.

For a more complete explanation of each of these features, see the appropriate sections in this chapter that describe these features.

**Table 4.1 Basic Mobile PC System Configuration**

| Feature | Logo requirement | Recommendation |
|---|---|---|
| CPU | 386 architecture | 486/33, minimum |
| RAM | 4 MB | 8 MB |
| Floppy disk drive, if present | Optional | 3.5", 1.44 MB |
| High-speed expansion bus (PCI or VL-bus) | No | Yes |
| Soft power-down | No | Yes |
| Connector icons | Yes | Yes |

**Table 4.2 Mobile PC System Plug and Play Capabilities**

| Feature | Logo requirement | Recommendation |
|---|---|---|
| Plug and Play BIOS 1.0a | Yes | Yes |
| Read back all resources | Yes | Yes |
| Soft-set all resources | No | Yes |
| 16-bit I/O decode (ISA bus) | No | Yes |
| Hot/warm docking | No | Yes |
| Locking or VCR dock/port replicator | No | Yes |

**Table 4.3 Mobile PC System Features**

| Feature | Logo requirement | Recommendation |
|---|---|---|
| Display adapter | VGA 640 × 480 × 8 bpp | VGA 640 × 480 × 8 bpp |
| Display monitor | 64-gray scale OK | 64 color |
| Parallel port | Standard (nibble mode) | ECP (P1284-I) |
| Serial ports | One (16550A compatible) | One 16550A |
| Pointing device | Yes | PS/2-style port |
| Integrated or separate port | Yes | Yes |
| Pen devices including barrel button | No | Yes |
| APM 1.1 | Yes | Yes |
| Option ROMs use PnP header format | Yes | Yes |
| SCSI-2 host adapter | No | Yes |
| Audio | No | 22 kHz, mono, output |
| Serial infrared devices | No | Follow IrDA specification |
| Network adapter | No | Optional |
| All devices/cards MCL certified | No | Yes |
| Motherboard device drivers | Windows 95 certifiable | Yes |

# Mobile PC 95 Hardware Compatibility Tests

The Windows 95 Hardware Compatibility Tests (HCT) verify the compatibility between the system hardware and Windows 95. The Hardware Compatibility Tests launch tests, keep track of test results, and provide an on-screen problem report form to communicate test results to the Microsoft HCT organization.

For information about obtaining the HCT, and about the system requirements for running the HCT, see Chapter 3, "The Desktop PC 95."

CHAPTER 5

# System Devices

This chapter discusses the many types of devices that can be designed for a Personal Computer for Microsoft® Windows™ 95 system, and covers the device requirements in detail, explaining how each relates to the system. This chapter also includes a set of recommendations for each type of device. As the device designer, you can use the recommended design criteria to optimize your devices for Windows 95 and Windows 95–applications.

Device designs discussed in this chapter can be used either on the motherboard or on a number of different types of expansion cards. In many cases, if you add the device to the motherboard, you may enable significant improvements in throughput, depending on the design. You, the device designer, should determine which devices to place on the motherboard and which to place on an expansion card.

# Requirements vs. Recommendations

For each device discussed in this chapter, there are two sections: device requirements and device recommendations. Requirements outline the features and functions required for a specific device to qualify for the Windows 95 Logo. Recommendations include additional features and functions that improve Windows 95 performance.

The recommendations in this chapter are a minimum "step up" from the required features. Far more advanced recommendations could have been made, but they would have been more expensive to implement and might have gone beyond the needs of the typical user.

You should determine how many enhancements to add to your devices. This guide does not intend to limit the technology that can be included in a PC 95.

# General Device Requirements

If a device on the motherboard of a PC 95 does not implement a bus-specific Plug and Play enumeration and configuration scheme, it must supply enough information so the Plug and Play system BIOS can, at a minimum, identify the device and its resources. To increase Plug and Play functionality, design the device with a variety of resource selections that can be configured in the event of conflict. The device must also be capable of being disabled if there is an irreconcilable conflict.

If a device is located on an expansion card, the card must support Plug and Play identification and configuration rules for the bus to which it is connected in order to qualify for the Designed for Windows 95 Logo for that device. For example, if you design a parallel port expansion card that plugs into an ISA card slot, the card must conform to the Plug and Play identification and configuration rules outlined in the *Plug and Play ISA Specification*. For information about the requirements for Plug and Play buses, see Chapter 6, "Plug and Play Cards and Buses."

For all devices on ISA expansion cards that require an option ROM to initialize, ensure that the option ROM meets all of the requirements documented in the *Plug and Play BIOS Specification*. These requirements include a means for a Plug and Play system BIOS to identify the Plug and Play capabilities of the option ROM, and enable the option ROM to determine whether the system BIOS is compatible with Plug and Play.

An expansion card with multiple devices must uniquely identify each device and its resources according to the specifications of the bus to which the card connects. For example, each device connected to a Plug and Play ISA bus must contain its own unique logical device tag. Each device connected to a PCI bus must have its own unique device identifier/vendor identifier. For information about this and other requirements for device identifiers, see Chapter 6, "Plug and Play Cards and Buses."

# Display Adapter

The display adapter on a PC 95 must meet a certain number of requirements to take advantage of the Windows 95 graphics display driver architecture.

## Display Adapter Requirements

The display adapter must meet the following requirements, at a minimum:

- The display adapter must support the VGA graphics standard for application compatibility and for the Windows 95 clean-boot error-recovery process.
- All non–VGA standard display resources (also known as extended resources, such as register sets and so on) must provide at least one alternate configuration in the event of conflict during initial program load (IPL) boot. The VGA BIOS and software drivers must be able to use alternate configuration register addresses.
- A memory-mapped packed-pixel frame buffer with 8 bpp, minimum, must be used.
- The adapter must support a 640 × 480 × 8-bpp display driver, at a minimum. Desktop systems must be able to display 256 colors, minimum. Mobile systems should support an 8-bpp driver and map colors into a 64-gray scale display, minimum.
- The adapter must support the VESA ergonomic timings.
- On an ISA Plug and Play display adapter expansion card used as a system boot device, the display adapter circuitry should come up active when power is turned on or the system is reset.
- The adapter must be able to be disabled if a conflicting VGA expansion card is added to the system.

## Extended Resources

Extended resources are additional I/O ports, direct-access frame buffers, or data transfer areas on a display adapter that use more resources than does a standard VGA. Most advanced display adapters, such as SVGA adapters, use extended resources. The configuration manager must be able to map the resources to avoid conflicts with other system devices in a Plug and Play environment. The Plug and Play system BIOS or a bus-specific resource allocation technique can perform this mapping.

Extended resources need not be relocatable if they use aliases of the standard VGA I/O addresses. The system BIOS can then lock these aliases as static resources. If aliases of the standard VGA I/O addresses are not used, the I/O addresses must be mappable to at least one other location.

Using memory mapping instead of I/O mapping for extended resources offers performance benefits in many implementations.

## Packed-Pixel Frame Buffer

Windows 95 is optimized for a display adapter with a packed-pixel frame buffer (at all resolutions supported by Windows 95). A packed-pixel frame buffer supports DCI, which Video for Windows, WinG, and other systems-level software use to improve performance of fast-motion video in Windows 95. For example, using a packed-pixel frame buffer, Video for Windows can transfer video frames directly to an adapter's frame buffer, increasing the speed at which images are displayed on the monitor.

Memory-mapped packed-pixel frame buffers also provide a fast and simple interface between Windows 95 and the display adapter. Windows 95 contains a new graphics component known as the DIB engine. The DIB engine provides a very fast display by writing directly to packed-pixel frame buffers. Because you must write only a small, simple minidriver to use the DIB engine, only minimal development time is needed to create fast, stable device drivers for a new display.

For optimized support with Windows 95, a linear packed-pixel frame buffer is recommended over a bank-switched frame buffer.

## Monitor Resolution Support

Monitor resolution should be 640 × 480 × 8 bpp, at a minimum, because this resolution is the most common for current portable system displays. Although the Windows 95 DIB engine supports 1 bpp, 4 bpp, 8 bpp, 15 bpp (5,5,5), 16 bpp (5,6,5), 24 bpp, and 32 bpp, a PC 95 must contain a display adapter that permits a color depth of 8 bpp, minimum.

## Ergonomic Timings

The display adapter must, at a minimum, support the ergonomic timings documented in the VESA specification titled *Monitor Timing Standards for 640 x 480, 800 x 600, 1024 x 768, and 1280 x 1024 at 75Hz* for all resolutions supported by the monitor. A display adapter that supports these timings provides a flicker-free, crisp-appearing image on the monitor.

Although this standard documents monitor timings at 75 Hz, higher scan rates are preferable. They should also meet standards published by VESA.

## Active ISA Display Adapters

A display adapter is one of the boot devices on a PC, and, as such, must be active when power is turned on or the system is reset. This allows the system BIOS to identify the adapter and reconfigure its resources, if necessary, before the adapter is initialized. In general, most expansion buses on the PC provide a means for activating a display adapter as an output device during the boot process.

The Plug and Play ISA specification requires most ISA expansion cards to power up inactive, allowing the system to isolate and identify the card before configuring its resources. Boot devices on ISA expansion cards are an exception. As a boot device, a display adapter on an ISA expansion card must come up active. For more information about Plug and Play ISA boot devices, see Chapter 6, "Plug and Play Cards and Buses."

## Resolving Conflicts

The system BIOS must have some means of automatically disabling or relocating the resources of a display adapter on the system motherboard if a display adapter expansion card is added to the system. With this capability, updating a display adapter on the system motherboard with a new, higher-resolution expansion card does not require changing jumpers or switches on either.

In the event of irreconcilable conflict with other devices on the system, the BIOS should disable the display adapter. This prevents the system from "hanging."

# Display Adapter Recommendations

The following set of features are recommended to enhance the capabilities of the display adapter on a PC 95:

- The standard VGA page frame and I/O address resources can be static (that is, not relocatable). The VGA BIOS, if it exists separately, should have its base address fixed at C000h.
- A linear frame buffer should be used and should be relocatable using software above the 16-MB boundary (where applicable).
- The adapter BIOS should meet the DDC1 host requirements documented in the VESA *Display Data Channel* standard.
- The display adapter option ROM or virtual display driver (VDD) should support the VESA BIOS extensions for power management (*VESA BIOS Extensions/Power Management Standard*).
- Color ordering should be BGR, with R as the high byte in 16-bpp and 24-bpp displays, to take advantage of the current Windows 95 graphics architecture capabilities.
- The VGA BIOS, if it exists separately, should be configurable to two addresses, at a minimum.
- Any 24-bit and higher displays should support downloadable *random access memory digital-to-analog converter* (RAMDAC) entries to perform gamma correction in hardware.
- The adapter should be connected to a high-speed expansion bus, such as a PCI bus or VL-bus.
- The adapter should be capable of supporting a monitor resolution of 1024 × 768 × 8 bpp. Optionally, it can support higher standard resolutions.
- If interrupt request 2 (IRQ2) is supported for VGA compatibility, it should be inactive when the system is powered up, and the system should not claim it as a static resource.
- If extended display resources are used, the adapter should be able to map the I/O addresses to seven locations and disable (minimum), unless the extended resource addresses are aliases of the standard VGA addresses.

## VGA Resources

Standard VGA page frame and I/O address resources should not be relocated. Instead, the resources can be reserved as static. They include the 0A000h page frame window into the frame buffer, the I/O ports at 3B0h through 3DCh, and, if a VGA BIOS is used, its base address of C000h.

## Linear Frame Buffer

The new protected-mode DIB engine in Windows 95 is optimized for systems using a high-speed expansion bus and packed-pixel, 32-bit, addressable linear frame buffers. The DIB engine, which contains fast assembly-language display code, requires the use of a packed-pixel frame buffer and runs even faster on linear packed-pixel frame buffers. The recommendation to use 32-bit addresses allows the linear frame buffer to be placed above the 16-MB ISA boundary, which enables a system to be populated with large amounts of RAM. A linear frame buffer is also important for the new DCI enhancements, which boost performance of full-motion video for multimedia applications and games. Pay special attention to video memory speed, because this is becoming the major bottleneck for graphics performance on high-speed expansion buses. Hardware acceleration should include bit-block transfer (BLT) engines for common raster operations, screen-to-screen copy, hardware cursor, and monochrome-to-color expansion.

Mapping of the frame buffer depends on the type of bus to which the adapter is connected. On non–ISA-based VGA adapters, the frame buffer should be mappable above the 16-MB boundary of the ISA bus. On an ISA system, if the system has a full 16 MB of RAM, the frame buffer is automatically accessed through the page frame address at 0A000h. If memory or other resources conflict with the frame buffer being mapped into a linear address space, the page frame address can be used with minimal degradation of performance.

## Display Data Channel Support

Display adapters should be designed to meet the requirements listed in the VESA *Display Data Channel* standard. This standard describes the mechanical and electrical specifications for a monitor and display adapter capable of communicating the monitor's identification and capabilities to the PC. If, for example, the system determines from the identification string it has retrieved from the monitor that the monitor is capable of 1024 × 786 × 256 color, it can automatically configure the display adapter to its highest resolution without intervention from the user. If another monitor with different capabilities is attached later, the system can configure that display adapter appropriately, as well, again without user intervention.

A display adapter on the PC 95 should meet the requirements for a DDC1 host, as described in the VESA standard. As a DDC1 host, the display adapter can only receive information from the monitor in Extended Display Identification (EDID) format.

A monitor connected to a PC 95 communicates to the display adapter through a VGA cable in which some of the connector pins have been redefined. The format of this cable is described in the VESA standard. Table 5.1 describes the pins on a DDC-compatible display adapter connector. Figure 5.1 shows the layout of the display adapter connector.

**Table 5.1 DDC1 Display Adapter Connector**

| Pin number | DDC1 display adapter connector |
|---|---|
| 1 | Red video |
| 2 | Green video |
| 3 | Blue video |
| 4 | Monitor ID bit 2 |
| 5 | DDC return (for pins 9, 12, and 15) |
| 6 | Red video return |
| 7 | Green video return |
| 8 | Blue video return |
| 9 | +5V supply (optional) |
| 10 | Sync return |
| 11 | Monitor ID bit 0 |
| 12 | Data from display |
| 13 | Horizontal sync |
| 14 | Vertical sync (VCLK) |
| 15 | Monitor ID bit 3 |

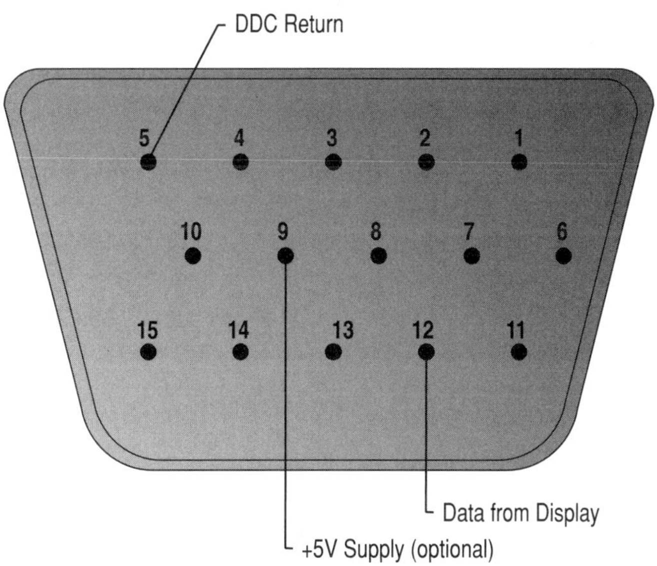


**Figure 5.1 DDC1 Display Adapter Connector Lines**

The VGA connector lines should be changed to comply with the VESA standard. For example, a DDC1 display adapter must provide a 15K ohm pull-up resistor on the Data from Display (Pin 12) line. (If the display adapter is DDC2 compatible, pin 15 also requires a 15K ohm pull-up resistor.) The display adapter should also supply +5V to the monitor through the optional +5V pin on the VGA adapter. This power enables the monitor circuit to inform the display adapter that power to the monitor is off. (When the monitor is turned on, the +5V from the display adapter is not needed.)

A DDC-compatible monitor begins sending EDID data to the system through pin 12 (bidirectional data) when the monitor is turned on, and it receives the first vertical sync (VCLK) signal from the display adapter. The monitor continues sending the EDID data until it is either turned off or receives a high-to-low transition on pin 15. A high-to-low transition indicates that the display adapter is DDC2 compatible, at which point the monitor goes into an idle state and waits for commands from the PC. On a DDC2 adapter, pin 15 is defined as the data clock line. For more information, see the VESA *Display Data Channel* standard.

## Power Management Option ROM Extensions

To provide applications with the ability to control the power state of a flat-panel or DPMS-compliant monitor, the display adapter option ROM or VDD should contain the VESA BIOS extensions for power management. For information about these extensions, see the *VESA BIOS Extensions/Power Management (VBE/PM) Standard.*

## Color Ordering

Display adapters that support packed-pixel frame buffers at color depths greater than 8 bpp should support the pixel orderings shown in Table 5.2. Color ordering in the table is shown from the most-significant bit (MSB) to the least-significant bit (LSB).

**Table 5.2 Color Ordering**

| Color depth | MSB LSB |
|---|---|
| 15 bpp | 1 undefined, 5 red, 5 green, 5 blue<br>(URRR RRGG GGGB BBBB) |
| 16 bpp | 5 red, 6 green, 5 blue<br>(RRR RRGGG GGGB BBBB) |
| 24 bpp | 8 red, 8 green, 8 blue<br>(RRRR RRRR GGGG GGGG BBBB BBBB) |
| 32 bpp | 8 undefined, 8 red, 8 green, 8 blue<br>(UUUU UUUU RRRR RRRR GGGG GGGG BBBB BBBB) |

Software drivers should be provided for these orderings because the first release of the Windows 95 DIB engine directly supports these modes.

## VGA BIOS

If a VGA BIOS exists on the display adapter, it should be able to configure its base address to C000h and one alternate address (minimum) to prevent conflicts.

## Downloadable RAMDAC Entries

Downloadable RAMDAC entries should be included to perform gamma correction in hardware. This recommendation applies only to display adapters that support 24-bit or higher displays.

## High-Speed Expansion Bus

The display adapter should be connected to a high-speed expansion bus to optimize performance of the packed-pixel frame buffer.

## Monitor Resolution Support

The display adapter should support monitor resolutions of $1024 \times 768 \times 8$ bpp, minimum. With these higher resolutions, a larger desktop area can be displayed, more applications can be shown on the display at once, individual windows can be larger, applications can be fully displayed side by side, and so on.

## Interrupt Request Support

---

**Note** Whenever IRQ2(9) is mentioned in this guide, it refers to the IRQ signal logically mapped to IRQ2 on the ISA bus (for historical reasons). From a hardware designer's point of view, however, IRQ9 refers to pin 19 of the slave 8259 PIC.

---

Some VGA-compatible adapters support ISA IRQ2 (PIC interrupt 9) as the hardware interrupt for vertical refresh, usually by means of a jumper on the display adapter. This interrupt, which can be used to synchronize updates to VGA registers during vertical refresh, exists mainly for compatibility with older, EGA-style adapters and is used by few modern display adapters. Windows 95 does not use it. Therefore, if IRQ2(9) capability is included on your display adapter (unless you use it during the card initialization), it should come up inactive when power is turned on and should not actively drive the bus. The adapter should also not claim IRQ2(9) when enumerating device resources to the Plug and Play system.

The Windows 95 resource arbitrator assigns devices to all other IRQs before using IRQ2(9), so it will most likely remain unused. Another device, however, can use the IRQ if it needs to.

### Mapping of Base I/O Addresses

If only standard VGA resources are used, the display adapter need not be mapped to seven I/O addresses and disable (minimum), because the display adapter I/O addresses can be reported as static. If extended resources are used on the display adapter, aliases of the standard VGA I/O addresses can be used and reported as static. As a shortcut, a display adapter could report its standard resources and declare itself to use 10-bit decodes, which will automatically grant it all the aliases. However, if aliases are not used for the extended resources, seven I/O address locations and disable (minimum) should be used, to prevent conflict with other devices on the system.

# Parallel (Printer) Port

Parallel ports are one of the most effective ways of moving data from the system to a variety of peripherals, primarily printers. Currently, the most common type of parallel port uses the Centronics interface.

To enhance the capabilities of the standard Centronics-style interface, improved parallel port protocols and device identification of peripherals have been defined. In most instances, these improvements should require few or no changes to the existing hardware.

## Parallel Port Requirements

A parallel port on a PC 95 must meet the following requirements, at a minimum:

- Support of the compatibility and nibble mode protocols described in the IEEE P1284 specification. Nibble mode is used to read the device identifier string from the peripheral for the initial enumeration of all devices.
- Mapping of the base I/O address to 378h and 278h, at a minimum. The port should also be capable of mapping the base I/O address to 3BCh; however, some *Enhanced Parallel Port* (EPP) implementations do not allow this, so a vendor-selected address can be substituted.
- Support of IRQ5 and IRQ7, at a minimum.
- Selection of two available DMA channels (minimum), if DMA is supported.
- Capability of being disabled in the event of conflict.

## Mode Support

Support for a parallel port must include the compatibility mode and nibble mode protocols described in the IEEE P1284 specification, *Standard Signaling Method for a Bi-directional Parallel Peripheral Interface for Personal Computer.* In most instances, a PC should need no new hardware to support these two modes.

Compatibility mode and nibble mode supply minimum support for Plug and Play peripherals as well as support for existing non–Plug and Play peripherals. Compatibility mode provides a byte-wide channel from the PC to the peripheral. This mode is backward compatible with the existing set of parallel peripherals that are not Plug and Play compatible. Nibble mode provides a channel from the peripheral to the host in which data is sent as 4-bit nibbles using four of the port's status lines. Together, these modes provide two-way communication between the host and the peripheral.

What is important to a PC 95 is that these modes give a peripheral attached to the parallel port a means to identify itself to the system using a device identifier. The device identifier resides in the peripheral and is sent to the PC using the parallel port's nibble mode. Windows 95 uses this device identifier to identify the peripheral and configure the system, and then uses the information to automatically load the proper device drivers for the peripheral.

A device driver must support the parallel port mode protocols. In most instances, the parallel port device driver shipped with Windows 95 will be sufficient to enumerate the port and the peripherals attached to the port. For information about designing alternate device drivers for the parallel port, see the *Microsoft Windows 95 Device Driver Reference*, supplied with the Windows 95 DDK.

## Mapping of Base I/O Addresses

A parallel port must be capable of mapping the base I/O address to 378h and 278h, at a minimum. Using these addresses ensures the proper functioning of software written for non–Plug and Play systems that address these locations directly (instead of using BIOS routines).

A parallel port should also be capable of mapping the base I/O address to 3BCh. However, some EPP parallel port implementations require eight contiguous I/O ports. Because VGA devices use I/O port 3C0h, an EPP parallel port cannot use 3BCh as a base I/O address. For this reason, a vendor-selected base I/O address can be used instead of 3BCh. The system BIOS must report the parallel port base I/O addresses in the BIOS data area (BDA).

The mapping of specific LPT I/O addresses to the device designations LPT1, LPT2, and LPT3 is controlled by the device ordering in the BDA. The BDA is located at address 40:0h. Windows 95 considers the parallel port base I/O address stored in the first BDA location to be LPT1. The base address stored in the second location is LPT2, and so on. Therefore, the system BIOS itself controls the mapping of LPT*x* to specific base I/O addresses for the first three parallel ports in the system. For more information, see Chapter 8, "System BIOS Design."

### Interrupt Request Support

The required set of IRQ signals for the parallel port are IRQ5 and IRQ7. Use of IRQ5 and IRQ7 ensures the proper functioning of software written for non–Plug and Play systems that use standard IRQ signals.

### DMA Support

If a parallel port design supports block data transfers to memory using the DMA controllers, the port must be capable of supporting at least two DMA channels. For information about DMA as a general resource requirement, see Chapter 3, "The Desktop PC 95."

Note that the DMA function will not work on a parallel port without an IRQ, because the end of a DMA transfer is signaled by an interrupt.

### Resolving Conflicts

In the event of irreconcilable conflict with other parallel ports on the system, the parallel port must be capable of being disabled by Plug and Play software to allow at least one of two conflicting parallel ports to operate correctly.

## Parallel Port Recommendations

A PC 95 should meet the needs of high-speed bidirectional parallel devices currently being designed. To meet these needs, Windows 95 supports parallel port hardware that conforms to the IEEE P1284 specification and includes enhancements to the standard requirements that provide hardware and software compatibility for a wider range of peripherals.

The following features are recommended to help increase the capabilities of the parallel port:

- Compliance with IEEE P1284-I.
- Support for ECP mode. EPP and byte mode can also be included.
- Ability to map the base I/O address to four locations other than the three required base I/O addresses, minimum.
- Support of five IRQ signals other than the two required IRQ signals, minimum.

## Compliance with the IEEE P1284 Specification

The parallel port of a PC 95 should comply with the IEEE P1284-I standard, at a minimum. An IEEE-P1284–compliant parallel port allows both P1284-compliant and P1284-compatible devices to be attached without problems. The P1284-compliance recommendation ensures that both P1284-compliant and P1284-compatible peripherals will operate correctly with the port.

The IEEE P1284 specification defines two different levels of compliance: 1284-I and 1284-II. These levels implement the compatibility and nibble modes as specified in IEEE P1284. A PC 95 should also implement the ECP mode, although this feature is optional for a P1284-compliant port. An IEEE P1284-compliant port should also support peripherals that conform to the older Centronics standard.

The two levels of compliance differ in mechanical and electrical specifications. P1284-I–compliant ports use a standard DB25 connector found on existing system parallel port designs, called a P1284-A connector in the specification. (P1284-I–compliant peripherals use the standard 36-pin 0.085 centerline connector found on existing peripherals, called a P1284-B connector in the specification.) P1284-II–compliant ports use a new 36-pin 0.050 centerline connector, called a P1284-C connector. This connector is used on both the port and the peripheral device. Figure 5.2 shows the P1284-I– and P1284-II–compliant connectors used on the parallel port. The parallel port design should provide enough space between the connectors and the surrounding enclosure to allow for a mating connector, the connector shell, and the latch assembly. The IEEE P1284 specification recommends a 1284-C connector for all new ports and devices.

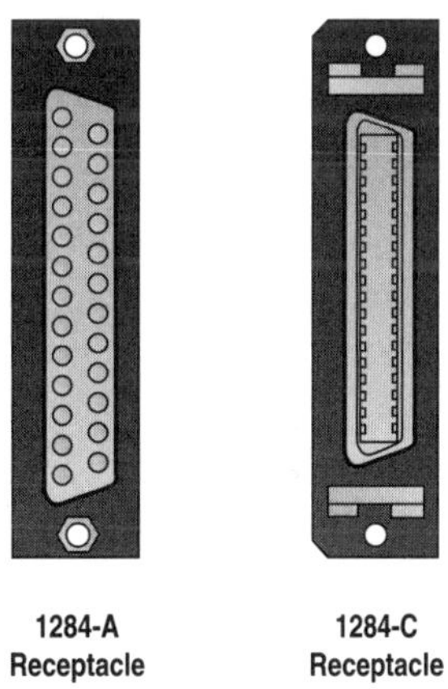


**Figure 5.2 P1284-I– and P1284-II–Compliant Connectors**

## Mode Support

The parallel port should provide support for the ECP mode. EPP and byte mode are optional.

Windows 95 includes built-in driver support for ECP mode. ECP mode offers the following advantages over existing parallel port standards:

- High-performance, half-duplex forward and reverse channel
- Interlocked handshake for fast, reliable transfer
- Optional single-byte run-length encoding (RLE) compression for improved throughput (64:1)
- Channel addressing for low-cost peripherals
- Maintains link and data layer separation
- Permits use of active output drivers
- Permits use of adaptive signal timing
- Peer-to-peer capability

You can include EPP mode to enable communication primarily with the Xircom™-style network adapters.

Byte mode provides basic bidirectional capabilities.

## Additional Base I/O Addresses

To provide additional Plug and Play functionality, the parallel port should map the base I/O address to four locations other than 3BCh (or the vendor-selected address), 378h, and 278h, at a minimum. The parallel port hardware should also allow the base I/O address to be disabled. For information about this general resource recommendation, see Chapter 3, "The Desktop PC 95."

## Additional Interrupt Request Support

The parallel port should provide interrupt request support to five IRQ signals other than IRQ5 and IRQ7, at a minimum. For example, the set of additional IRQ signals for a parallel port located on an ISA expansion card could be IRQ2(9), IRQ10, IRQ11, IRQ12, and IRQ15. The parallel port hardware should also allow interrupt requests to be disabled independently.

System expansion buses other than the ISA bus may not support enough IRQ signals to meet these recommendations. For information about mapping IRQ signals, and other general resource recommendations for various system buses, see Chapter 3, "The Desktop PC 95."

# Additional Parallel Port Information

For information about design of parallel peripherals, see Chapter 7, "Designing Peripherals." For information about cable design for the IEEE P1284 port, see Chapter 3, "The Desktop PC 95."

# High-Speed Serial Ports and Internal Modems

Serial ports have been used on computers for decades. In the past, standard baud rates for most serial ports ranged up to 19.2K baud. Now that systems and peripherals have become more demanding, higher-speed devices must be used to meet the needs of the newest generation of serial ports.

Most of the information in this section also pertains to internal modem adapters that are contained on the motherboard, or are supplied as an expansion card for ISA and PCMCIA buses.

## Serial Port Requirements

A serial port on a PC 95 must meet the following requirements:

- Support of baud rates up to 115.2K baud
- Mapping of the base I/O address to 3F8h, 2F8h, 3E8h, and 2E8h, at a minimum
- Support of IRQ3 and IRQ4
- Capability of being disabled in the event of conflict

### 115.2K Baud Support

A serial port circuit must be able to deliver up to 115.2K baud on a PC 95. A standard 8250-compatible UART is capable of supporting this data rate, but the CPU needs significant bandwidth to accommodate that rate on a non–FIFO buffered UART.

### Mapping of Base I/O Addresses

The serial port must be capable of mapping the base I/O address to the standard AT-style default serial port addresses 3F8h, 2F8h, 3E8h, or 2E8h. Using these addresses ensures the proper functioning of software written for non–Plug and Play systems that address these locations directly (rather than using BIOS routines). The system BIOS must report the serial port addresses in the BDA.

### Interrupt Request Support

The serial port must be able to support IRQ3 and IRQ4. Support of these IRQ signals ensures the proper functioning of software written for non–Plug and Play systems that use standard IRQ signals.

### Resolving Conflicts

In the event of irreconcilable conflict with other serial ports on the system, a serial port must be capable of being disabled by the Plug and Play software to allow at least one of the two conflicting serial ports to operate correctly.

## Serial Port Recommendations

The following features are recommended to take advantage of the built-in serial functions in Windows 95:

- Use of a 16550A UART (or equivalent)—required for a mobile PC 95
- Mapping of the base I/O address to three other locations and disable (minimum), in addition to the four required base I/O addresses
- Support of five other IRQ signals and disable (minimum), in addition to the two required IRQ signals

### 16550A Support

A PC 95 should support high-speed communications while permitting smooth multitasking in the operating system software. To meet these needs, use a 16550A buffered UART with any new serial port.

The primary benefit for designing serial ports with the 16550A UART is derived from its 16-byte FIFO. Older UARTs required that an interrupt be sent to the CPU each time a character was received. With a 16-byte FIFO, the CPU has more time to serve other processes before it turns its attention to the serial port. It can also service multiple characters in a single interrupt routine, so there is lower overhead from fewer context or task switches. In a multitasking environment, the extra time provided by the 16550A UART is invaluable.

Figure 5.3 shows one possible implementation of a serial port circuit using the 16550A UART. Because the 16550A UART is one of several devices in the super I/O chip, discrete chips are kept to a minimum. Note the Plug and Play mapping circuits for the interrupt request signals and DMA channels.

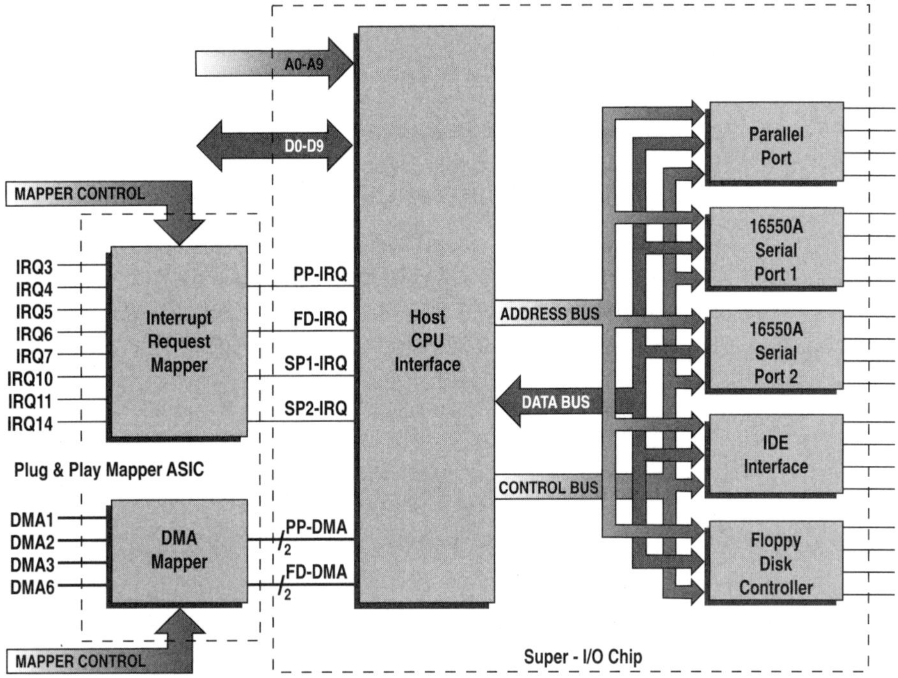


**Figure 5.3 Typical 16550A Serial Port Circuit**

Note how the use of a single "crossbar" mapping circuit ASIC can be used to meet the resource relocation requirements of all the integrated motherboard circuits. Thus, for little cost, this capability can be added to existing super I/O chips and motherboard chip sets with no change in the super I/O design or pinouts. Use caution to ensure that additional timing delays introduced by a specific mapper circuit implementation do not affect system performance.

## Additional Base I/O Addresses

To increase Plug and Play functionality, be sure that the serial port maps the base I/O address to three locations other than 3F8h, 2F8h, 3E8h, or 2E8h, minimum. The serial port hardware should also allow the base I/O address to be disabled. For information about this general resource recommendation, see Chapter 3, "The Desktop PC 95."

## Additional Interrupt Request Support

The serial port should provide interrupt request support to five IRQ signals other than IRQ3 and IRQ4, minimum. For example, the set of additional IRQ signals for a serial port located on an ISA expansion card can be IRQ2(9), IRQ5, IRQ10, IRQ11, and IRQ15. The serial port hardware should also allow interrupt requests to be disabled.

Other system expansion buses may not support enough IRQ signals to meet these recommendations. For information about mapping IRQ signals, and other general resource recommendations for various system buses, see Chapter 3, "The Desktop PC 95."

## Nonstandard Serial Port Interfaces

Nonstandard serial port interfaces (that is, not 8250 compatible) can be used on the PC 95 if they meet the general requirements for Plug and Play devices. Windows 95 drivers that properly support the nonstandard interface must be included with the hardware products, and must be preinstalled on systems that ship with Windows 95.

# Floppy Disk Drive Controller

A floppy disk drive controller (FDC) is not a requirement for a PC 95. Although most systems ship with some form of floppy disk drive, some systems, such as diskless workstations that are backed up over the network, do not need one. It is strongly recommended, however, that you include a floppy disk drive, except in special systems designed for diskless environments.

## Floppy Disk Controller Requirements

An FDC on a PC 95 must meet the following requirements, at a minimum:

- Use of the static I/O addresses 3F2h, 3F4h, and 3F5h, minimum
- Support of IRQ6
- Support of DMA2 (minimum), if DMA is used
- Capability of being independently disabled

### Base I/O Addresses

The FDC must use, at a minimum, the static I/O addresses 3F2h, 3F4h, and 3F5h, which are conventionally used by FDCs. Using these addresses ensures the proper functioning of software written for non–Plug and Play systems that directly address these locations (rather than using BIOS routines).

Although most FDCs use 3F7h as a partial FDC port, the address also contains registers used by the primary channel of the ATA (IDE) adapter. To prevent resource conflicts from occurring because of the dual nature of this address, 3F7h must not be claimed by the controller (or the ATA [IDE] adapter) as a resource in device registers. Because this address is a standard legacy resource port, Windows 95 will use it properly when communicating with the floppy and ATA (IDE) drives.

### Interrupt Request Support

The FDC must support IRQ6. Using IRQ6 ensures proper functioning of software written for non–Plug and Play systems that expect this IRQ signal to be used.

### DMA Support

If an FDC supports block data transfers to memory using the DMA controllers, the FDC must be capable of supporting DMA channel 2, at a minimum.

### Resolving Conflicts

The FDC must be capable of being disabled. For example, if the FDC is located on the motherboard, and an ATA (IDE) adapter card with a built-in FDC is added to the system, the on-board adapter must be disabled to prevent conflicts with the new card.

If the FDC is located on an ATA (IDE) adapter expansion card, the expansion card must be capable of independently disabling the FDC and the hard disk controller (HDC). In this case, the ATA (IDE) adapter will continue to function if the FDC is disabled because of conflicts, and vice versa.

## Floppy Disk Controller Recommendations

The following features are recommended to enhance the capabilities of an FDC on a PC 95:

- Mapping of I/O addresses to 372h, 374h, and 375h
- Reports "write protect" when no floppy disk is in the floppy drive
- Supports six other IRQ signals and disable, minimum, in addition to IRQ6
- Able to select two other available DMA channels, minimum, either 8 bit or 16 bit

### Additional I/O Addressing

The FDC should be capable of mapping its I/O addresses to addresses 372h, 374h, and 375h to provide secondary address space. Additional addresses can be provided for more address selection, in the event of conflict.

Although some FDCs use 377h as a partial secondary channel for the FDC port, the address also contains registers used by the secondary channel of the ATA (IDE) adapter. To prevent conflicts from occurring because of the dual nature of this address, 377h must not be claimed by the controller (or the ATA [IDE] adapter) as a resource in device registers. Because this address is a standard legacy resource port, Windows 95 will use it properly when communicating with the floppy and ATA (IDE) drives.

To provide further Plug and Play functionality, ensure that the FDC maps its I/O addresses to six other locations, at a minimum. The controller should also allow the I/O addresses to be disabled. This allows several FDCs to coexist peacefully. For more information about this general resource recommendation, see Chapter 3, "The Desktop PC 95."

### Report Write Protect

The FDC should be capable of reporting "write protect" to the operating system whenever a floppy disk is not in the floppy disk drive. This allows Windows 95 to detect when a write-enabled floppy disk is inserted into the floppy drive.

### Additional Interrupt Request Support

The FDC should be capable of supporting six different IRQ signals other than IRQ6 and disable, at a minimum. System expansion buses other than ISA may not support enough IRQ signals to meet these recommendations. For information about mapping IRQ signals, and other general resource recommendations for various system buses, see Chapter 3, "The Desktop PC 95."

## ATA (IDE) Adapter

An ATA (IDE) adapter is currently the most common type of HDC for the PC.

## ATA (IDE) Adapter Requirements

An ATA (IDE) adapter on a PC 95 must meet the following requirements, at a minimum:

- Use of the first device attached to the adapter as the boot device.
- Use of the standard I/O addresses 1F0h through 1F7h and 3F6h.
- Support of IRQ14, at a minimum.
- Capability to select at least three available DMA channels, either 8 bit or 16 bit, if DMA is supported.
- Capability to be disabled if an ATA (IDE) expansion card is added to the system. If a single adapter card contains an FDC, the adapter must be capable of independently disabling the FDC if a conflict occurs.

### Boot Device

The ATA hard disk is the standard boot device in most systems. If the ATA HDC is located on a Plug and Play ISA expansion card, it should initialize actively as the system IPL boot device.

## Mapping of Base I/O Addresses

The ATA (IDE) adapter must be capable of using the static I/O addresses 1F0h through 1F7h and 3F6h, at a minimum. Using these addresses ensures the proper functioning of software written for non–Plug and Play systems that directly address these locations (rather than using BIOS routines).

Although most ATA (IDE) adapters use 3F7h as a partial primary channel HDC port, the address also contains registers used by the FDC. To prevent conflicts from occurring because of the dual nature of this address, 3F7h must not be claimed by the ATA (IDE) adapter (or the FDC) as a resource in device registers. Because this address is a standard legacy resource port, Windows 95 will use it properly when communicating with the floppy and ATA (IDE) drives.

## Interrupt Request Support

The standard interrupt request line for the ATA (IDE) adapter is IRQ14. If the design of the ATA (IDE) adapter includes an FDC, you must also support IRQ6. Use of IRQ14 and IRQ6 ensures the proper functioning of software written for non–Plug and Play systems that expect these IRQ signals to be used.

## DMA Support

If the ATA (IDE) adapter supports block data transfers to memory using the DMA controller, the adapter must be capable of supporting three DMA channels, at a minimum. For more information about this general resource requirement, see Chapter 3, "The Desktop PC 95." The initial Windows 95 IDE driver code will not use DMA transfers, but this may change in future versions.

## Resolving Conflicts

The ATA (IDE) adapter must be capable of being disabled. For example, if an expansion card with added ATA capabilities is added to the system, the on-board adapter must be disabled to prevent conflicts with the new card.

If the ATA (IDE) adapter contains an FDC, it must be able to independently disable the FDC and the HDC. For example, if the ATA (IDE) adapter is designed on the motherboard, a non–Plug and Play ATA (IDE) adapter expansion card might be added that conflicts with one controller or the other. To ensure that the adapter will continue to function in this situation, the controllers should be capable of being independently disabled by the system BIOS.

In cases of irreconcilable conflict with other devices on the system, the ATA (IDE) adapter must be capable of being disabled by either the BIOS or the software to prevent the system from "hanging."

# ATA (IDE) Adapter Recommendations

The following recommended features add power management capabilities, greater numbers of drives and capacities, and more Plug and Play functionality to the ATA (IDE) adapter on a PC 95:

- Proper implementation of the ATA STANDBY command, to support power management
- Support of enhanced (advanced) IDE
- Mapping of the I/O address range to 170h through 177h and five other ranges and disable (minimum)
- Support of IRQ15 and at least five other IRQ signals and disable (minimum) in addition to the required IRQ signal

## Power Management

The ATA (IDE) adapter should properly implement the ATA STANDBY command to ensure that ATA (IDE) drives are able to spin up properly when power returns. With the increase in the number of new systems on the market that support the EPA's Energy Star program, the demand for this functionality will increase, even for desktop systems.

## Enhanced IDE

The ATA (IDE) adapter should provide enhanced (advanced) IDE capabilities that support four internal IDE devices, higher-capacity drives, and higher-speed transfer of data.

The ATA (IDE) adapter should be designed to share primary and secondary channels. Each channel supports one master and one slave device. With dual channels, slower peripherals—such as CD-ROM drives—and faster peripherals—such as hard drives—can be separated so the slower peripherals don't slow down the faster peripherals. Using this configuration, you can maximize concurrent I/O processing.

Currently, ATA (IDE) drive capacity is limited to less than 528 MB because of the structure of the system BIOS and the IDE interface. By extending the system's Int 13h BIOS interface and the peripheral's firmware, you can expand the maximum capacity to support 8.4-GB drives.

You can speed throughput by connecting the ATA (IDE) adapter to a high-speed bus, such as a PCI bus or VL-bus.

### Additional Base I/O Addresses

To provide support for enhanced IDE, the adapter should support alternate I/O addresses 170h through 177h. For further Plug and Play functionality, the ATA (IDE) adapter should map the I/O address range to a minimum of five other locations. The adapter hardware should also allow the base I/O address to be disabled. For more information about this general resource recommendation, see Chapter 3, "The Desktop PC 95."

Although some ATA (IDE) adapters use 377h as a partial secondary channel HDC port, the address also contains registers used by an FDC. To prevent conflicts from occurring because of the dual nature of this address, 377h must not be claimed by the ATA (IDE) adapter (or the FDC) as a resource in device registers. Because this address is a standard legacy resource port, Windows 95 will use it properly when communicating with the floppy and ATA (IDE) drives.

### Additional Interrupt Request Support

To provide support for enhanced IDE, the adapter should support IRQ15. The adapter should also be capable of supporting at least five other IRQ signals and disable, at a minimum. System expansion buses other than the ISA bus may not support enough IRQ signals to meet these recommendations. For information about mapping IRQ signals, and other general resource recommendations for various system buses, see Chapter 3, "The Desktop PC 95."

## SCSI Host Adapter

The SCSI host adapter is the circuitry that serves as an interface between the system and one or more SCSI peripherals. A host adapter can be a card that plugs into the system's expansion bus, such as an ISA card or a PCI card, or it can be designed directly into the system motherboard.

## SCSI Host Adapter Requirements

A SCSI host adapter for a PC 95 must meet the following requirements, at a minimum:

- Meeting of standards described in the current version of the *Plug and Play SCSI Specification*
- Selection of three available DMA channels (minimum), either 8 bit or 16 bit, if DMA is supported
- Capability of being disabled in the event of conflict

## Hardware Standards

A SCSI host adapter must follow these standards, described in the current version of the *Plug and Play SCSI Specification*:

- Support of the SCAM level 1 protocol for automatic SCSI assignment, at a minimum. The SCAM protocol is documented in the *SCSI Configured AutoMatically* proposal, in the SCSI-3 Parallel Interface (SPI) draft standard.
- The adapter must contain an internal SCSI connector and an external SCSI connector. The internal SCSI connector should be keyed for proper insertion. The external connector must be a 50-pin, high-density shielded connector, as specified in the SCSI-2 standard. (For information about shielded connector alternative 1-A cable, see section 5.3.2.1.) All external SCSI connectors must display the SCSI icon defined in SPI Annex F (and shown in Chapter 3, Table 3.4).
- Use automatic termination that allows a user to add external devices without removing the PC case and disabling the host-adapter *exit-point terminator*. Terminators used in the SCSI host adapter for a PC 95 must be regulated terminators, also known as active, SCSI-3 SPI, SCSI-2 alternative 2, or Boulay terminators. The motherboard must supply terminator power (TERMPWR) to the SCSI bus. Only terminators can use TERMPWR. A positive-temperature-coefficient device must be used, instead of a fuse, to limit the maximum amount of current sourced. This type of device opens the circuit when an too much current is drawn and closes the circuit when the device cools.
- Use of the single-ended alternative for the SCSI bus.
- Support of logical block addressing by host-adapter option ROMs, as defined in the Int 13h BIOS extensions document in the *IBM BIOS Technical Reference Manual*.
- Support of the current Int 13h functions by option ROMs, for backward compatibility.

## Mapping of Base I/O Addresses

The SCSI host adapter must be capable of mapping the base I/O addresses to two different locations (minimum) for minimal Plug and Play I/O address support.

## Interrupt Request Support

The SCSI host adapter must also be capable of supporting four different IRQ signals (minimum) for minimal Plug and Play IRQ support.

### DMA Support

If the SCSI host adapter supports block data transfers to memory using the DMA controllers, the adapter must be capable of supporting at least three DMA channels. For more information about this general resource requirement, see Chapter 3, "The Desktop PC 95."

### Resolving Conflicts

Two different methods can be used to resolve conflicts between a SCSI host adapter and other devices on the system. These conflicts may arise from non–Plug and Play cards or because a SCSI host-adapter card inserted into the system's expansion bus conflicts with a SCSI host adapter built on the system motherboard.

In the event of irreconcilable conflict, the host adapter must be capable of being disabled. This method prevents the system from "hanging."

The second method allows both devices to remain active, while resolving any conflict by relocating the resources on each device. For example, if a Plug and Play SCSI host-adapter card is plugged into a system with a built-in host adapter on the system motherboard, both devices' resources can be relocated such that both can be used at the same time without causing the system to hang.

## SCSI Host-Adapter Recommendations

You can add the following recommended features to enhance the capabilities of the on-board SCSI host adapter:

- Improvement of signal quality on SCSI host-adapter designs by locating the SCSI protocol chip and SCSI connectors as close as possible to the exit-point terminator
- Use of default SCSI identifier assignments for non–Plug and Play systems
- Mapping of the base I/O address to seven locations and disable, minimum
- Support of seven IRQ signals and disable, minimum

### Host-Adapter Layout

The SCSI protocol chip and cable connectors should be located as close as possible to the exit-point terminator. This layout lessens the chances that the SCSI bus will experience transients from other devices. As an example, the positions of the protocol chip, the connectors, and the terminator for an expansion card layout are shown in Figure 5.4.

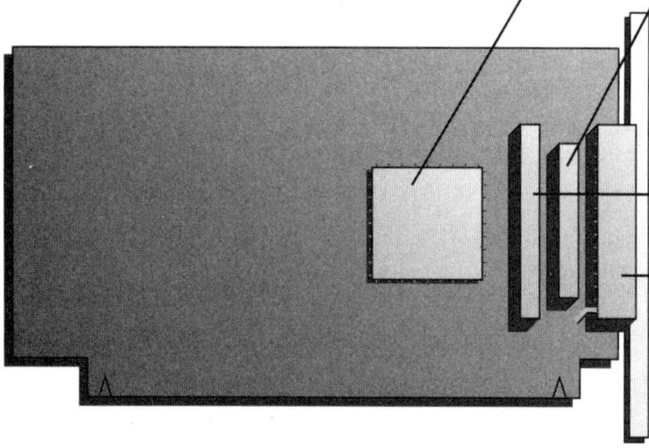


**Figure 5.4 SCSI Host-Adapter Expansion Card Layout**

### Default SCSI ID Assignments

The SCSI host adapter should contain a default SCSI identifier assignment of 7. This default identifier reduces the risk that older SCSI peripherals that don't contain the SCAM protocol will not work with a Plug and Play SCSI host adapter.

### Additional Base I/O Addresses

SCSI host adapters should be designed to be as flexible as possible. To minimize conflicts with other devices, an adapter should be capable of mapping the base I/O addresses to seven different locations, at a minimum. The adapter hardware should also allow the base I/O address to be disabled. For more information about this general resource recommendation, see Chapter 3, "The Desktop PC 95."

### Additional Interrupt Request Support

The SCSI host adapter should be capable of supporting seven different IRQ signals and disable, at a minimum. System expansion buses other than the ISA bus may not support enough IRQ signals to meet these recommendations. For information about mapping IRQ signals, and other general resource recommendations for various system buses, see Chapter 3, "The Desktop PC 95."

## Additional SCSI Information

For information about designing SCSI peripherals for the PC 95, see Chapter 7, "Designing Peripherals."

# Audio

Historically, the audio section of a PC has generally contained an 8254 programmable timer, an audio amplifier, and the speaker. The old audio section reproduces tones created by dividing the timer chip's 1.19318 MHz clock. Although this circuit has served its purpose over the years, it is inadequate for modern audio reproduction.

As the features of audio chip sets have increased, their cost has decreased. Although audio functionality has increased greatly, not all systems require all of the capabilities of the best audio reproduction. Audio on a PC 95 should, however, support a minimum set of requirements for improved sound quality.

# Audio Requirements

An audio circuit in a PC 95 must meet the following requirements, at a minimum:

- Capability to produce 22 kHz, 8-bit, monaural, output-only sound, minimum.
- Support of either Sound Blaster™ or Microsoft Windows Sound System compatibility to use built-in Windows 95 drivers.
- Use of a 1/8" miniphone jack wired for stereo, as the output connector.
- Mapping of the base I/O address to configurations compatible with either Sound Blaster or the Microsoft Windows Sound System.
- Support of the IRQ signals used with either Sound Blaster or the Microsoft Windows Sound System.
- Selection of three available DMA channels (minimum), either 8-bit or 16-bit channels, if DMA is supported.
- Capability of resolving conflicts with other devices. At a minimum, the conflict can be resolved by disabling the on-board audio circuit.

## Minimum Audio Performance

The audio circuit must be capable of 22 kHz, 8-bit, monaural, output-only sound, which is considered a minimum set of sound capabilities.

The 22 kHz frequency was chosen because it balances a minimum acceptable frequency with a reasonable implementation cost. Audio standards are usually set at 5.5, 11, 22, and 44 kHz. 22 kHz wave files are fairly standard for Windows 95. The codec and multimedia software automatically drive a 22 kHz output as easily as a 44 kHz output. The secondary consideration for the 22 kHz output was cost. In general, a 22 kHz capability is less costly to implement than higher frequencies.

The 8-bit minimum requirement was chosen because 8-bit A/D converters are readily available and inexpensive.

Monaural eliminates the need for additional circuitry beyond one channel.

Output-only eliminates the need to design an additional A/D converter circuit for input conversion to digitized sound.

## Compatibilities

The audio circuit should be compatible with either Sound Blaster or Microsoft Windows Sound System. If the circuit is Sound Blaster compatible, it can take advantage of the driver supplied with Windows 95. If it is not Sound Blaster compatible, the device designer must supply a driver for the audio and include it with the preinstall program.

As an alternative to Sound Blaster compatibility, the on-board audio can support capabilities required for the Microsoft Windows Sound System, including IRQ signals, DMA channels, and I/O port addresses. For information about the Microsoft Windows Sound System, see the *Microsoft Windows Sound System Developer's Assistance Kit*. The Microsoft Windows Sound System drivers must be licensed separately from Windows 95.

## Output Connector

The output connector must be a 1/8" stereo miniphone jack. For monaural output, hardwire both sides of the stereo jack together, so it can supply sound to both sides in a set of stereo headphones.

## Mapping Base I/O Addresses

The audio circuit must support the base I/O addresses associated with either Sound Blaster or Microsoft Windows Sound System, at a minimum. For minimum Sound Blaster compatibility, base I/O addresses 220h and 240h must be supported. For minimum Microsoft Windows Sound System compatibility, 388h, 530h, 604h, 0E80h, and 0F40h must be supported.

## Interrupt Request Support

The audio circuit must support the IRQ signals required for compatibility with either Sound Blaster or Microsoft Windows Sound System, at a minimum.

Of this recommended set of IRQ signals, IRQ3, IRQ5, IRQ7, IRQ9, and IRQ10 are used for Sound Blaster compatibility. IRQ7, IRQ9, IRQ10, and IRQ11 are used for the Microsoft Windows Sound System. Your audio card can implement either subset, as appropriate, for compatibility.

### DMA Support

If your audio design includes support of block data transfers between the audio circuits and memory using the DMA controllers, the circuit must be capable of supporting three DMA channels, at a minimum. For more information about this general resource requirement, see Chapter 3, "The Desktop PC 95."

The Microsoft Windows Sound System can use any of the DMA channels 0 through 3.

### Resolving Conflicts

Two different methods can be used to resolve conflicts between the audio circuit and other devices on the system. These conflicts may arise from non–Plug and Play cards or because an audio card is inserted into a system with audio capabilities designed on the motherboard.

In the event of irreconcilable conflict, the audio circuit must be capable of being disabled. This method prevents the system from "hanging."

The second method allows both devices to remain active, while resolving any conflict by relocating the resources on each device. For example, if a Plug and Play audio card is plugged into the expansion bus, either device's resources can be relocated such that both can be used at the same time without causing the system to hang.

## Audio Recommendations

You can add the following recommended features to increase the capabilities of the sound system on a PC 95:

- Support of 44 kHz, 16-bit, stereo codec, Microphone-In, Line-In, Line-Out, and Headphones-Out, with volume controlled by the software
- Support of CD-ROM DA passthrough to play Redbook audio, so standard audio CDs can be played through the computer
- Capability of passing through old audio tones formerly produced by the programmable timer
- Support of seven base I/O addresses and disable, at a minimum
- Support of seven IRQ signals and disable, at a minimum

### Enhanced Audio

The audio adapter should support enhanced capabilities that improve the overall quality of audio reproduction. Additional hardware should be included that adds standard audio features, such as the availability of microphones for audio input.

### Redbook Audio Passthrough

Using Redbook audio passthrough, the audio adapter can play standard CD-ROM audio disks.

### Tone Passthrough

The audio circuit should be capable of handling tones such as those generated by the 8254 programmable timer, in older systems. This allows software that uses only these tones to function properly.

### Additional Base I/O Address Support

To provide more Plug and Play functionality, the audio circuit should map the base I/O address to seven different locations, at a minimum. For an audio circuit that is Sound Blaster compatible, this includes the two Sound Blaster base I/O addresses and two others. The serial port hardware should also allow the base I/O address to be disabled. For more information about this general resource recommendation, see Chapter 3, "The Desktop PC 95."

### Additional Interrupt Request Support

The audio circuit should provide interrupt request support to seven IRQ signals, at a minimum. For example, the recommended set of IRQ signals for an audio circuit that supports Sound Blaster compatibility on an ISA expansion card is the five required IRQ signals and two more of your choice. The audio adapter hardware should also allow interrupt requests to be disabled.

System expansion buses other than the ISA bus may not support enough IRQ signals to meet these recommendations. For information about mapping IRQ signals, and other general resource recommendations for various system buses, see Chapter 3, "The Desktop PC 95."

## Optional Features

You can also add the following optional features to enhance the audio capabilities of the PC 95:

- Use hardware music synthesis to reduce file sizes associated with re-creating digital music. Two types exist: FM synthesis and wave table synthesis.
- Use a *digital signal processor* (DSP) to offload the system CPU from audio-intensive tasks. A DSP can compress and decompress digital audio (wave files), and can be used as a dedicated wave table synthesis chip.

# Additional Audio Information

For information about requirements and recommendations for audio support on a desktop system, see Chapter 3, "The Desktop PC 95." This chapter includes recommendations for design of the audio output jacks on the system case and for accessories that can be shipped with the system.

# Network Adapter

Connectivity is one of the most important capabilities for many PC users. A network can be as small as a local area network consisting of a few computers, printers, and other devices, or it can consist of many small and large computers distributed over a vast geographic area. Small or large, a computer network exists to provide computer users with the means of communicating and transferring information expeditiously.

## Network Adapter Requirements

A network adapter on a PC 95 must meet the following requirements:

- Capability of automatically enabling the adapter as a boot device or enabling the adapter as a nonboot device, if the network adapter is designed for RIPL capability
- Support for the NDIS 3 network device driver
- No hooking of Int 18h or Int 19h on ISA bus systems until instructed by the system BIOS
- Mapping of the I/O addresses to seven locations and disable, minimum
- Support of seven IRQ signals and disable, minimum
- Selection of three available DMA channels (minimum), either 8 bit or 16 bit, if DMA is supported
- Capability of being disabled in the event of conflict

### Network Adapter and IPL Boot

If the network adapter is designed with the capability to boot the system through a remote network, the adapter must contain some means of automatically enabling the adapter either as a boot device or as a nonboot device.

## NDIS 3.1 Support

The network adapter must fully support the NDIS 3.1 device driver. NDIS support provides the PC 95 with the capability of dynamically starting and stopping the network card. This capability is critically important in systems that incorporate advanced power management. When the system suspends, the network essentially treats the suspension as the removal of a device. When the system resumes, the network dynamically restarts the network adapter.

For more information about NDIS 3.1 support for the network adapter, see the *Microsoft Windows 95 Device Driver Reference*, supplied in the Microsoft Windows 95 DDK.

## Hooking Int 18 and Int 19

Plug and Play ISA cards must not hook Int 18 or Int 19 until the Plug and Play system BIOS calls the boot connection vector in the network adapter's option ROM expansion header. If you attempt to hook them before the boot connection vector is called, the Plug and Play system BIOS on a PC 95 will automatically recapture these interrupts from the network adapter option ROM, rendering any routines you have written for these interrupts inactive. For more information about the Plug and Play BIOS control of Int 18 and Int 19, see the *Plug and Play BIOS Specification* and Chapter 9, "Option ROM Design."

## Mapping Base I/O Addresses

The network adapter must be designed to be as flexible as possible. To minimize the chances that the adapter will conflict with other devices, it must be able to map the base I/O addresses to seven different locations and disable (minimum). For more information about this general resource requirement, see Chapter 3, "The Desktop PC 95."

## Interrupt Request Support

The network adapter must also be capable of supporting seven different IRQ signals and disable (minimum) to prevent conflicts with other devices in the system. System expansion buses other than the ISA bus may not support enough IRQ signals to meet these recommendations. For information about mapping IRQ signals, and other general resource recommendations for various system buses, see Chapter 3, "The Desktop PC 95."

## DMA Support

If your design includes support of block data transfers from the network adapter to memory using the DMA controllers, the adapter must be capable of supporting three DMA channels, at a minimum. For more information about this general resource recommendation, see Chapter 3, "The Desktop PC 95."

### Resolving Conflict

In the event of irreconcilable conflict, the adapter must be capable of being disabled. This method prevents the system from "hanging."

## Network Adapter Recommendations

You can add the following recommended features to enhance the capabilities of a network adapter on a PC 95:

- Automatic sensing of whether a net cable is connected or not
- Automatic sensing of the transceiver type
- Automatic sensing of whether a docking station network adapter is available or not (during hot docking and undocking)
- Support of at least 15 I/O addresses

### Sensing the Network Connection

The network adapter should be capable of automatically sensing whether a net cable is connected or not. For a network adapter that is designed onto the motherboard or is used as a boot device (RIPL), the system BIOS should be capable of determining whether or not a cable is connected to the adapter. If the network adapter is on an expansion card that is not used as a boot device, the presence of the cable can be determined by device drivers.

If a cable is not attached, a message should be displayed informing the user that there is a problem with the connection.

### Sensing the Transceiver Type

The display adapter should automatically sense the transceiver type. In some current network adapter designs, a jumper is used to determine the transceiver type. However, the user must manually enter the information to inform the operating system of the transceiver type.

Network adapters should be designed such that software can detect the transceiver type, at a minimum. For a network adapter that is designed onto the motherboard or is used as a boot device (RIPL), the system BIOS should be capable of determining the transceiver type. If the network adapter is on an expansion card that is not used as a boot device, device drivers can determine the transceiver type.

### Network Adapter Availability

During hot docking, the network adapter device driver should sense the presence of the network adapter to determine whether the commands sent to and received from the network adapter are appropriate. One possible way to provide this service in hardware is to create a register address that contains a known value, and query this value occasionally to see if it is still valid. When the portable system is undocked (and the network card is not available), the value that is read back from this register will be incorrect, and the device driver can behave appropriately (including informing the user that the network is not available at that time).

### Additional Base I/O Addresses

The network adapter should support 15 I/O port addresses. Because network adapters are usually placed in systems that already contain a large number of logical devices, using more than the standard seven I/O addresses is a good idea to lessen the chances that conflicts will occur between network adapters and other devices on the system.

For information about this general resource recommendation and its exceptions, see Chapter 3, "The Desktop PC 95."

# Mouse Port

Because the effectiveness of Windows 95 is greatly enhanced by the inclusion of a pointing device in the system, a motherboard in a PC 95 should include an auxiliary port for a pointing device (most commonly, a mouse).

## Mouse Port Requirements

Mouse port requirements differ somewhat, depending on the type of port. However, all types of mouse ports on a PC 95 must meet the following requirements, at a minimum:

- Use of either a PS/2-style port, a serial mouse port, or an *ACCESS.bus* port
- Capability of being disabled or relocated when conflicts with other devices occur

In addition to these requirements, a variable set of requirements must be met, depending on the type of port designed on the motherboard.

## PS/2-Style Mouse Port

PS/2-style mouse ports must meet the following requirements:

- Meeting of the requirements documented in the *Personal System/2® Specifications* published by IBM.
- Use of an 8042 chip (or equivalent) to ensure compatibility with Windows 95. (In most instances, the existing keyboard port 8042 is sufficient.) The 8042 initiates an IRQ12 when the mouse is connected to the port. An 82C710 can also be used.
- Support of IRQ12 to enable the proper functioning of software written for non–Plug and Play systems that expect this IRQ signal to be used.
- Mapping of the I/O addresses to 60h and 64h.

## Serial Mouse Port

A serial mouse port must meet all the requirements described under the heading "Serial Port Requirements" earlier in this chapter. If a port meets the requirements of a standard PC 95 serial port, a device other than a mouse can be connected to the port and operate correctly.

For information about the design of the icon for a serial mouse port, see Chapter 3, "The Desktop PC 95." For information about the Plug and Play design for a serial mouse, see Chapter 7, "Designing Peripherals."

## ACCESS.bus Port

If the mouse is connected to the system through an ACCESS.bus port, it must meet all the requirements for identification and configuration listed in the *ACCESS.bus Specifications*. The OEM must supply the ACCESS.bus device drivers, because Windows 95 does not supply them.

## Resolving Conflicts

One of two methods can be used to resolve the conflict when more than one mouse is detected on the system.

The first method is to completely disable the mouse port. For example, if an expansion card, such as a display adapter with a built-in mouse port, is added to a desktop system with a motherboard mouse port, the expansion card overrides the motherboard mouse port. Using this method, the system disables the mouse port on the motherboard and only accepts mouse input from the expansion card.

The second method allows both mouse ports to remain active, while resolving any conflict by relocating the resources on one or both ports. For example, in a docking system, the mouse on the portable PC and the mouse on the docking station can be allowed to share pointing responsibilities. Using this method, either mouse can be used as a pointing device, although only one mouse pointer will be used by the software.

# Mouse Port Recommendations

You can add the following recommended features to take advantage of the built-in mouse port functions in Windows 95:

- Use of a PS/2-style mouse port.
- No permanent damage if a mouse is "hot-plugged" into the port with the PC fully powered. The overcurrent circuit should not require that the user open the case and replace parts if an overcurrent condition occurs.

## PS/2-Style Mouse Port

Although you can include a serial, ACCESS.bus, or PS/2-style mouse port on the PC 95, a PS/2-style mouse port is recommended. A serial mouse port could confuse the user, if more than one serial port is included with the system. Because the connectors for a standard serial port and a serial mouse port are the same, the user could plug the mouse into the wrong port and wonder why the mouse didn't work. Although the ACCESS.bus port allows *dynamic detection* and identification of the mouse, the system designer must supply device drivers for the ACCESS.bus port. Windows 95 provides built-in drivers for a PS/2-style mouse port.

## Dynamic Detection

A Plug and Play mouse can be detected on a serial mouse port whenever the DSR line on the serial port goes high. For information about this method of detection, which is part of the Plug and Play serial mouse requirements, see the *Plug and Play External COM Device Specification.*

On the ACCESS.bus, the specifications require dynamic detection of any device. The operating system polls the ACCESS.bus occasionally to see whether the configuration of the devices has changed. If a change has occurred, the bus reconfigures the devices on the bus and informs the operating system about these changes.

### Hot-Plugging

The user should be able to connect and disconnect a mouse from a fully powered PC 95 with the assurance that no permanent damage to the mouse or the system will occur. Neither the overcurrent circuit in the mouse nor the one in the system should require the user to open the case and replace parts if an overcurrent condition occurs. Using a fuse that must be replaced each time an overcurrent condition occurs, for example, is unacceptable.

## Additional Mouse Port Information

For information about mouse port drivers, see the *Microsoft Windows 95 Device Driver Reference*, supplied with the Microsoft Windows 95 DDK.

# Keyboard Port

The primary input device for a PC is the keyboard. The keyboard port on the motherboard has traditionally been controlled by an 8042 microcontroller or the equivalent.

## Keyboard Port Requirements

Keyboard port requirements differ, depending on what type of keyboard port is being designed. However, all keyboard ports must meet the following requirements, at a minimum:

- Use of either a PS/2-style or ACCESS.bus port
- No interference between a keyboard in a portable PC and a docking station keyboard, if present, when it is docked

### Type of Keyboard Port

A keyboard port on a PC 95 can be designed either as a PS/2-style port or as an ACCESS.bus port. (For the purposes of this guide, a "PS/2-style keyboard port" refers to a keyboard port that uses either the PS/2 connector or the standard AT keyboard connector.) Whichever type you choose, you must design additional features into the port to meet the requirements of the port interface.

If you design a PS/2-style keyboard port in the system, it must meet the following requirements:

- Support of IRQ1 to ensure the proper functioning of software written for non–Plug and Play systems that expect to use this IRQ signal
- Mapping of the I/O address ports to 60h and 64h

If the keyboard uses the ACCESS.bus, the bus must meet all of the requirements for identification and configuration listed in the *ACCESS.bus Specifications*. The OEM must supply the ACCESS.bus device drivers, because Windows 95 does not provide them.

### Resolving Conflicts

When a portable PC is connected to a docking station, more than one keyboard at a time can be attached to the system. The keyboard ports on a portable PC and the docking station must be able to resolve conflicts between the two ports when the portable PC is docked. Windows 95 supports multiple configurations through the registry and will determine which keyboard to enable.

## Keyboard Port Recommendations

The following features are recommended to enhance the capabilities of the keyboard port on a PC 95. They take advantage of the built-in Plug and Play features in Windows 95 and add protection to the hardware:

- Dynamic detection when a keyboard is connected or disconnected.
- No permanent damage from "hot-plugging" a keyboard to a fully powered PC. The overcurrent protection circuit on the motherboard should not require that the user open the case and replace parts if an overcurrent condition occurs.

### Dynamic Detection

For the ACCESS.bus, the specifications require dynamic detection of any device. The system polls the ACCESS.bus occasionally to see whether the configuration of the devices has changed. If a change has occurred, the bus reconfigures the devices on the bus and informs the system about the changes. Although the ACCESS.bus port does allow dynamic detection and identification of the keyboard, the system designer must supply device drivers for the ACCESS.bus port.

### Hot-Plugging

The user should be able to connect and disconnect a keyboard from a fully powered PC 95 with the assurance that no permanent damage to either the keyboard or the system will occur. Neither the overcurrent circuit in the keyboard nor the one in the system should require the user to open the case and replace parts if an overcurrent condition occurs. Using a fuse that must be replaced each time an overcurrent condition occurs is unacceptable.

## Additional Keyboard Port Information

For information about device drivers for keyboards, see the *Microsoft Windows 95 Device Driver Reference*, supplied with the Microsoft Windows 95 DDK.

# Windows 95 Logo Device Feature Set

A system must provide a minimum set of basic device features to qualify to receive the Windows 95 Logo. These device features, which have been described throughout this chapter, are summarized in Table 5.3 through Table 5.10. More advanced recommended features are also included, which optimize the devices for Windows 95.

For a more complete explanation of each of these features, see the appropriate device section in this chapter.

**Table 5.3 Display Adapter Requirements**

| Feature | Logo requirement | Recommendation |
|---|---|---|
| Bus-specific PnP identifier | Yes | Yes |
| VESA DDC1 (PnP) | No | Yes |
| VGA 640 × 480 × 8 bpp | Yes | No |
| VGA 1024 × 768 × 8 bpp, noninterlaced | No | Yes |
| Packed-pixel frame buffer | Yes | Yes |
| Linear | No | Yes |
| Relocatable > 16-MB address | No | Yes |
| Color ordering | N/A | BGR |
| Resource configurations | | |
| VGA BIOS | Fixed at C000h OK | One alternate address |
| Standard VGA registers | Static | Static |
| Extended registers | 2 options | 8 options |
| IRQ2(9)[1] | | No |
| Memory-mapped extended registers | | Yes |
| Disable | Yes | Yes |
| VESA DPMS | Yes | Yes |
| VESA ergonomic timings | Yes | Yes |
| High-speed expansion bus | No | Yes |

1 IRQ2(9) is generally not used on modern display adapters. However, if you use it, it should come up inactive when power is turned on, and should not actively drive the bus. The adapter should not claim it as a resource.

**Table 5.4 Parallel Port**

| Feature | Logo requirement | Recommendation |
|---|---|---|
| Parallel port | Yes | Yes |
| Compatibility and nibble mode | Yes | Yes |
| ECP (IEEE P1284-I) | No | Yes |
| EPP | No | Yes |
| 378h, 278h, (3BCh or vendor) | Yes | Yes |
| IRQ5, IRQ7 | Yes | Yes |
| Disable | Yes | Yes |
| Additional configurations (that is, five base addresses, five IRQs for ISA) | No | Yes |

**Table 5.5 Serial Port**

| Feature | Logo requirement | Recommendation |
|---|---|---|
| Serial port | Yes | Yes |
| 16550A | No | Yes |
| 3F8h, 2F8h, 3E8h, 2E8h | Yes | Yes |
| IRQ3, IRQ4 | Yes | Yes |
| Disable | Yes | Yes |
| Additional configurations | No | Yes |

**Table 5.6 Floppy Disk Drive Interface**

| Feature | Logo requirement | Recommendation |
|---|---|---|
| Floppy disk drive interface | No | Optional |
| Write-protect detection | No | Yes |
| Disable | Yes | Yes |

**Table 5.7 IDE/ATA Hard Disk Interface**

| Feature | Logo requirement | Recommendation |
|---|---|---|
| IDE/ATA hard disk interface | No | Optional |
| Spin-down | No | Yes |
| Enhanced IDE | No | Yes |
| Disable | Yes | Yes |

**Table 5.8 SCSI Host Adapter**

| Feature | Logo requirement | Recommendation |
|---|---|---|
| SCSI host adapter | No | Optional |
| Plug and Play SCSI specification | Yes | Yes |
| Plug and Play bus–type identifier | Yes | Yes |
| SCAM level 1 | Yes | Yes |
| Basic configurations (that is, two I/O, four IRQs for ISA) | Yes | Yes |
| Alternate resource configurations | No | Yes |
| Disable | Yes | Yes |
| Automatic termination | Yes | Yes |
| 50-pin SCSI-2 connector | Yes | Yes |
| SCSI-2 | Yes | Yes |
| SCSI-3 | No | Yes |

**Table 5.9 Audio Adapter**

| Feature | Logo requirement | Recommendation |
|---|---|---|
| Audio adapter | No | Yes |
| Plug and Play bus–type identifier | Yes | Yes |
| Alternate resource configurations | No | Yes |
| Disable | Yes | Yes |
| Sampling rate | 22 kHz | 44.1 kHz |
| Stereo | No | Yes |
| Input | No | Yes |
| DSP | No | Yes |

**Table 5.10 Net Adapter**

| Feature | Logo requirement | Recommendation |
|---|---|---|
| Net adapter | No | Optional |
| Plug and Play bus–type identifier | Yes | Yes |
| Plug and Play software configuration | Yes | Yes |
| NDIS 3.1 | Yes | Yes |
| XCVR sense | No | Yes |
| Cable sense | No | Yes |
| Disable | Yes | Yes |
| Alternate resource configurations | Yes | Yes |

CHAPTER 6

# Plug and Play Cards and Buses

This chapter discusses Plug and Play motherboard buses, Plug and Play ISA expansion cards, and Plug and Play on expansion cards that connect to advanced buses.

You'll need to make few, if any, changes to the expansion bus on the motherboard of a Personal Computer for Microsoft® Windows™ 95 to make it comply fully with Plug and Play. For some designs, however, you may need to update each expansion card slot so that all slots share the same capabilities. This chapter examines these general changes, as well as design suggestions to optimize the bus to Windows 95.

Most hardware changes to a Plug and Play bus will need to be made to the expansion cards connected to the bus. Because the ISA bus expansion card is an older design and lacks identification techniques, it will require more changes, compared to other types of cards, when you incorporate Plug and Play. Although most of this chapter discusses expansion cards on the ISA bus, a smaller part discusses changes required for other motherboard buses and the expansion cards that connect to them. In most cases, these buses and cards will require few changes, because their specifications already include some form of device identification. The discussion of these buses focuses on their Plug and Play aspects.

# Motherboard Buses

One of the most important considerations in motherboard design is the type of bus that runs the system. Some buses, such as the ISA bus, have a long history with the PC; others, such as the VL-bus, Micro Channel, and the PCI bus, are relatively new, and offer improved performance. Some of these advanced buses allow the system to pass configuration information to devices attached to the bus, making Plug and Play implementations much easier.

In most cases, if you follow the guidelines in the bus specifications, the bus will comply with Plug and Play, meaning it meets the requirements for a PC 95. For information about obtaining a copy of these specifications, see Appendix D, "References."

The motherboard bus hardware should comply with the written specifications for each bus. In the past, some bus designs did not fully implement all of the bus requirements on every expansion card connector. For example, some designs did not allow bus master privileges for all connectors on a PCI expansion bus. Such designs could result in the failure of a PCI expansion card that required bus master privileges, a result not compatible with the Plug and Play initiative. To ensure full Plug and Play functionality on a PCI bus with expansion cards, all PCI connectors on the motherboard must be able to allow any PCI expansion card to have bus master privileges.

# PCMCIA Socket Controllers

The built-in Plug and Play PCMCIA software in Windows 95 includes drivers for Intel® PCIC–compatible and Databook TCIC–compatible socket controllers. To be compatible with these drivers, socket controller implementations must support the Intel PCIC (365) or Databook TCIC base-register set. Many controllers do not fully implement the base-register set, and are incompatible. Also, some controllers implement extended registers or enhancements. The built-in Windows 95 drivers do not exploit these features, even though the controller may be compatible.

It is also recommended that compatible implementations:

- Adhere to the PCIC or TCIC mapping of system IRQ lines to controller interrupt pins. This means that the IRQ*x* pin on the controller is wired to the IRQ*x* signal on the system board, and not some other IRQ line. This is because the Plug and Play software maps the IRQs through registers whose bits correspond to the pins on the chip. When connecting the chip into the system, the system designer must maintain this mapping.
- Support all possible system IRQ lines for mapping of the slot interrupt (or interrupts) and the socket controller interrupt. The PCIC provides 10 IRQ pins (IRQ*x*), and the TCIC provides 7 (HIRQ*x*). The dedicated socket controller interrupt pin (INTR or SKTIRQ) should not connect to a system IRQ line, because the driver cannot determine this system-specific mapping.

# Device Identification

For proper Plug and Play functionality, each device connected to the expansion bus must be able to supply its own unique identifier. This identifier is constructed from the logical device identifier structures documented in the specifications for a particular bus. Although each type of bus contains different amounts of information for devices on expansion cards, there is sufficient information available for deriving a unique device identifier.

The following information is required to create a device identifier for each device on a particular bus:

- ISA: A 32-bit EISA identifier for each Plug and Play ISA device.
- EISA: A 32-bit EISA identifier for each EISA device. This identifier consists of a leading zero followed by three compressed ASCII characters and a unique 16-bit identifier for each logical device design.

- PCI: A 40-bit value consisting of the 16-bit vendor identifier, the 16-bit device identifier, and the 8-bit revision identifier defined in the PCI specification for each PCI device.
- VL-bus: A 32-bit EISA identifier for each VL-bus device.
- PCMCIA: A device identifier is created from the tuples documented in this chapter.
- Micro Channel: A 16-bit vendor adapter identifier assigned by IBM for each Micro Channel device.
- ACCESS.bus: A 23-byte value consisting of the 8-byte vendor name, the 8-byte module name, and the 7-byte module revision defined in the ACCESS.bus specification for each ACCESS.bus device.

---

**Note** EISA identifiers can be obtained from BCPR Services, Inc. For information about contacting BCPR Services, Inc., see Appendix D, "References."

---

If a peripheral attaches to the expansion card, such as a SCSI drive to a host adapter or a printer to a parallel port expansion card, it must be able to supply enough information to create a device identifier. For more information, see Chapter 7, "Designing Peripherals."

Expansion cards can contain more than one device per card. In such cases, each device requires its own device identifier and must be able to independently configure its resources. The system BIOS and Windows 95 must be able to access each logical device separately, configure the device resources independently, and disable individual logical devices in the event of a conflict. The system BIOS and Windows 95 depend on the device identifiers and resources for each device being independent in order to properly identify each device node. If more than one device shares a device identifier or resources, neither device can have its functions separated; for example, if one device is disabled, all devices with the same device identifier will be disabled. To receive the Windows 95 Logo, each device must have an independent device identifier and resources.

# Requirements vs. Recommendations

For each bus discussed in this chapter, there are two sections: requirements and recommendations. Requirements outline those features and functions required so that a specific bus, or expansion card that connects to that bus, will qualify for the Windows 95 Logo. Recommendations include additional features and functions that improve Windows 95 performance.

The recommendations in this chapter are a minimum "step up" from the required features. More advanced recommendations could have been made, but they would have been more costly to implement and might have exceeded the needs of the typical user.

You, the designer, must decide how many enhancements to add to your design. This guide does not intend to limit the technology that can be added to a PC 95.

## Expansion Card Requirements

Expansion cards for the PC 95 can be designed using many different types of buses and can contain a variety of devices, but all expansion cards must meet a minimum set of requirements. You must implement the following features on all expansion cards that connect to the PC 95:

- Support of the Plug and Play identification and configuration criteria for the bus to which the card is connected. Bus requirements for Plug and Play compatibility are described elsewhere in this chapter.
- Capable, at a minimum, of being disabled in the event that all resources available on the card conflict with the resource requirements of other devices.
- No DIP switches or jumpers, except in the case of certain boot devices.
- DIP switches on boot devices can be used for an initial power-on default state or for non–Plug and Play system compatibility, but must be able to be overridden by software configuration after power-up.
- All expansion card devices must use 16-bit decoding for their I/O port addresses. This makes full use of the I/O address range for devices that may be added to the system. (On static and integrated motherboard devices, 16-bit decoding is recommended, but not required.)
- Option ROMs must be able to map their base address to at least eight different locations. VGA option ROMs are the exception to this rule and must be able to map their base address to at least two locations.
- Option ROMs must contain the Plug and Play expansion headers described in the *Plug and Play BIOS Specification*. The header contains information that identifies the type of boot device connected to the expansion card and allows the system BIOS to prioritize the boot devices. Shadowed copies of the option ROM must also contain the Plug and Play expansion headers.

# ISA Expansion Cards

ISA cards are currently the most commonly purchased type of card and are the most well known by users. They are also the most uncontrollable. When the PC was originally designed, there was no need for cards to identify themselves to the system, because most PC users were knowledgeable, to some extent, about setting jumpers and switches. As users with less technical knowledge have become the more common buyers of PC equipment, new techniques that automatically configure the system have become necessary.

---

**Note** The information in this section is based on the *Plug and Play ISA Specification*, Version 1.0a, dated May 5, 1994. Obtain the current version of this specification before implementing Plug and Play ISA designs, and verify that your card complies with the latest specification version.

---

## ISA Card Requirements

In addition to meeting the general expansion card requirements, ISA cards must meet the following specific requirements:

- Implementation of the standards described in the current version of the *Plug and Play ISA Specification.*
- Option ROMs must only be used on cards with boot devices.
- Cards with option ROMs must not hook primary boot interrupts (Int 9h, Int 10h, Int 13h, Int 18h, and Int 19h) until the Plug and Play system BIOS calls the boot connection vector in the selected option ROM expansion header.
- On cards with option ROMs, the default configuration must be able to be disabled after the card has been isolated.
- Implementation of the full 16-bit I/O address decode logic. This can be a simple circuit limiting them to the 0h to 3FFh range, or can be flexible enough to use the upper address regions.

One of the limitations of the original PC design was the incomplete I/O address decoding of 10 bits, rather than 16 bits. This limited the number of usable I/O addresses to 1024 unique values. One of the benefits of Plug and Play is the ability to map a Plug and Play ISA expansion card into different address locations in the full 16-bit I/O address space. Plug and Play cards must implement this full 16-bit I/O decode to qualify for the Windows 95 Logo. The card vendor or chip set designer can implement this simply and inexpensively using a logical AND gate to combine address lines A15:A10 with *AEN, *IOR, and *IOW to create new signals *AEN10, *IOR10, and *IOW10. To increase flexibility, full address decoding can be implemented.

For more information about option ROM support for ISA cards, see Chapter 9, "Option ROM Design."

## Plug and Play ISA Standards

The ISA bus is the most popular expansion bus standard in the PC industry. The ISA bus architecture allows allocation of memory and I/O address spaces, DMA channels, and interrupt levels among multiple ISA cards. But the ISA interface has no defined hardware or software mechanism for allocating these resources. As a result, configuration of ISA cards is typically done with jumpers that change the decode maps for memory and I/O space and steer the DMA and interrupt signals to different pins on the bus. Further, system configuration files may need to be updated to reflect these changes. Users typically resolve sharing conflicts by referring to documentation provided by each card manufacturer. For many users, this configuration process can be difficult and frustrating.

A Plug and Play–compliant system can identify the Plug and Play ISA cards and the resources they use and then program these resources so they do not conflict. The conflict-resolution scheme used on Plug and Play ISA cards essentially puts all cards "to sleep," then reads the card identification and the information about what the card can do and the resources it requires. This information can include what resources are programmable and over what ranges they can be programmed. With this information, the system can configure the card in a way that prevents conflicts with other cards in the ISA bus.

Figure 6.1 contains a logic flow diagram of the auto-configuration sequence for a Plug and Play ISA card. The sections that follow discuss the design criteria for and a breakdown of these local elements.

---

**Note** Although many of the schematic examples in this chapter are shown using discrete logic for clarity, most practical implementations would use programmable logic or gate arrays to implement these functions.

---

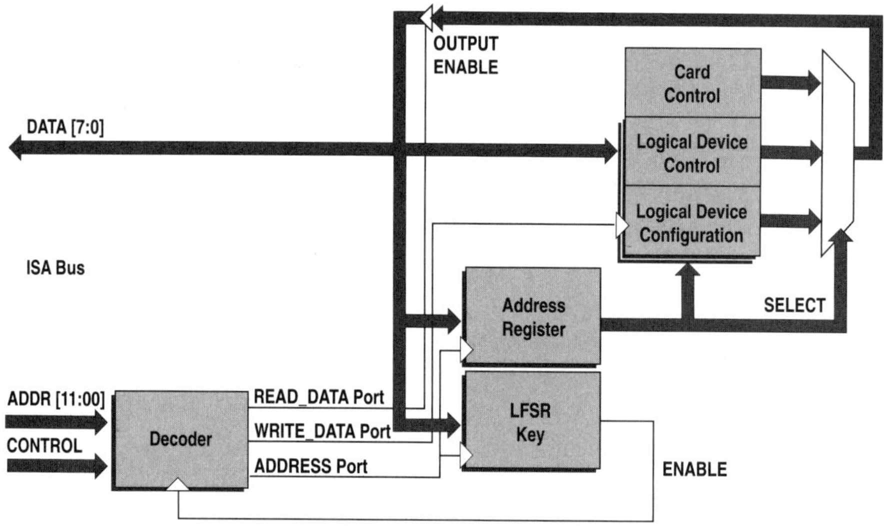


**Figure 6.1 Logic Flow for Auto-Configuration**

## Plug and Play ISA Card Configuration Sequence

Before reading about implementing the hardware changes needed to make Plug and Play–compliant ISA cards, you should become familiar with the steps in the configuration sequence. Although not all of these steps require unique hardware, it is a good idea to know what is required of the hardware for each step.

The major steps of the configuration sequence are:

- Initiation. Put all Plug and Play ISA cards in configuration mode.
- Isolation. Isolate one Plug and Play ISA card at a time.
- Read resources. Assign a handle and read the card's resource data structure.
- Arbitration. After the resource requirements and capabilities have been determined for all cards, use the handle to assign conflict-free resources to each card.
- Activation. Activate all Plug and Play ISA cards and remove them from configuration mode.

The Plug and Play software identifies and configures devices using a set of commands defined in the *Plug and Play ISA Specification*. The commands are executed using three 8-bit I/O ports called auto-configuration ports. A sequence of writes to one of the ports (the ADDRESS port, 0279h) is used as an *initiation key* to enable the Plug and Play logic on all cards in the system. For more information about the initiation key, see "Initiation Key Sequence" later in this chapter.

Because all Plug and Play cards respond to the same I/O port addresses, some type of *isolation* mechanism must be used to single out the cards. This mechanism, called the isolation protocol, uses a unique number on each card to isolate one card at a time. After a card has been isolated, the Plug and Play software assigns it a handle, which is then used to select that Plug and Play card. Using this handle makes it unnecessary to repeat the isolation protocol when an individual card must be accessed. For more information about the isolation protocol, see "Isolating the Plug and Play ISA Cards" later in this chapter.

Each card supports a readable resource data structure that describes the resources supported and those requested by the functions on that card. The structure supports the concept of multiple functions on each ISA card, with each function defined as a logical device. Plug and Play resource information is provided for each logical device, and each logical device is independently configured through the Plug and Play standard registers. After the cards are isolated, the Plug and Play software reads the resource data structure on each card. When all resource capabilities and demands are known, a process of resource arbitration is carried out to determine resource allocation to each ISA card.

ISA cards are configured using the command registers specified for each resource type. Some ISA functions may not be able to be reconfigured, however. In these instances, the resources requested will be equivalent to the resources supported. Other resources on the system will be assigned around these static resources.

After the resources are assigned, an I/O conflict–detection mechanism may be invoked. This mechanism ensures that I/O resources assigned do not conflict with standard ISA cards.

After configuration has been completed, Plug and Play cards are removed from configuration mode. To reenable configuration mode, the initiation key must be issued again so the configuration information is not accidentally erased.

## Auto-Configuration Ports

A Plug and Play ISA card communicates with the system through the auto-configuration ports. The auto-configuration ports (listed in Table 6.1) are three 8-bit ports the software uses to access the configuration space on each Plug and Play ISA card; 16-bit accesses (IOCS16* asserted) to the configuration ports are not supported. The configuration space accessed by the ports is implemented as a set of 8-bit registers. For information about the contents of the configuration space, see "Reading the Resource Data" later in this chapter.

---

**Note** All Plug and Play ISA cards must decode and use these three I/O ports.

---

**Table 6.1 Auto-Configuration Ports**

| Port name | Location | Type |
|---|---|---|
| ADDRESS | 0279h (Printer status port) | Write only |
| WRITE_DATA | 0A79h (Printer status port + 0800h) | Write only |
| READ_DATA | Relocatable in range 0203h to 03FFh | Read only |

The ADDRESS and WRITE_DATA ports are located at fixed addresses. The WRITE_DATA port is located at an address alias of the ADDRESS port. All three auto-configuration ports use a 12-bit ISA address decode.

The READ_DATA port can be relocated within the I/O range 0203h through 03FFh. READ_DATA is the only auto-configuration port that can be read.

These three ports were chosen to avoid conflicts in the installed base of ISA functions, and to minimize the number of ports needed in the ISA I/O space.

**Note** The ISA card hardware must be able to decode the I/O addresses for the new configuration ports. It must also be able to disable the WRITE_DATA and READ_DATA ports on reset and then reenable them after the initiation key sequence has finished successfully.

### ADDRESS Port

To access the Plug and Play registers, first write the address of the appropriate register to the ADDRESS port. Then, read from the READ_DATA port or write to the WRITE_DATA port. A write to the ADDRESS port can be followed by any number of WRITE_DATA or READ_DATA accesses to the same register location; it is not necessary to write to the ADDRESS port before each access.

The ADDRESS port is also the write destination of the initiation key; see "Initiation Key Sequence" later in this chapter.

### WRITE_DATA Port

The WRITE_DATA port writes information to the Plug and Play registers. The last setting of the ADDRESS port determines the destination of the data.

### READ_DATA Port

The READ_DATA port reads information from the Plug and Play registers. The last setting of the ADDRESS port determines the source of data.

The address of the READ_DATA port is set by writing the proper value to the Plug and Play control register. The isolation protocol verifies that the location selected for READ_DATA is free of conflict. Bits 0 and 1 of the READ_DATA port address are fixed at 1. For information about setting the READ_DATA port address and a description of the conflict resolution of the address, see "Isolating the Plug and Play ISA Cards" later in this chapter.

## Plug and Play Registers

Each Plug and Play ISA card must contain enough register space to perform the functions needed to isolate, identify, and configure the card. Plug and Play card standard register space (shown in Figure 6.2) is divided into three parts: card control, logical device control, and logical device configuration.

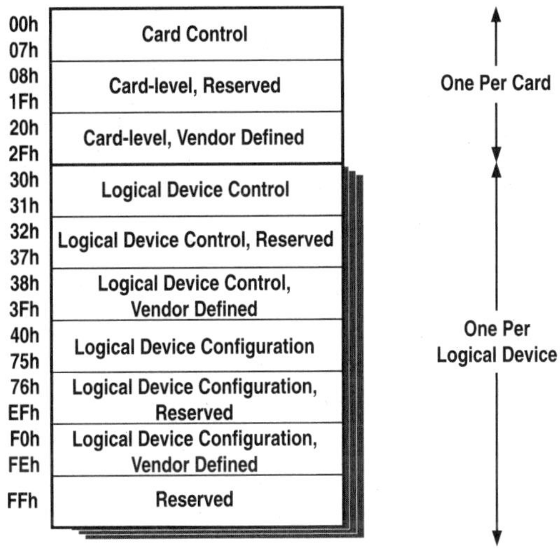


**Figure 6.2 Plug and Play Standard Register Space**

One set of card control registers is located on each ISA card. Card control registers are used for global functions that control the entire card.

Logical device control registers and logical device configuration registers are repeated for each logical device. Logical device control registers control device functions, such as enabling the device onto the ISA bus. Logical device configuration registers are used to program the device's ISA bus resource use.

Several vendor-defined registers exist in all three register locations so vendors can configure nonstandard ISA resources using the Plug and Play mechanism.

You must provide these register spaces and the logic that accesses each register location and data in your Plug and Play ISA card design.

Before reading about what happens to Plug and Play ISA cards after a reset, you should become familiar with the card control registers. Many of the events that occur after a reset are dependent on these registers, which collect and store information about the events as they take place. For information about each of the card control registers, see Table 6.2.

**Note** Any unimplemented registers in the range 00h through 2Fh must return a 0 when they are read. Unimplemented configuration registers must return the "disabled" or "unused" value when they are read.

**Table 6.2 Card Control Registers**

| Name | Address port value | Definition |
|---|---|---|
| Set RD_DATA port | 00h | Writing to this location modifies the address of the port used for reading from the Plug and Play ISA cards. Bits[7:0] become I/O read port address bits[9:2]. Reads from this register are ignored. |
| Serial isolation | 01h | A read to this register causes a Plug and Play card in the Isolation state to compare one bit of the board's identifier. This register is read only. |
| Config control | 02h | Bit[2]. Reset CSN to 0.<br>Bit[1]. Return to the Wait for Key state.<br>Bit[0]. Reset all logical devices and restore configuration registers to their power-up values.<br>A write to bit[0] of this register performs a reset function on all logical devices. This resets the contents of configuration registers to their default state. All cards' logical devices enter their default state, and the CSN is preserved.<br>A write to bit[1] of this register causes all cards to enter the Wait for Key state, but all CSNs are preserved and logical devices are not affected.<br>A write to bit[2] of this register causes all cards to reset their CSN to zero.<br>This register is write only. The values in this register must be automatically cleared by hardware, so software does not need to clear the bits. |

**Table 6.2 Card Control Registers (*continued*)**

| Name | Address port value | Definition |
|---|---|---|
| Wake[CSN] | 03h | A write to this port causes all cards that have a CSN matching the write data[7:0] to go from the Sleep state to either the Isolation state, if the write data for this command is zero, or the Config state, if the write data is not zero. The pointer to the byte-serial device is also reset. This register is write only. |
| Resource data | 04h | A read from this address reads the next byte of resource information. The status register must be polled until bit[0] is also set before this register can be read. This register is read only. |
| Status | 05h | Bit[0], when set, indicates it is okay to read the next data byte from the Resource Data register. This register is read only. |
| Card select number | 06h | A write to this port sets a card's CSN value. The CSN is a unique value assigned to each ISA card after the serial identification process so that each card can be individually selected during a Wake[CSN] command. This register is read-write. |
| Logical device number | 07h | Selects the current logical device. All reads and writes of memory, I/O, interrupt, and DMA configuration information access the registers of the logical device written here. The I/O Range Check and Activate commands operate on the selected logical device only. This register is read-write. If a card has only one logical device, this location should be a read-only value of 00h. |
| Card level reserved | 08h–1Fh | Reserved for future use. |
| Card level, vendor defined | 20h–2Fh | Vendor defined. |

## Initiation Key Sequence

The initiation key sequence is a series of writes to the ADDRESS port that is used as a key to enable the Plug and Play logic on all cards in the system (including boot devices). This sequence occurs after each system reset, whether it is a hardware or a software reset. If the proper series of I/O writes is detected, the Plug and Play auto-configuration ports are enabled and the configuration sequence begins.

All Plug and Play ISA cards, except boot devices, start up inactive and must go through the initiation key sequence. Boot devices must come up active to boot correctly on systems with a non–Plug and Play system BIOS. When the initiation key sequence has ended, boot devices are also deactivated and isolated with the rest of the Plug and Play cards, as described later in this chapter.

After Plug and Play ISA cards power up or are reset using RESET DRV on the ISA bus, they must be set to a known state in preparation for the initiation key sequence. These events occur on every ISA card (including boot devices) immediately after the RESET DRV line on the ISA bus goes low:

- The WRITE_DATA port is disabled.
- The *card select number* (CSN) register is reset to 00h, which places the cards in the Wait for Key state.
- The initial value of the *linear feedback shift register* (LFSR) is set to 6Ah.
- A delay of 2 ms occurs between the end of RESET DRV and any Plug and Play port access to allow a card to load initial configuration information from a nonvolatile device. (This could include setting the CSN register to 00h.)
- The card waits until it detects the first write at the ADDRESS port.

After the Plug and Play ISA cards are in the Wait for Key state, the system software begins to send a sequence of writes to the ADDRESS port. These writes consist of the 32 values that make up the initiation key, and are compared to those generated on each of the ISA cards.

The Plug and Play ISA cards use an LFSR to generate the values that verify the initiation key. The LFSR is an 8-bit shift register that resets to the value 6Ah. Figure 6.3 contains a diagram of the LFSR.

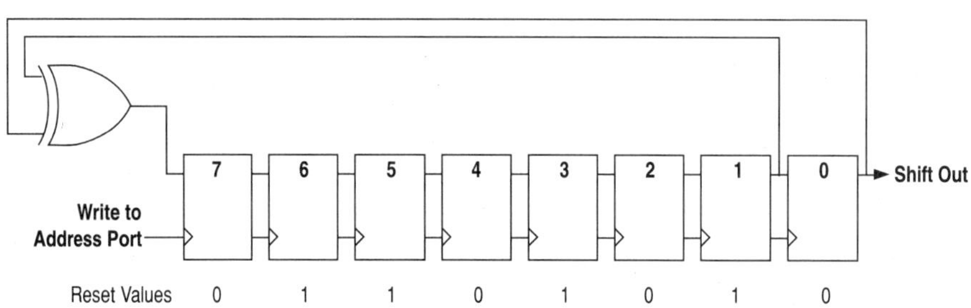


**Figure 6.3 Initiation Key Linear Feedback Shift Register**

The LFSR resets to its initial state (6Ah) any time the Plug and Play card is in the Wait for Key state and receives a write to the ADDRESS port that does not match the value currently in the LFSR. To ensure that the LFSR is in the initial state, the system software performs two write operations of the value 00h to the ADDRESS port before sending the initiation key. (The second of the two values sent to the ADDRESS port does not match the number in the LFSR, which means that the LFSR value is reset to 6Ah.)

The system software now begins writing the values of the initiation key to the ADDRESS port. The sequence of values for the initiation key in hexadecimal notation are:

```
6A, B5, DA, ED, F6, FB, 7D, BE,
DF, 6F, 37, 1B, 0D, 86, C3, 61,
B0, 58, 2C, 16, 8B, 45, A2, D1,
E8, 74, 3A, 9D, CE, E7, 73, 39
```

The ISA cards compare each value to the value located in their shift registers. If the values match, the shift register compares the two least-significant bits in the shift register, performs an eXclusive OR on the bits, and places the results back into the most-significant bit while performing a shift right. Figure 6.4 shows how the second value, 0B5h, is derived from the first value, 6Ah.

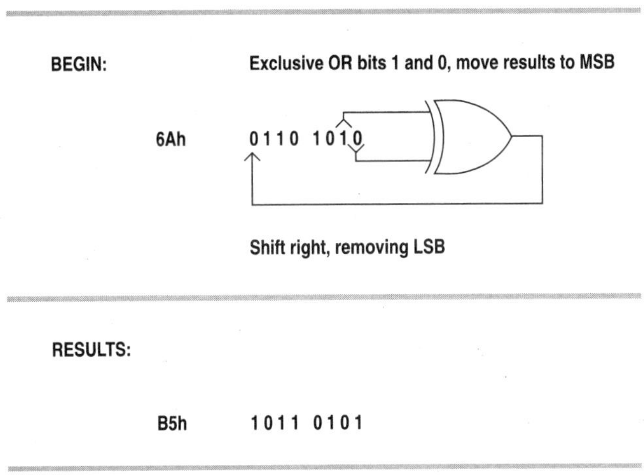


**Figure 6.4 Deriving Values for the Initiation Key**

The value determined after each of these shifts is then compared to the value available at the ADDRESS port. If the two values match, the next shift occurs. This sequence continues until all numbers in the key have been compared. At the end of a successful initiation key sequence, the value in the LFSR is 39h.

After the initiation key sequence has successfully finished, the hardware enables the WRITE_DATA port. Data can now be written to each of the cards' internal registers. (The design of these registers is described later in this chapter.) Boot device cards must also become inactive so their resources can be allocated. For more information about this process, see "Plug and Play ISA Boot Devices" later in this chapter. An LFSR signal also enables the circuitry for the READ_DATA port, although the actual address of the port will be determined later in the Plug and Play initialization sequence. All cards are now in the Sleep state.

If the value in the LFSR does not match the value at the ADDRESS port, the shift register value is returned to its initial state (6Ah). This means the value in the shift register at the end of the initiation key sequence will be 6Ah, because all values after the failed value will most likely also fail. Because the card does not enable its WRITE_DATA port, it cannot communicate with the system and is ignored throughout the rest of the configuration sequence.

Figure 6.5 contains a block diagram of a possible hardware configuration for the initiation key sequence.

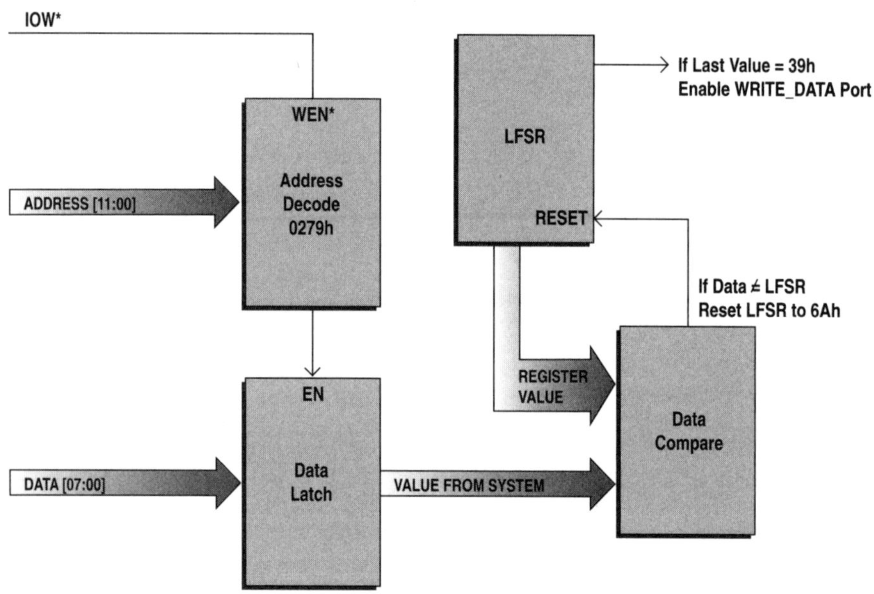


**Figure 6.5 Initiation Key Block Diagram**

## Isolating the Plug and Play ISA Cards

Because all Plug and Play ISA cards respond to the same I/O port address, it must be possible to differentiate between cards. This is done by isolation. As each card is isolated, it is given a unique CSN, which is used from then on as a means of identifying the card.

After the cards have successfully completed the initiation key, they enter the Sleep state (including boot devices). In this state, the cards wait for a Wake[CSN] software command with the write data set to 00h. The Wake[CSN] command is generated by first writing 03h (the address of the correct card control register) to the ADDRESS port. Next, 00h is written to the WRITE_DATA port, which loads 00h in each card's Wake[CSN] card control register. This sequence places all cards in the Isolation state, resets the serial identifier resource pointer to the beginning of its serial data, and disables the IOCHRDY line on the ISA bus. For more information about the card control registers, see "Plug and Play Registers" earlier in this chapter.

If the cards are entering the Isolation state for the first time, the READ_DATA port address must be set somewhere in the range 0203h through 03FFh using the Set RD_DATA port software command. The value 00h is written to the ADDRESS port, selecting the card control register that sets the READ_DATA port address. This address is then written to the WRITE_DATA port, which loads the address into the card control register. (The hardware must be able to determine the address of the number set in the card control register so that it can enable reads at that address.) The data stored in the register is located in bits[7:0]. When an address comparison occurs, this data is shifted so that it sets the bits[9:2] on the address bus. Bits[1:0] are fixed at binary 11, which sets the READ_DATA port address to any multiple of four. If the address selected for the READ_DATA port conflicts with another device, the address is changed during the isolation sequence and the sequence begins again. This process is described later in this section.

Each of the Plug and Play ISA cards now begins the isolation sequence. The key element of this isolation sequence is the serial identifier contained on each card. The serial identifier is a 72-bit, unique, nonzero number made up of two 32-bit fields and an 8-bit checksum. The first 32-bit field is a vendor identifier. The other 32 bits can be any value—for example, a serial number, part of a LAN address, or a static number—as long as no two cards in a single system contain the same 64-bit number.

The hardware on each of the cards expects 72 pairs of I/O accesses to the READ_DATA port. A card's response to these reads depends on the value of each bit of the serial identifier, which is being examined one bit at a time starting at bit 0 of byte 0 of the vendor identifier and continuing to bit 7 of the checksum. This method is shown in Figure 6.6.

| Check-sum | Serial Number | | | | Vendor ID | | | |
|---|---|---|---|---|---|---|---|---|
| Byte 0 | Byte 3 | Byte 2 | Byte 1 | Byte 0 | Byte 3 | Byte 2 | Byte 1 | Byte 0 |
| 7:0 | 7:0 | 7:0 | 7:0 | 7:0 | 7:0 | 7:0 | 7:0 | 7:0 |

SHIFT

**Figure 6.6 Shifting the Serial Identifier**

The vendor identifier and serial number for the Plug and Play ISA card can be saved in a nonvolatile source, such as a serial ROM, and can be read out during the isolation sequence. The checksum can also be calculated beforehand and saved in this serial ROM, where it is compared to a checksum calculated by the system software after a single card is isolated. The checksum can also be generated using an LFSR similar to the one used in the initiation key sequence. For a complete description of the serial identifier, see "Reading the Resource Data" later in this chapter.

As an example of a serial identifier, consider a card with a vendor abbreviation of "PXQ", a product number of "0443h", and a serial number of 04000100h. The vendor abbreviation is created using a 5-bit compressed ASCII format. See "Reading the Resource Data" later in this chapter.

The serial identifier in this example would be saved in the following order:

| | |
|---|---|
| Vendor identifier byte 0: | 43h |
| Vendor identifier byte 1: | 11h |
| Vendor identifier byte 2: | 04h |
| Vendor identifier byte 3: | 43h |
| Serial number byte 0: | 00h |
| Serial number byte 1: | 01h |
| Serial number byte 2: | 00h |
| Serial number byte 3: | 04h |

The isolation sequence begins when the system software performs a write to the ADDRESS port with the value 01h to select the serial isolation card control register. Next, the system software reads the value in the register. Performing the read clocks the first bit, causing the hardware to examine the first value of the serial identifier.

If the current bit of the serial identifier is 1, the card drives the data bus to 55h to complete the first I/O read cycle. If the bit is 0, the card places its data bus driver into a high-impedance state. All cards in a high-impedance state check the data bus during the I/O read cycle to find out if another card is driving D[1:0] to 01h.

The system software now performs a second read. (Serial ROM is not clocked, so the value of the serial identifier remains the same.) During this second I/O read, the card (or cards) that drove the 55h now drives the data bus to 0AAh. All high-impedance cards then check the data bus to find out if another card is driving D[1:0] to 10.

If a high-impedance card senses another card driving the data bus with the appropriate data during both cycles, that card ceases to participate in the current iteration of card isolation. Cards that stop participating participate in future iterations of the isolation sequence.

---

**Note** During each read cycle, the Plug and Play hardware drives the entire 8-bit data bus, but checks only the lower two bits.

---

All cards that were driving the bus should now prepare for the next pair of I/O reads. In some instances, the cards in a high-impedance state did not sense another card driving the bus. If none of the participating cards contain a 1 bit, each card that is still participating should continue to the next pair of I/O reads. The card increments the serial identifier by one bit and uses the shifted bit to decide its response.

This sequence is repeated for the entire 72-bit serial identifier.

At the end of this process, one card remains. This card is assigned a value in the CSN control register, which is later used to select the card. Cards that have been assigned a CSN do not take part in subsequent iterations of the isolation sequence.

Figure 6.7 contains a block diagram of one possible way to implement the isolation sequence. In this example, the card is placed in the Isolation state by writing to the Wake[CSN] port (03h) with a value of 00h. The serial ROM is reset to the beginning of the serial identifier.

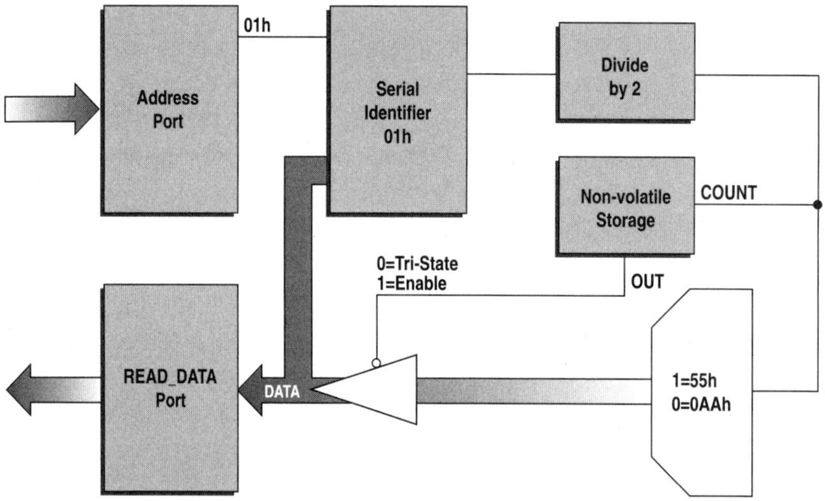


**Figure 6.7 Isolation Sequence Block Diagram**

Next, the ADDRESS port selects the serial identifier register (01h). During the first read cycle to the card, the output of a divide-by-two counter goes high, which selects the first bit in the serial ROM and places 55h on the card's internal data bus. If the value of the first bit in the serial ROM is 1, the 55h is sent to the READ_DATA port, where the system software can read it. If the first bit in the serial ROM is 0, the data bus is tri-stated, and the 55h is not detected at the READ_DATA port. During the second read cycle to the card, the output of the divide-by-two counter goes low, which causes no change in the serial ROM, but places 0AAh on the card's internal data bus. Because the serial identifier bit remains the same, the 0AAh is placed on the data bus in the same manner as the 55h. On the third read cycle to the card, the output of the divide-by-two counter goes high, clocking the next bit of the serial identifier. This process continues until 72 pairs of reads have occurred.

While the isolation sequence is taking place, any card that contains a 0 in the current bit position must be able to detect whether any other card contains a 1 in that position. If it does, the card that contains the 0 goes into the Sleep state, dropping out of the current iteration of the isolation sequence.

As noted, the 8-bit checksum can be stored in nonvolatile memory on the card or generated by the on-card logic in real time. An LFSR similar to the one described in the initiation key sequence can generate the checksum. This circuit is shown in Figure 6.8. The LFSR resets to 6Ah when it receives the Wake[CSN] command. The next shift value for the LFSR is calculated as LFSR[1] XOR LFSR[0] XOR Serial Data. The LFSR is shifted right one bit at the conclusion of each pair of reads to the serial isolation register. LFSR[7] is assigned the next shift value.

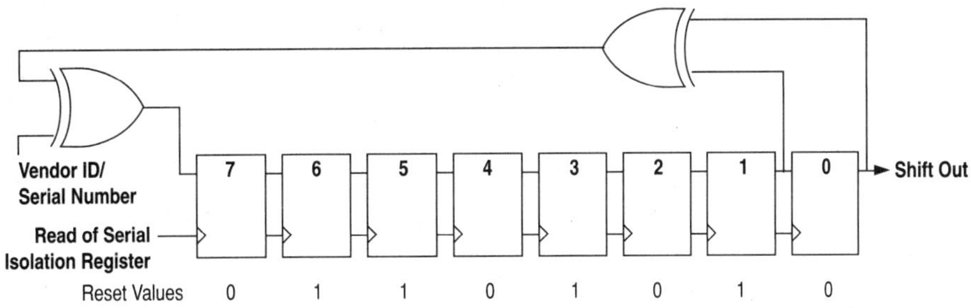


**Figure 6.8 Checksum Linear Feedback Shift Register**

For example, using the serial identifier discussed earlier (with a vendor abbreviation of "PXQ", a product number of "0443h", and a serial number of 04000100h), the bits of the serial identifier sent to the LFSR would be:

```
43h (Bit 0 to bit 7, 1 1 0 0 0 0 1 0)
11h                  1 0 0 0 1 0 0 0
04h                  0 0 1 0 0 0 0 0
43h                  1 1 0 0 0 0 1 0
00h                  0 0 0 0 0 0 0 0
01h                  1 0 0 0 0 0 0 0
00h                  0 0 0 0 0 0 0 0
04h                  0 0 1 0 0 0 0 0
```

The LFSR is reset to 6Ah when this card receives a Wake[CSN] command. After 64 pairs of reads of the serial isolation register, the LFSR contains the value 18h.

While the Plug and Play ISA cards are performing the isolation sequence, system software is reading back the results from the READ_DATA port. The software checks the data returned from each pair of I/O reads for the 55h and 0AAh driven by the ISA card hardware. If both 55h and 0AAh are read back, the software assumes the hardware had a 1 bit in that position. All other results are assumed to be a 0.

During the first 64 bits, software generates a checksum using the received data. The checksum is compared with the checksum read back in the last 8 bits of the sequence.

The system software must respond to two special conditions during an iteration. In the first iteration, if the software does not detect the 55h and 0AAh combination or the checksum does not match, the software assumes the READ_DATA port is in conflict, and the READ_DATA port is relocated. This process is repeated until a nonconflicting location for the READ_DATA port is found. The entire range between 0203h and 03FFh is available, but the software tries only a few locations before determining that no Plug and Play cards are present.

During subsequent iterations of the isolation sequence, the software interprets the occurrence of either of these two special conditions as meaning that no more Plug and Play cards are present (that is, the last card was found in the previous iteration). The isolation sequence is then terminated.

---

**Note** The system software delays 1 ms before starting the first pair of isolation reads, and waits 250 µs between each subsequent pair of isolation reads. This delay gives the ISA card time to access information from slow storage devices.

---

At this point, the IOCHRDY line on the ISA bus can be reenabled.

In this state, Plug and Play cards wait for a Wake[CSN] software command. This command selectively places one or more cards in either the Isolation or Config states, based on the write data and the value of the CSN on each card. Cards leave the Sleep state in response to a Wake[CSN] command when the value of write data bits[07:00] of the Wake[CSN] command matches the card's CSN. If the write data for the Wake[CSN] command is 00h, all cards that have not been assigned a CSN enter the Isolation state. If the write data for the Wake[CSN] command is any value other than 00h, the one card whose assigned CSN matches the parameter of the Wake[CSN] command enters the Config state.

### Reading the Resource Data

The resource data for a Plug and Play ISA card can be read while the card is in the Config state. This card can enter the Config state either after it has been isolated during the isolation sequence, or whenever it receives a Wake[CSN] software command in which the CSN matches the CSN assigned to the card. Only one card at a time can be in the Config state.

Resource data describes what resources must be available for each logical device on the card (for example, number of available IRQ numbers, address ranges of memory, and so on). Resource data can be stored in the same nonvolatile storage device (such as a serial ROM) that contained the serial identifier. The contents of a typical storage device are shown in Figure 6.9.

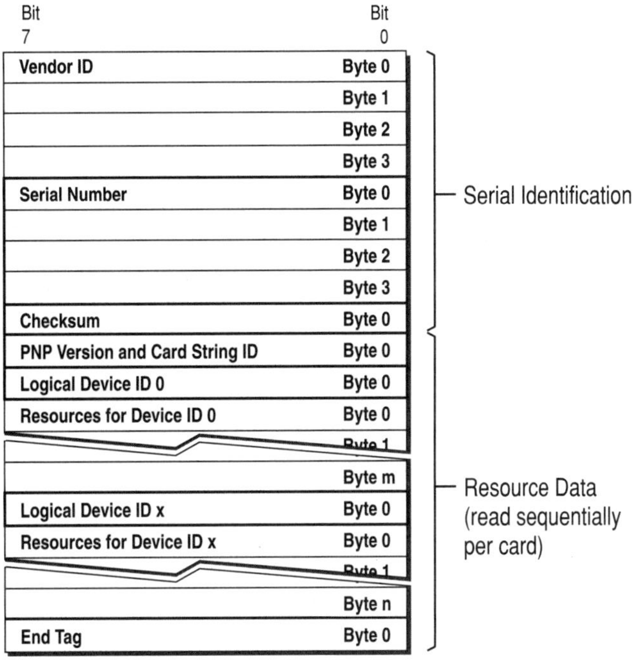


**Figure 6.9 Serial Identifier and Resource Data**

The resource data in the nonvolatile storage device must be sequentially loaded into the resource data register (04h). While the resource data is being loaded, the system software continues to read the status register (05h) until bit[0] is set, indicating that a byte of data is available at the resource data register. The system software can then retrieve the byte of resource data. When the read is performed on the resource data register, the status bit[0] is cleared, eight more bits are accumulated in the resource data register, and the status bit[0] is set again. When all of the resource data has been retrieved from the nonvolatile device, the device sends an End tag to the resource data register, letting the system software know that it has all of the information.

The contents of the nonvolatile storage device must be programmed with the information that the system needs to interpret which resources the card requires. The structure of the data contained in the storage device is variable, depending on what resources are needed.

The first nine bytes of the nonvolatile storage device contain the serial identifier for the card used during the isolation sequence, discussed earlier. Table 6.3 shows the construction of the serial identifier.

**Table 6.3 Plug and Play Serial Identifier**

| Field name | Length | Definition | |
|---|---|---|---|
| Vendor identifier byte 0 | 8 bits | Bit[7] | 0. |
| | | Bits[6:2] | First character in compressed ASCII. |
| | | Bits[1:0] | Second character in compressed ASCII bits[4:3]. |
| Vendor identifier byte 1 | 8 bits | Bits[7:5] | Second character in compressed ASCII bits[2:0]. |
| | | Bits[4:0] | Third character in compressed ASCII. |
| Vendor identifier byte 2 (high byte) | 8 bits | (Vendor assigned.) | |
| | | Bits[7:4] | First hexadecimal digit of product number. (Bit 7 is the most-significant bit.) |
| | | Bits[3:0] | Second hexadecimal digit of product number. (Bit 3 is the most-significant bit.) |
| Vendor identifier byte 3 (low byte) | 8 bits | (Vendor assigned.) | |
| | | Bits[7:4] | Third hexadecimal digit of product number. (Bit 7 is the most-significant bit.) |
| | | Bits[3:0] | Hexadecimal digit of revision level. (Bit 3 is the most-significant bit.) |
| Serial/Unique number byte 0 | 8 bits | Unique device number so the system can differentiate between multiple cards of the same type in one system. Bits[7:0]. | |
| Serial number byte 1 | 8 bits | Serial number bits[15:8]. | |
| Serial number byte 2 | 8 bits | Serial number bits[23:16]. | |
| Serial number byte 3 | 8 bits | Serial number bits[31:24]. | |
| Checksum | 8 bits | Checksum of identifier and serial number verifies that the information has been correctly read from a Plug and Play ISA card. | |

The 32-bit vendor identifier is constructed in the same way as an EISA identifier. This identifier consists of:

- Bits[15:0]. Three-character compressed ASCII EISA product identifier.
- Compressed ASCII is defined as five bits per character, "00001" = "A" ... "11010" = "Z".
- Bits[31:16]. Manufacturer-specific Product Number. The vendor must select the unique values for this field.

The vendor identifier field serves as a unique board identifier for selecting the Plug and Play card during the isolation sequence described earlier.

A 32-bit serial number is used only in the isolation process for selection of individual Plug and Play ISA cards. This number must be unique to support multiple cards in one system with the same vendor identifier. If this feature is not supported, this field must be returned as "FFFFFFFF". Lack of a unique serial number implies that only one instance of a vendor identifier can be supported in a system.

The checksum field ensures that no conflicts occurred while reading the device identifier information. The checksum generation is described earlier in this chapter. Note that if the checksum field is zero (0), the header is treated as if the checksum is correct, and the configuration proceeds normally.

Immediately following the serial identifier is a complete description of the resource requirements of the Plug and Play card.

Card resource data can only be read from cards in the Config state. A card can enter the Config state one of two different ways: in response to "winning" the serial isolation protocol and having a CSN assigned, or in response to receiving a Wake[CSN] command that matches the card's CSN.

Plug and Play cards function as if their 72-bit serial identifier and their resource data come from a single byte-serial device. The pointer to the data in the byte-serial device is reset in response to any Wake[CSN] command. This implies that if a card enters the Config state directly from the Sleep state in response to a Wake[CSN] command, the 9-byte serial identifier must be read first before the card resource data is accessed. The vendor identifier and unique serial number are valid, but the checksum byte, when read in this way, is not valid. For a card that enters the Config state from the Isolation state (that is, after the isolation protocol has been run and all 72 bits of the serial identifier have been read), the first read of the resource data register returns resource data.

The resource data is programmed as a set of "tagged" structures; that is, each resource is given a 1-byte tag at the beginning that describes the type of resource data, the name of the resource, and how long the description of that resource is. Each resource listed in the storage device begins with a tag. Two different tag types exist, one for small *resource data type functions* and one for large resource data type functions. Using the small resource data type tag minimizes the amount of storage needed in the nonvolatile device. The large resource data type tag can be used if large amounts of information must be kept on the storage device.

A Plug and Play logical device can use any number of resources and any combination of small resource data types or large resource data types. The general format of the resource data in the storage device is:

1. Plug and Play version number.
2. Identifier string resource.
3. Logical device identifier resource.
   - Any compatible device identifier resource for this logical device.
   - Resource data that matches the functions the card uses (IRQ, memory, I/O, DMA). No particular order is required.
   - Any dependent functions of the Plug and Play card can be configured. The order of the resource data establishes the binding to configuration registers.
4. End tag resource indicates the end of the resources for this Plug and Play card.

Step 3 is repeated for each logical device on the card.

For information about the resource data type functions and their format, see Appendix A, "Resource Data Type Functions." The examples in Appendix A demonstrate the format of the resource information that is programmed into a nonvolatile storage device.

## Configuring the Plug and Play ISA Card

The configuration of the Plug and Play ISA card is stored in a set of registers on the card. These registers are part of the standard registers described earlier in this chapter. The registers are divided into three parts—card control, logical device control, and logical device configuration—as shown in Figure 6.10.

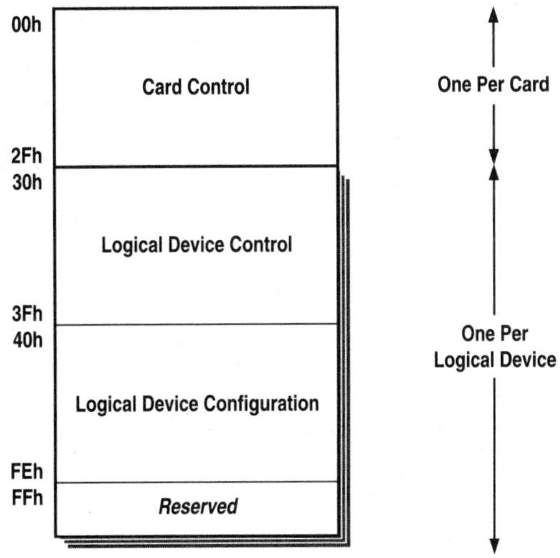


**Figure 6.10 Plug and Play Standard Register Map**

The logical device configuration portion of the standard registers must be loaded with the configuration information for whatever resources are assigned to that logical device. The logical device configuration registers are:

- Memory address base registers (up to four noncontiguous ranges)
- I/O address base registers (up to eight noncontiguous ranges)
- Interrupt level select registers (up to two separate interrupt levels)
- DMA channel select registers (up to two DMA channels )

The resource assignments of the Plug and Play ISA cards are programmed through the ADDRESS, WRITE_DATA, and READ_DATA ports using the same method that was used to access the card control registers.

The following paragraphs describe each of the logical device configuration registers in detail. These configuration registers are all based on the current logical device selected. They are read-write registers, and always reflect the current operation of all logical devices on the Plug and Play ISA card.

### Memory Configuration Registers

Tables 6.4 and 6.5 describe how memory resources are programmed. If the configuration software does not allocate memory for any reason, memory resource registers (for example, 40h, 41h, 43h, and 44h for descriptor 0) are written with a zero value, disabling the memory range. Registers must accurately reflect the resources in use at all times. Reading these registers is the only way operating system software can learn what resources are in use by an activated card (in the case where the card is activated by the system BIOS before the system loads).

**Table 6.4 Memory Space Configuration**

| Name | Register index | Definition |
|---|---|---|
| Memory base address bits[23:16] descriptor 0 | 40h | Read-write value indicating the selected memory base address bits[23:16] for memory descriptor 0. |
| Memory base address bits[15:08] descriptor 0 | 41h | Read-write value indicating the selected memory base address bits[15:8] for memory descriptor 0. |
| Memory control | 42h | Bit[1] specifies 8/16-bit control. This bit is set to indicate 16-bit memory and is cleared to indicate 8-bit memory.<br>Bit[0], if cleared, indicates the next field can be used as a range length for decode (implies that range length and base alignment of memory descriptor are equal).<br>Bit[0], if set, indicates the next field is the upper limit for the address.<br>Bit[0] is read only. |
| Memory upper-limit address bits[23:16] or range length bits[23:16] for descriptor 0 | 43h | Read-write value indicating the selected memory high address bits[23:16] for memory descriptor 0.<br>If bit[0] of memory control is 0, this is the range length.<br>If bit[0] of memory control is 1, this is the upper limit for memory address (equal to memory base address plus the range length allocated). |
| Memory upper-limit address bits[15:8] or range length bits[15:8] for descriptor 0 | 44h | Read-write value indicating the selected memory high address bits[15:8] for memory descriptor 0, either a memory address or a range length, as described above. |
| Filler | 45h–47h | Reserved. |
| Memory descriptor 1 | 48h–4Ch | Memory descriptor 1. |
| Filler | 4Dh–4Fh | Reserved. |
| Memory descriptor 2 | 50h–54h | Memory descriptor 2. |
| Filler | 55h–57h | Reserved. |
| Memory descriptor 3 | 58h–5Ch | Memory descriptor 3. |
| Filler | 5Dh–5Fh | Reserved. |

**Table 6.5 32-Bit Memory Space Configuration**

| Name | Register index | Definition |
|---|---|---|
| 32-bit memory base address bits[31:24] descriptor 0 | 76h | Read-write value indicating the selected memory base address bits[31:24] for 32-bit memory descriptor 0. |
| Memory base address bits[23:16] descriptor 0 | 77h | Read-write value indicating the selected memory base address bits[23:16] for 32-bit memory descriptor 0. |
| Memory base address bits[15:8] descriptor 0 | 78h | Read-write value indicating the selected memory base address bits[15:8] for 32-bit memory descriptor 0. |
| Memory base address bits[7:0] descriptor 0 | 79h | Read-write value indicating the selected memory base address bits[7:0] for 32-bit memory descriptor 0. |
| 32-bit memory control | 7Ah | Bits[7:3] reserved.<br>Bits[2:1] specify memory control. These bits are set to indicate 8-bit, 16-bit, or 32-bit memory as follows:<br>00 8-bit memory<br>01 16-bit memory<br>10 Reserved<br>11 32-bit memory<br>If bit[0] of memory control is 0, this is the range length.<br>If bit[0] of memory control is 1, this is the upper limit for memory address (equal to memory base address plus the range length allocated).<br>Bit[0] is read only. |
| Memory upper-limit address bits[31:24] or range length bits[31:24] for descriptor 0 | 7Bh | Read-write value indicating the selected memory high address bits[31:24] for memory descriptor 0.<br>If bit[0] of memory control is 0, this is the range length.<br>If bit[0] of memory control is 1, this is the upper limit for memory address (equal to memory base address plus the range length allocated). |
| Memory upper-limit address bits[23:16] or range length bits[23:16] for descriptor 0 | 7Ch | Read-write value indicating the selected memory high address bits[23:16] for memory descriptor 0, either a memory address or a range length, as described above. |
| Memory upper-limit address bits[15:8] or range length bits[15:8] for descriptor 0 | 7Dh | Read-write value indicating the selected memory high address bits[15:8] for memory descriptor 0, either a memory address or a range length, as described above. |
| Memory upper-limit address bits[7:0] or range length bits[7:0] for descriptor 0 | 7Eh | Read-write value indicating the selected memory high address bits[7:0] for memory descriptor 0, either a memory address or a range length, as described above. |
| Filler | 7Fh | Reserved. |
| 32-bit memory descriptor 1 | 80h–88h | 32-bit memory descriptor 1. |
| Filler | 89h–8Fh | Reserved. |
| 32-bit memory descriptor 2 | 90h–98h | 32-bit memory descriptor 2. |
| Filler | 99h–9Fh | Reserved. |
| 32-bit memory descriptor 3 | A0h–A8h | 32-bit memory descriptor 3. |

Four memory descriptors, maximum, are available for each logical device.

Memory range length registers are defined as a mask of address bits[23:8] (or [31:0] for 32-bit memory space). If a bit in the mask is set, this indicates that the memory address bit is used in a comparator to determine an address match. If a bit is clear, this indicates that the memory address bit is not used in determining an address match. For example, a logical device that requests 64K of memory would have a range length of:

Memory range length [23:16] = FFh
Memory range length [15:8] = 00h

This indicates that address bits[23:16] are used to compare for a matching address, and address bits[15:8] and bits[7:0] are not used. This 64K address range must be aligned on a 64K or higher boundary.

Memory upper-limit registers are defined as being one byte greater than the memory resource assigned. For example, a logical device that requests 64K of memory assigned at a base address of 1 MB would have:

Memory base [23:16] = 10h
Memory base [15:8] = 00h
Memory upper limit [23:16] = 11h
Memory upper limit [15:8] = 00h

The memory control register, 42h (or 7Ah for 32-bit memory), can be implemented as a read-only register in devices that do not support programmable 8/16/32-bit operation and use only one type of memory decode. Memory registers 43h and 44h (or 7Bh through 7Eh for 32-bit memory) need not be supported by devices that support only a fixed-length memory range aligned on a natural boundary.

### I/O Configuration Registers

Registers 60h through 6Fh are used for I/O range configuration, as shown in Table 6.6. Eight I/O descriptors, maximum, are available for each logical device. Writing a base address of 0000h disables the I/O range. Reading these registers is the only way operating system software can "learn" what resources are in use by an activated card (in the case where the system BIOS activates the card before the operating system loads).

**Table 6.6 I/O Configuration Registers**

| Name | Register index | Definition |
|---|---|---|
| I/O port base address bits[15:8] descriptor 0 | 60h | Read-write value indicating the selected I/O lower-limit address bits[15:8] for I/O descriptor 0. If a logical device indicates it only uses 10-bit decoding, bits[15:10] need not be supported. |
| I/O port base address bits[7:0] descriptor 0 | 61h | Read-write value indicating the selected I/O lower-limit address bits[7:0] for I/O descriptor 0. |
| I/O port address descriptors[1–6] | 62h–6Dh | I/O base addresses for I/O descriptors 1–6 |
| I/O port base address bits[15:8] descriptor 7 | 6Eh | Read-write value indicating the selected I/O base address bits[15:8] for I/O descriptor 7. If a logical device indicates it only uses 10-bit decoding, bits[15:10] need not be supported. |
| I/O port base address bits[7:0] descriptor 7 | 6Fh | Read-write value indicating the selected I/O base address bits[7:0] for I/O descriptor 7. |

### Interrupt Configuration Registers

Each logical device in a Plug and Play ISA card can use up to two interrupt requests. These can be selected by writing to the appropriate configuration register. Table 6.7 describes the interrupt configuration registers.

**Table 6.7 Interrupt Configuration Registers**

| Name | Register index | Definition |
|---|---|---|
| Interrupt request level select 0 | 70h | Read-write value indicating selected interrupt level. Bits[3:0] select which interrupt level is used for Interrupt 0. 1 selects IRQL 1; 15 selects IRQL 15. IRQL 0 is not a valid interrupt selection and represents no interrupt selection. 9 specifies IRQL 2(9). IRQL 2 is reserved and is not a valid interrupt selection. |
| Interrupt request type select 0 | 71h | Read-write value indicating which type of interrupt is used for the request level selected above.<br><br>Bit[1] : Level, 1 = high, 0 = low<br>Bit[0] : Type, 1 = level, 0 = edge<br><br>If a card supports only one type of interrupt, this register can be read only. |
| Interrupt request level select 1 | 72h | Read-write value indicating selected interrupt level. Bits[3:0] select which interrupt level is used for Interrupt 0. 1 selects IRQL 1; 15 selects IRQL 15. IRQL 0 is not a valid interrupt selection and represents no interrupt selection. 9 specifies IRQL 2(9). IRQL 2 is reserved and is not a valid interrupt selection. |
| Interrupt request type select 1 | 73h | Read-write value indicating which type of interrupt is used for the request level selected above.<br><br>Bit[1] : Level, 1 = high, 0 = low<br>Bit[0] : Type, 1 = level, 0 = edge |

### DMA Configuration Registers

Each logical device in a Plug and Play ISA card can use up to two DMA channels. These channels can be selected by writing to the appropriate configuration register. Table 6.8 describes the DMA configuration registers.

**Table 6.8 DMA Configuration Registers**

| Name | Register index | Definition |
|---|---|---|
| DMA channel select 0 | 74h | Read-write value indicating selected DMA channels. Bits[2:0] select which DMA channel is in use for DMA 0. Zero selects DMA channel 0; 7 selects DMA channel 7. DMA channel 4, the cascade channel, indicates no DMA channel is active. |
| DMA channel select 1 | 75h | Read-write value indicating selected DMA channels. Bits[2:0] select which DMA channel is in use for DMA 1. Zero selects DMA channel 0; 7 selects DMA channel 7. DMA channel 4, the cascade channel, indicates no DMA channel is active. |

### Reserved and Vendor-Defined Configuration Registers

Registers 0A9h through 0EFh are reserved for future Plug and Play ISA use. Registers in the range of 0F0h through 0FEh are vendor defined and can be used for any purpose. These registers are shown in Table 6.9.

**Table 6.9 Reserved and Vendor-Defined Configuration Registers**

| Name | Register index | Definition |
|---|---|---|
| Logical device configuration reserved | 0A9h–0EFh | Reserved. |
| Logical device configuration vendor defined | F0h–FEh | Vendor defined. |
| Reserved | 0FFh | Reserved. |

## Accessing the Configuration Information

Figure 6.11 and Figure 6.12 show how the configuration registers can be used to direct specific information to and from the ISA bus. In each case, the configuration information contained in the logical device configuration register is compared with signals on the ISA bus.

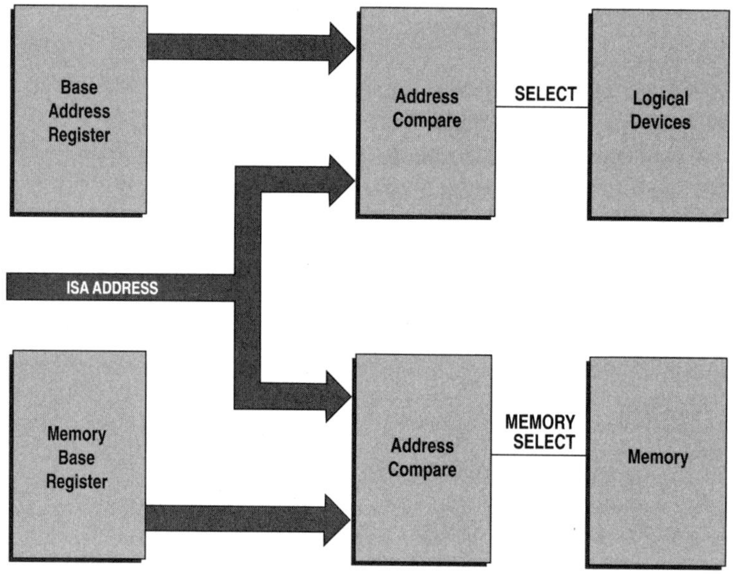


**Figure 6.11 Using the Address Configuration Registers**

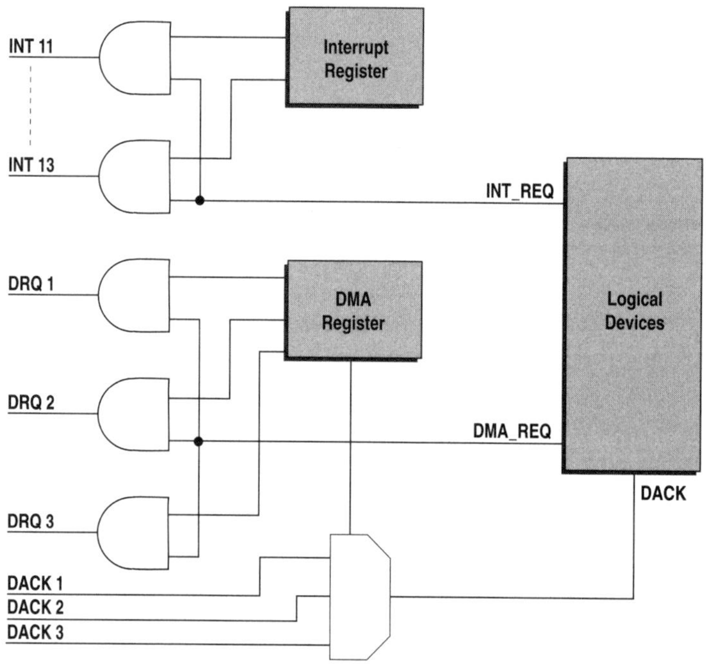


**Figure 6.12 Using Interrupt and DMA Configuration Registers**

The base address register is compared to the address on the ISA bus and, if the two match, is used as the chip select line to the ISA card. The memory base address register is also connected to the ISA address bus, and when the two match, a memory chip select line can be activated.

When an interrupt request or a DMA request occurs on the card, these signals are gated through a set of AND gates whose other input is connected to the interrupt and DMA registers, which select the proper ISA bus lines to use, depending on the configuration information loaded into the registers. The DMA register is also used to select the DACK line that sends the DMA acknowledge to the ISA card.

## Plug and Play ISA Boot Devices

The types of devices required for the boot process include the primary input (generally a keyboard), the primary output (generally a display adapter and a monitor), and any IPL devices.

The Plug and Play ISA expansion card must power up active. This gives systems without a Plug and Play system BIOS the means of using Plug and Play ISA devices during a "legacy" boot process.

Plug and Play ISA expansion cards that contain boot devices require some special considerations to properly boot the system. The system BIOS is primarily responsible for isolating, identifying, and configuring devices required in the boot process. The system BIOS can override the default resource configuration to prevent conflicts.

In some instances, a Plug and Play ISA expansion card can be used in a system that cannot configure the Plug and Play registers until after the system has booted (because the system contains a non–Plug and Play system BIOS). In these cases, the card should include a means of setting a default resource configuration at power-up, whether this mechanism is provided by jumpers, switches, or a configuration EEPROM (the preferred method).

If a boot card is plugged into a motherboard that does not contain a Plug and Play system BIOS, the card must be capable of responding to the system BIOS as though it were a non–Plug and Play card. A non–Plug and Play system BIOS will not perform the isolation sequence, but will instead perform a *ROM scan* to detect the presence of a boot device. After the ROM scan detects the presence of an option ROM on the boot device, the system ROM will jump to the option ROM to initialize the device. A Plug and Play option ROM will detect that the system BIOS is not Plug and Play compatible, and should respond accordingly. For more information about option ROMs, see the *Plug and Play BIOS Specification* and Chapter 9, "Option ROM Design." Although an initial set of static resources must be provided during this "legacy" boot, the Plug and Play ISA card must be capable of changing these resources, or of completely disabling the device, if the system contains a Plug and Play–compliant operating system. When the operating system is loaded, it will isolate, identify, and configure any resources available on Plug and Play ISA cards that the system BIOS has not yet enumerated.

Default resource usage of a card is always reflected in the card's configuration registers. This information allows the Plug and Play configuration or a driver to easily determine the default settings of a Plug and Play boot device, regardless of which operating system the device driver was written for. The resource use of the boot devices can be overridden by the operating system–dependent Plug and Play configuration with full cooperation of the device driver. This functionality, coupled with the fact that nonboot Plug and Play devices do not power up active, decreases the amount of user intervention needed to configure a system, and increases the chance the system will boot.

Some devices are always boot devices. For this class of device, except for disable, no user-selectable options need be included on the card to control booting.

Another class of device, such as a network interface card, may be a boot device in some situations and not a boot device in others. For this type of device, a user-selectable option should be included on the card that allows the user to choose whether the device is active at boot time or not.

### BIOS Support for Plug and Play ISA Devices

A system BIOS can support Plug and Play ISA devices two basic ways. One way is to implement a full Plug and Play BIOS 1.0a, as defined in the *Plug and Play BIOS Specification*, Version 1.0a. This is the recommended solution because it also provides similar configuration capabilities for motherboard devices.

An alternate solution, which is primarily an interim step to implementing a full Plug and Play BIOS 1.0a, is to add Plug and Play ISA extensions to a standard BIOS (for ISA cards only). For example, the Intel BIOS extensions and the corresponding Intel configuration utility are the most common means of implementing this solution. Windows 95, however, will treat this type of BIOS as a legacy BIOS with legacy ISA cards, and will not provide the full benefits of Plug and Play.

## Option ROM Support

For more information about option ROM support for ISA expansion cards, see Chapter 9, "Option ROM Design."

# ISA Card Recommendations

In addition to the ISA card requirements, you can also implement the following recommendations:

- The serial identifier and resource data for each logical device on the card should be stored in a nonvolatile storage device, such as a serial ROM.
- ISA cards should support non–Plug and Play systems using a combination of power-up active boot devices and software configuration utilities and drivers.
- Standard settings for IRQs, DMA channels, I/O ports, and base memory addresses (where appropriate) generally associated with the device in a non–Plug and Play system should be available at power-up. However, these resources must be able to be configured by software after the system boots.
- If your Plug and Play system BIOS is using Functions 42h and 43h to store information about non–Plug and Play ISA devices and their resources, it may be necessary to add more nonvolatile memory to handle the Extended System Configuration Data (ESCD) contents. How much extra memory is required depends on the amount of data the system BIOS will save. For more information, see Chapter 8, "System BIOS Design."

# PCI Cards

To be Plug and Play compliant, PCI cards attached to the PCI bus must comply with the hardware and timing specifications in the *PCI Local Bus Specification,* Revision 2.0. You may also need to make changes to PCI bus bridges to propagate the Plug and Play attributes of a secondary bus connected to a PCI bridge.

The PCI specification describes the configuration register space used by the system to identify and configure each device attached to the bus. This configuration space is made up of a 256-byte field for each device, and contains sufficient information for the system to identify the capabilities of the device. Configuration of the device is also controlled from this register space.

The configuration register space is made up of a header region and a device-dependent region. Each configuration space must have a 64-byte header at offset 0. All of the device registers the device circuit uses for initialization, configuration, and catastrophic error handling must fit within the space between byte 64 and byte 255. All other registers the device uses during normal operation must be located in normal I/O or memory space. Reads to reserved or unimplemented registers must complete normally and return 0. Writes to reserved registers must complete normally, and the data must be discarded.

*Expansion ROM* can also be placed on the PCI card to provide for device-specific requirements, or for the system boot.

If you are using an ISA bus in conjunction with a PCI bridge, the Plug and Play ISA Write Data Port address must be propagated through the bridge to the ISA bus at power-up and system reset. This will ensure that a Plug and Play BIOS or operating system can isolate, identify, and configure Plug and Play ISA cards plugged into the ISA bus during the boot process.

The PCI SIG has been working on a new board vendor level of identification for PCI adapters. The new ID registers should be included in the PCI Local Bus Specification Revision 2.1, available from the PCI SIG. These registers should be used on all PCI boards to enable Plug and Play and specifically Windows 95 to correctly identify the PCI adapter rather than the chip on the adapter. This will enable a more correct driver installation to take place without user intervention.

The adapter-level identification registers work in conjunction with the device-level identification registers to completely identify the PCI adapter. The new IDs, which have been added to the configuration space header, are located at offsets 02Ch and 02Eh. Subsystem Vendor ID (offset 02Ch) is the ID of the manufacturer of the PCI adapter/subsystem and is assigned by the PCI SIG. Subsystem ID (offset 02Eh) is the ID of the adapter and is assigned by the manufacturer.

Adapter manufacturers should implement the ID fields in this proposal as soon as possible to enable Plug and Play systems to correctly identify and configure their adapters.

# PCMCIA Cards

Generally, PCMCIA cards can be broken down into two categories: I/O cards and memory cards. Both types must meet the requirements documented in the *PCMCIA Standard* to qualify for the Windows 95 Logo.

For all PCMCIA cards to work effectively with Windows 95, you must implement a minimum set of tuples documented in the PCMCIA standard. Windows 95 uses these tuples to identify and configure any PCMCIA cards connected to the PC 95.

## Assigning I/O or Memory Regions

Windows 95 determines what type of card is plugged into the PCMCIA socket by examining the tuples on the card. If the card contains no tuples, Windows 95 attempts to detect the card as a memory card. Memory cards that do not have tuples are detected by checking the common memory area to determine the size of the memory on the card, because there is no device information tuple that would contain the memory size. After the size is determined, Windows 95 sets up the card to have a single drive number assigned. If the card contains tuples, Windows 95 examines the tuples to determine the type of device, I/O, and/or memory that exists on the card. It uses the configuration and configuration table entry tuples to determine whether the card is an I/O device. It uses the device information tuple to determine whether the card is a memory device and the size of the memory, and sets up the card to be assigned appropriate drive numbers.

---

**Note** Although Windows 95 will detect and configure memory cards that contain no tuples, this feature exists only for backward compatibility. Memory cards that qualify for the Windows 95 Logo must contain the minimum set of memory card tuples discussed later in this chapter.

---

A PC card can have a single function, such as a single-function memory card or a single-function SCSI card, or it can contain multiple functions, such as a memory card and a SCSI card combined. Because of this, Windows 95 must be able to gather information about these multiple functions from the tuples on the card (if it contains tuples). However, a single-function SCSI card, for example, could also contain a small amount of memory that buffers reads and writes to the disk. This memory should be included in the tuples. If it is identified in the tuple as RAM or flash memory, Windows 95 will treat it as it would any other memory region, and set it up to be assigned a drive number. To prevent this from happening, memory regions on the card that are not intended for normal RAM or flash memory should be defined as function-specific memory regions in the device information tuple. Otherwise, Windows 95 will configure it as a memory device.

## PCMCIA I/O Card Requirements

For Plug and Play functionality in a PC 95, PC I/O cards must support a set of required information and configuration tuples. The PCMCIA bus enumerator uses these tuples to identify the card, load the correct device driver, and indicate all the possible configurations to the Plug and Play configuration manager. The configuration manager then dynamically assigns a valid configuration based on this information.

You must implement the following items for any PCMCIA I/O card that connects to a PC 95:

- The PC card must contain the device information tuple (CISTPL_DEVICE, 01h), the level 1 version/product information tuple (CISTPL_VERS_1, 15h), the configuration tuple (CISTPL_CONFIG, 1Ah), and the configuration table entry tuple (CISTPL_CFTABLE_ENTRY, 1Bh).
- The level 1 version/product information tuple must contain the name of the manufacturer and the name of the product in the product information string (TPLLV1_INFO, byte 4).
- The name of the manufacturer and the name of the product in the level-1 version/product information tuple must be composed only of ASCII characters greater than ASCII 20h and less than ASCII 7Fh.

At a minimum, a PCMCIA I/O card for the PC 95 must support the tuples shown in Table 6.10. Windows 95 uses the information contained in the required (and recommended) tuples to create a unique device identifier for the card, and assimilate configuration information for the device. Windows 95 uses the device configuration tuples to determine the general characteristics of the card.

**Table 6.10 Required I/O Card Tuples**

| Tuple | Tuple code | Tuple identifier | Comments |
|---|---|---|---|
| Device information (common memory) | CISTPL_DEVICE | 01h | For nonmemory cards, this tuple must be present, but the device type will be NULL. |
| Level 1 version/ product information | CISTPL_VERS_1 | 15h | Product information string<br>Product name<br>Product number<br>Other manufacturer information |
| Configuration | CISTPL_CONF | 1Ah | Indicates the location of configuration registers and the registers that are present. |
| Configuration table entry | CISTPL_CE | 1Bh | Appropriate configuration requirements for I/O space, interrupts, memory, and so on should be specified. |

The device information tuple provides information about the memory devices used in the card's common memory space. The device type, size, and speed are used to configure the socket for efficient accesses to the card. This tuple must be present on PCMCIA I/O cards, but the device type must be NULL.

The level 1 version product information tuple contains human-readable information about the product and its manufacturer. This information is intended to be displayed, where necessary, to the user. Windows 95 uses the information contained in the product information and product name strings to construct the device identifier for that card. It also scans through the tuple, starting at the very beginning and going to the end of the product name string. The information gathered from the scan is one source for creating a 16-bit cyclic redundancy check (CRC) that Windows 95 uses to construct the device identifier. Because the optional third and fourth strings in the tuple are not used in the CRC scan, devices that require unique numbers on each card can use these strings to store that information.

The configuration tuple tells the software where to locate the configuration registers that program the card's configuration, and which registers are present on the card.

Each configuration table entry tuple completely describes one valid configuration in which the card can operate. Each entry describes power, timing, I/O space, interrupt, and memory space requirements for the given configuration. Configuration software selects one of these configurations for the card based on the resources currently available in the system.

# PCMCIA I/O Card Recommendations

You can implement the following recommended features to help Windows 95 better identify the PC card and make the identification and configuration process more efficient:

- The manufacturer identifier tuple (CISTPL_MANFID, 20h) and the function identification tuple (CISTPL_FUNCID, 21h) should be included.
- In the configuration entry tuples, place the configuration information in the preferred order for configuring the device.
- At least one configuration table entry should provide complete flexibility of IRQs, I/O ports, and memory space.

## Additional Tuples

The manufacturer identifier tuple (CISTPL_MANFID, 20h) and the function identification tuple (CISTPL_FUNCID, 21h) add extra flexibility to a PC card that connects to the PC 95. These two tuples are described in Table 6.11.

**Table 6.11 Additional Recommended Tuples**

| Tuple | Tuple code | Tuple identifier | Comments |
|---|---|---|---|
| Manufacturer identifier | CISTPL_MANFID | 20h | Card manufacturer identifier code. Defines manufacturer for this card. |
| Function identification | CISTPL_FUNCID | 21h | Provides function information about the card. Also includes system initialization information. |

The manufacturer identifier tuple provides a unique identifier for the manufacturer of this card. This code is registered with PCMCIA. Windows 95 uses the manufacturer identifier tuple as one source for creating a 16-bit CRC used in the construction of the device identifier.

The function identification tuple provides information about the class of device, or what function the card provides (for example, memory, modem, disk, and so on). This information helps the software perform necessary installation tasks and locate compatible drivers. Windows 95 uses the function identification tuple internally to determine what type of device is on the PC card (although it is not required to make this determination).

## Placing Configuration Information

In the configuration entry tuples, place the configuration information in the preferred order for configuring the device. Windows 95 processes the tuples in the order they are placed in the card's card information structure (CIS). From these tuples, the PCMCIA bus enumerator creates logical configurations in the same order. The configuration manager also processes them in this order.

## Resource Flexibility

Many current PCMCIA cards specify "fixed" configurations to address compatibility with existing software. However, this is not the intended use for tuples; the configuration software should be responsible for compatibility. The tuples should be used only to rule out configurations not supported by the hardware. If you must provide fixed configurations for an operating system other than Windows 95, you should still provide one or more entries that specify the maximum configurability the hardware can handle.

# PCMCIA Memory Card Requirements

A PCMCIA memory card must also meet a set of standards identified in the *PCMCIA Standard*, at a minimum. For Plug and Play functionality in a PC 95, memory cards must support a set of required device, memory information, and configuration tuples.

You must implement the following tuples for any new PCMCIA memory cards designed to be used with a PC 95:

- The device information tuple (CISTPL_DEVICE, 01h)
- The JEDEC-C tuple (CISTPL_JEDEC-C, 18h)
- The device geometry information tuple (CISTPL_DEVICE_GEO, 1Eh)
- The format tuple (CISTPL_FORMAT, 41h)
- The organization tuple (CISTPL_ORG, 46h)

The PCMCIA bus enumerator uses these tuples to identify the type and size of each memory region on the card. The type of memory determined is used to load the Memory Technology driver (MTD), which handles all access to the memory card. The tuples also describe the configuration of the memory available on the card. These required tuples are described in Table 6.12.

**Table 6.12 Required Memory Card Tuples**

| Tuple | Tuple code | Tuple identifier | Comments |
|---|---|---|---|
| Device information (common memory) | CISTPL_DEVICE | 01h | Card Services uses the device size and type to configure the socket interface. Extended device speeds are not required to be supported by host systems. |
| JEDEC-C | CISTPL_JEDEC-C | 18h | Programmability information. |
| Device geometry information | CISTPL_DEVICE_GEO | 1Eh | Device-level architecture information. |
| Format | CISTPL_FORMAT | 41h | Data recording format information. |
| Organization | CISTPL_ORG | 46h | Partition information. |

The device information tuple provides information about the memory devices used in the card's common memory space. The device type, size, and speed are used to configure the socket for efficient accesses to the card.

The JEDEC-C tuple provides specific information (in conjunction with the device information tuple) about programmable memory devices. Software can use this information to identify the specific programming algorithm to use with the devices. New types of flash memory cards must contain a JEDEC ID tuple for Windows 95 to determine the proper MTD to load for the device.

The device geometry information tuple provides low-level (physical) device organization information relating to block or sector size or both. This information can be used to configure low-level drivers for access to the media.

The format tuple describes how data is laid down on the media (for example, formatted as for a disk, for memory, and so on) including error detection and correction methods. This information allows low-level drivers to reliably read and write the media.

The organization tuple provides information about the file system format of the data on the media. With this information, the correct file system can be used to interpret the data on the media.

## Additional Information

The DTPL.EXE program displays information derived from the tuples on a PCMCIA I/O card. This program interprets the tuples on the PC card, then displays the Plug and Play device identifier, the Plug and Play logical configurations, and a display of each tuple on the card.

DTPL.EXE is available in the Windows 95 DDK and in the CompuServe Plug and Play forum library (enter "go plugplay").

# VL-Bus Cards

A VL-bus for the PC 95 must meet the requirements described in the current version of VESA's VL-bus standard. It must also meet the Plug and Play requirements as defined by VESA. VESA is currently determining the Plug and Play characteristics that must be added to VL-bus expansion cards for identification and configuration. For more information, see the preliminary VESA *VL-Bus Plug and Play Addendum*. For more information about where to obtain this documentation, see Appendix D, "References."

# EISA Cards

The EISA bus is a 32-bit extension of the original ISA bus. A card that plugs into the EISA bus must meet the EISA hardware and timing standards documented in the *EISA Specification*. The card must also contain the EISA product identifier and the expansion bus control bits.

Within the I/O address locations required by the EISA bus specification, five specific addresses contain identification information and control bits for the card. The addresses are 0*x*C80h to 0*x*C84h, where the *x* stands for the slot number in which the card is plugged. Addresses 0*x*C80h to 0*x*C83h contain platform and expansion card manufacturers' product and revision codes. Address 0*x*C80h also contains a not-ready indicator.

When the system is turned on or reset, the system should write an 0FFh to address 0*x*C80h and then perform a read at the same address to precharge the system identifier register. The card must support a readable identifier at 0*x*C80h through 0*x*C83h, and should return the most-significant bit of 0*x*C80h as a zero. The system then reads the four identifier registers.

The system must contain some form of nonvolatile memory that stores the identifier information retrieved from the card. This information is then compared against the contents of the cards located on the bus each time the system is reset. A match of the contents of the nonvolatile memory with the hardware identifier confirms that no change has occurred in the bus configuration.

The register at location 0*x*C84h contains control bits. The register allows cards to be individually enabled and reset. Errors on the card are indicated by one of the control bits being set, which also lets the system know which card was the source of an active IOCHCK* signal.

# Micro Channel Cards

IBM designed the Micro Channel bus to support their line of PS/2-compatible computers. All card designs for the Micro Channel bus must meet the physical and design guidelines outlined in the *Micro Channel Interface Specification* published by the Micro Channel Developers Association. Any Plug and Play–compatible hardware and software guidelines added to the *Micro Channel Interface Specification*, after it has been defined by IBM, must also be met.

# ACCESS.bus Devices

The ACCESS.bus is a serial bus that links a variety of slower-speed devices, such as keyboards, mice, printers, and so on, to the PC. Each device is connected to a single cable that attaches to the PC.

Devices attached to the ACCESS.bus must conform to the ACCESS.bus hardware and timing standards documented in the *ACCESS.bus Specifications*. The system requires that the devices contain enough hardware to accommodate identification and capabilities strings. These strings are used to identify the resources of the device; the bus hardware uses them to arbitrate messages the devices send at power-up or after a reset. The system then assigns a new address for each device using the identification strings. The devices use their assigned addresses to communicate with the system.

Although Windows 95 does not contain specific internal drivers and enumerators for ACCESS.bus devices, the basic Plug and Play architecture and VCOMM architecture enable easy implementation of vendor-specific ACCESS.bus hardware and drivers. Because a number of PC systems vendors are considering implementing the ACCESS.bus, this guide contains many references to this bus. These should enable an OEM implementing the ACCESS.bus to do so in a way that is highly compatible with Windows 95.

In some areas, the ACCESS.bus is an acceptable alternative interface to current standard interfaces. Therefore, a system that uses the ACCESS.bus should not be disqualified from using the Windows 95 Logo. For example, a vendor who implements an ACCESS.bus port should not also be required to implement a PS/2-style or serial port just to qualify for the Windows 95 Logo.

CHAPTER 7

# Designing Peripherals

This chapter discusses the following topics:

- General peripheral changes
- Display monitors
- Storage devices
- Common input devices
- Modems, mice, and other devices attached to serial ports
- Printers and other devices attached to parallel ports
- Power management
- Peripheral cabling

Peripherals—devices attached to the basic PC system—can either be mounted inside the PC case or inside their own cases, with external cables that attach to the circuitry inside the PC. Peripherals can be storage devices, display monitors, and many types of hardware that attach to the serial and parallel ports.

The main goal of this chapter is to guide you in designing peripheral devices that are easy to configure. The user should be able to change a peripheral or add a new peripheral to the system without changing jumpers and switches or manually configuring the software. Adding a peripheral should be as easy as pulling the device out of the box, plugging it in, and running the software.

This chapter describes design criteria for specific peripheral devices that must be modified for a Personal Computer for Microsoft® Windows™ 95. A peripheral should be able to identify itself to the system. After the peripheral has identified itself, the system can load whatever device drivers are appropriate, and communicate intelligently with the peripheral without user intervention. For example, if the user attaches a Plug and Play laser printer to the parallel port, the printer identifies itself to the system when the system boots. The system loads the correct printer driver, and the printer can print pages immediately. If the type of printer is later changed, the new printer identifies itself, and the system loads a new set of drivers the next time it boots up.

Another consideration when designing peripherals is cabling. The PC hardware environment includes many different types of cables to internal and external devices. There are few standards to help the user identify which cable attaches to which device. This chapter describes a method of identifying cables that allows the user to see at a glance which cables are needed for specific devices.

This chapter also discusses power management of attached peripherals.

# Requirements vs. Recommendations

For each peripheral discussed in this chapter, there are two sections: peripheral requirements and peripheral recommendations. The requirements outline those features and functions required for a specific peripheral to qualify for the Windows 95 Logo. The recommendations include additional features and functions that improve Windows 95 performance.

The recommendations in this chapter are a minimum "step up" from the required features. Far more advanced recommendations could have been made, but they would have been more expensive to implement and might have gone beyond the needs of the typical user.

You, the designer, should decide how many enhancements to add to your peripherals. This guide does not intend to limit the technology you can add to a PC 95.

# General Peripheral Changes

Peripherals that connect to a PC 95 must contain a minimum set of Plug and Play features. These features give the system a means to download the correct drivers without user intervention, and prevent the user from damaging the peripheral or the system:

- The peripheral should be able to identify itself to the system.
- A peripheral that plugs into the system using external connectors should be capable of hot-plugging without causing damage. Windows 95 will dynamically recognize some peripherals; it will not recognize others.

These are general requirements for every peripheral that connects to a PC 95. The sections that follow discuss individual requirements for specific peripherals.

## Peripheral Identification

All peripherals must have some method of identifying themselves to the system so the system can either load the device driver from an available set on the system or ask the user to insert a floppy disk containing the driver and download it to the system. If the peripheral connects to either the serial or parallel port, it must contain an identification string that it can send to the system through the port when the peripheral is turned on, or, in some cases, when the peripheral receives a reset command.

If the peripheral is connected to the system using an expansion card, more than one method can be used to identify the peripheral. If the expansion card contains a common port (such as a standard serial or parallel port), the peripheral must supply an identification string that is passed through the expansion card to the system. If the peripheral connection to the card uses a proprietary bus, the peripheral can either supply an identification to the system through the expansion card, or the expansion card can supply all the necessary information about the peripheral.

This chapter discusses the method for identifying the peripheral attached to the PC 95.

## Hot-Plugging

A user should be able to connect and disconnect peripherals that attach to connectors on the outside of the PC without having to turn off the PC. This is known as hot-plugging. Hot-plugging a Plug and Play peripheral should not cause damage to the system.

Any extra protection you can add to internal peripherals to prevent accidental damage, without substantially increasing production costs, is recommended, though not required.

## Cable Icons

For information about connector icons for the PC end of peripheral cables, see Chapter 3, "The Desktop PC 95."

# Display Monitors

The display monitor is one of the most important components of the PC 95. The monitor conveys most of the information the user sees, and helps the user visualize data in a way that is easy to comprehend.

To properly use Windows 95, display monitors must be capable of displaying, at a minimum, VGA-compatible 640 × 480 graphics. To enhance this minimum capability, you can add the following recommended features:

- Support of VESA's *Display Power Management Signaling (DPMS)* standard.
- Support of resolutions higher than 640 × 480.
- Support of VESA's *Monitor Timing Standards for 640 x 480, 800 x 600, 1024 x 768 and 1280 x 1024 at 75Hz*, and future timing standards published by VESA.

- Compliance with the standards of a DDC1/2B display type, at a minimum, as documented in the VESA *Display Data Channel* standard.
- Hot-plugging to a fully powered PC should not cause permanent damage to the monitor or the display adapter. The overcurrent protection circuit on the monitor should not require that the user open the case and replace parts if an overcurrent condition occurs.

## Display Power Management

A monitor for a PC 95 should be capable of power management for the "green" systems now coming to market. Monitor design should follow the guidelines described in VESA's *Display Power Management Signaling (DPMS)* standard. This document provides a standard method of signaling display power management states. These states, along with the relative power savings and recovery times, are shown in Table 7.1.

**Table 7.1 Advanced Power Management States**

| APM state | Power savings | Recovery time |
|---|---|---|
| On | None | Not applicable |
| Standby | Minimal | Short recovery |
| Suspend | Substantial | Longer recovery allowed |
| Off | Maximum | System dependent |

## Display Monitor Resolution

Because of its visibility to the user, the monitor should be visually pleasing, as well as easy to install and configure. The PC 95 should incorporate a VGA display capable of resolutions greater than 640 × 480. A desktop system monitor subsystem should have 256-color capability, minimum. Mobile systems should support an 8-bpp driver, and map into a 64-gray scale display, minimum. To enhance the clarity even more, especially for monitors whose display surface measures 17 inches or more, standard resolutions higher than 1024 × 786 can also be included.

The monitor should comply with the ergonomic monitor timing standards in VESA's *Monitor Timing Standards for 640 x 480, 800 x 600, 1024 x 768, and 1280 x 1024 at 75Hz*. These standards provide a clear, flicker-free monitor display. Although this standard documents monitor timings at 75 Hz, higher scan rates are preferable and should also meet published VESA standards.

## Display Data Channel Specifications

Display monitors should be designed to meet the requirements listed in the VESA *Display Data Channel* standard. This standard describes monitors that can send an identification string to the display adapter and receive instructions from the BIOS and operating system through the display adapter. If, for example, Windows 95 determines from the identification string retrieved from the monitor that the monitor is capable of 1024 × 786 color, it can automatically change the display adapter to this resolution without the user intervening. If another monitor with different capabilities is later attached, Windows 95 can identify the monitor, determine its capabilities, and configure the display adapter for the new monitor, again without user action. More importantly, however, Windows 95 will use the monitor EDID information to prevent the user from selecting a resolution not supported by a specific monitor.

A monitor that connects to a PC 95 communicates to the display adapter through a modified VGA cable, which is described in the VESA standard. At a minimum, the monitor should meet the requirements for a DDC1/2B display. A DDC1/2B display monitor returns its identification string in EDID format. The format of this string is described in the VESA standard. The display adapter should be able, at a minimum, to receive DDC1 unidirectional information from the monitor.

A DDC1/2B monitor uses the standard 15-pin, VGA-type connector with the following modifications:

- Pin 9 of the VGA connector is moved back 50/1000 inch for DDC compatibility. This change ensures the proper sequencing of power and ground if the PC display adapter is supplying +5V to the monitor.
- The color of the connector is royal blue, which indicates that it is DDC compatible.

Some of the pins on the VGA connector have also been redefined to meet the DDC requirements. Table 7.2 describes the pins on a DDC-compatible VGA monitor connector. Figure 7.1 shows the layout of the VGA monitor connector.

**Table 7.2 DDC-Compatible VGA Connector**

| Pin number | Monitor VGA connector |
|---|---|
| 1 | Red video |
| 2 | Green video |
| 3 | Blue video |
| 4 | Optional |
| 5 | DDC return (for pins 9, 12, and 15) |
| 6 | Red video return |
| 7 | Green video return |
| 8 | Blue video return |
| 9 | +5V load (optional) |
| 10 | Sync return |
| 11 | Optional |
| 12 | Bidirectional data (SDA) |
| 13 | Horizontal sync |
| 14 | Vertical sync (VCLK) |
| 15 | Data clock (SCL) |

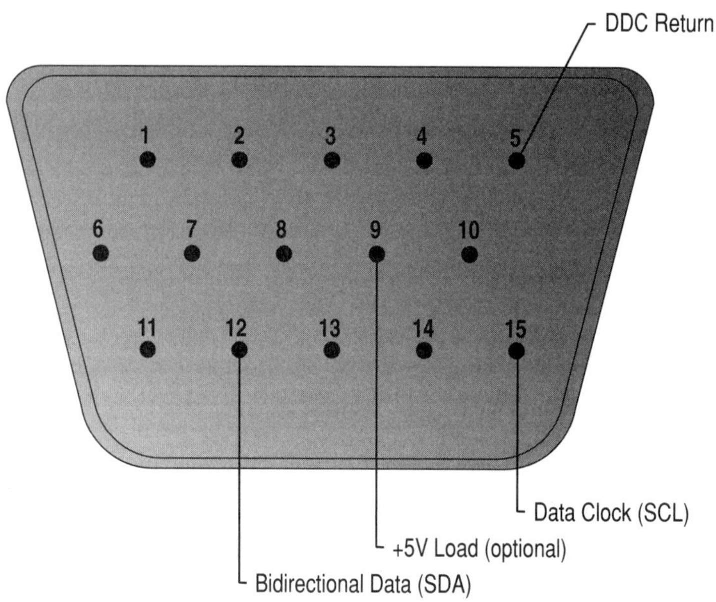


**Figure 7.1 DDC Pins on the Monitor Connector**

A DDC-compatible monitor must also have a 47K ohm pull-up resistor added to its data clock (SCL) line.

The DDC-compatible monitor begins sending EDID data to the system through pin 12 (bidirectional data) when the monitor is turned on and it receives the first vertical sync (VCLK) signal from the display adapter. The monitor continues sending the EDID data until it is either turned off or receives a high-to-low transition on its data clock line. (A high-to-low transition indicates that the display adapter is DDC2 compatible. After the high-to-low transition, the monitor goes into an idle state and waits for commands from the PC.)

### Hot-Plugging

Hot-plugging is not a required Plug and Play feature but is highly recommended for the monitor included with a PC 95. The nontechnical PC user may not know that damage is possible as a result of plugging or unplugging a monitor while power is on, and will value a monitor able to withstand hot-plugging.

## SCSI Peripherals

The SCSI is an extremely flexible I/O bus that is used in the design of a wide variety of peripherals, including disk drives, CD-ROM drives, tape drives, scanners, and magneto-optical drives.

Unfortunately, configuring the SCSI bus has always been a challenge to users. To connect a SCSI peripheral to the SCSI bus requires changing cables, moving termination hardware, and configuring new identifier assignments. The number of variables required to add, connect, and configure a SCSI bus can prove formidable to a user without a background in PC hardware.

On a PC 95, a user plugs a new peripheral into the SCSI bus, and the bus automatically adjusts. Changes to the SCSI identifier, enabling or disabling the termination on peripherals, and other variables that require physically changing peripherals must be as simple as possible for the user.

Basic changes to the design of host adapters and SCSI peripherals are needed to make the SCSI bus and its peripherals comply with the requirements of the PC 95. The design requirements and recommendations for SCSI peripherals follow. For information about changes to motherboard and expansion card SCSI host adapters, see Chapter 5, "System Devices."

# SCSI Peripheral Requirements

The *Plug and Play SCSI Specification* lists the requirements for SCSI peripherals —the hardware and software changes that will create an easy-to-use environment for the user. To design SCSI peripherals for the PC 95, follow the requirements listed in the *Plug and Play SCSI Specification* and the general peripheral requirements listed under "General Peripheral Changes" earlier in this chapter.

The *Plug and Play SCSI Specification* lists a number of changes and requirements for Plug and Play compatibility. These changes are also required for SCSI peripherals that connect to the PC 95:

- Support of the *SCSI Configured AutoMatically* (SCAM) Level 1 protocol for automatic SCSI identifier assignment. The SCAM protocol is documented in the SCAM proposal in the *SCSI-3 Parallel Interface (SPI)* draft standard.
- Use of drivers and receivers that meet the specifications defined in the single-ended alternative of the SPI.
- Cables must conform to the cable requirements defined in clause 6 of the SPI specification.
- External SCSI peripheral subsystems must use the 50-pin, high-density shielded device connector defined in the *Small Computer Interface (SCSI-2)* standard.
- External SCSI peripherals must contain two connectors for the SCSI cable: a SCSI-In connector and a SCSI-Out connector. The last peripheral in the chain uses a terminator on the SCSI-Out connector.
- Attachment of a permanent terminator to the end of the cable, for internal SCSI peripherals.
- Internal SCSI peripherals must not terminate the SCSI bus.
- Terminations must use regulated terminators (conforming to the requirements in the SCSI-3 SPI specification) over the TERMPWR voltage range of 4.0 to 5.25 VDC. Regulated terminators are also known as active, SCSI-3 SPI, SCSI-2 alternative-2, or Boulay terminators.
- Terminators must be powered from the TERMPWR line on the SCSI bus. Exceptions may be necessary for battery-operated peripherals and PCMCIA cards.
- Provision of overcurrent protection for the TERMPWR line or lines. The overcurrent protection circuit must not require that the user open the peripheral or system case and replace parts if an overcurrent condition occurs.
- Only terminators can draw power from TERMPWR.
- Implementation of the SCSI bus parity signal defined in the SCSI-2 specification, for all SCSI peripherals.

## Identifier Assignments

SCSI peripherals are identified by the unique SCSI identification number assigned to each device. Up to eight peripherals can be attached to the SCSI bus, including the SCSI host adapter. For SCSI peripherals on the PC 95, some method of automatically assigning identifiers must be used. The SCAM proposal provides methods for automatically configuring the identifier assignments.

SCAM SCSI peripherals should also contain a default identifier (generally set with jumpers or switches) for older systems in which the host adapter does not support automatic identifier assignment.

### Automatic SCSI Identifier Assignment

A new identifier assignment protocol called SCAM allows a master device to assign SCSI identification numbers to other peripherals on the system. SCAM is fully backward compatible with existing SCSI peripherals with a manually configurable SCSI identifier.

Under the SCAM protocol, a SCSI peripheral can contain either a hard identifier or a soft identifier. A hard identifier is generally set with either a jumper or a switch. A soft identifier is configured with the SCAM protocol.

A SCSI peripheral can implement either Level 1 SCAM or Level 2 SCAM protocols. Many existing SCSI peripherals can implement Level 1 SCAM with no changes to the hardware and limited changes to the firmware. Level 2 SCAM is meant to be used with new SCSI peripherals, and requires both hardware and firmware changes. Level 1 SCAM support is required to qualify for the Windows 95 Logo.

Level 1 SCAM SCSI buses can contain only one SCAM initiator, which must use a hard identifier. Level 2 SCAM buses can contain more than one SCAM initiator and can use either hard or soft identifiers. If the system contains an ATA boot device, Windows 95 will allow late power-up of a SCAM Level 1 device that is already connected to the bus, and will autoconfigure this device. Run-time SCSI configuration requires that the SCSI device driver maintain current SCSI ID assignments. If all devices on the bus are Level 2, any device can be powered up independently. SCSI target devices can also contain a default identifier so they can be run on SCSI systems that do not contain the SCAM protocol.

SCAM devices contain a device identification string that provides information about the device. The first two bytes are a type field that shows the current priority flag of the device in its first bit, the bus width supported by the device, and the peripheral's default identifier. These bytes are followed by an 8-byte vendor identification string, then a number consisting of 23 or fewer bytes representing the model number, serial number, or other unique number chosen by the vendor. The entire length of the device identification string is 32 bytes.

### Default SCSI identifiers

To be Plug and Play compatible, SCAM SCSI peripherals must contain a default identifier assignment. With a default identifier, a SCAM-capable Level 1 peripheral can be used in a non–Plug and Play system that contains a legacy host adapter. The SCSI peripheral manufacturer must ensure that the default identifier assignment is set when the peripheral is shipped. Table 7.3 contains the required SCSI identifier assignments for each type of SCSI device.

**Table 7.3 Recommended SCSI Identifiers**

| SCSI identifier | Default identifier assignment |
|---|---|
| 7 | Host adapter |
| 6 | Disk drive |
| 5 | |
| 4 | Tape or r/w optical |
| 3 | CD-ROM |
| 2 | Scanner/printer |
| 1 | |
| 0 | |

Initially, SCAM devices will need switches or jumpers to set the default identifier for compatibility with non-SCAM systems. Users of the PC 95 may occasionally need to change the SCAM default identifier to control which device becomes the boot device. It is expected that BIOS or operating system enhancements, or both, will eventually overcome this need.

## SCSI Cable Configuration

SCSI configuration in a PC involves connecting one or more internal or external SCSI peripherals to the host adapter, and terminating the ends of the bus.

One of the aspects of the SCSI bus that can be confusing to the user is termination. The principle of termination is fairly simple, but the number of different methods used by current SCSI peripherals is formidable. Termination in peripherals can be turned on or off by jumpers or switches, or by adding or removing resistor packs. The user may even find it hard to tell whether or not a peripheral is enabled or disabled. This can be especially difficult if the end of the SCSI cable is inside the peripheral case where the user can't see it easily.

In all instances, both ends of the SCSI bus must be terminated. In the past, users have been confused about what constitutes the "end" of the bus when installing SCSI peripherals on a PC, which has given the SCSI bus the reputation of being difficult to install. With this in mind, you should provide some method of simplified termination.

There are a number of types of configurations for the SCSI bus. The bus may consist only of peripherals inside the PC case, peripherals outside the PC case, or a combination of the two.

## Internal Configuration

For an internal configuration, one end of the internal SCSI bus cable is plugged into a 50-position, shrouded and keyed connector on the host adapter, which ensures that the cable is positioned properly. This connector must comply with the SPI specification. The cable is then routed to the various internal peripherals in the system. At the opposite end of the cable, as close as possible to the last peripheral in the chain, is the internal terminator. You should use some means (such as written instructions on the cable) to ensure that the user always plugs in internal peripherals starting with the plug closest to the terminator.

Internal termination of the SCSI bus consists of an internal terminator at the end of the SCSI cabling to the internal peripherals, and an automatic exit-point terminator located on the host adapter. An example of the internal cabling and termination of an expansion card host adapter and the internal peripherals is shown in Figure 7.2.

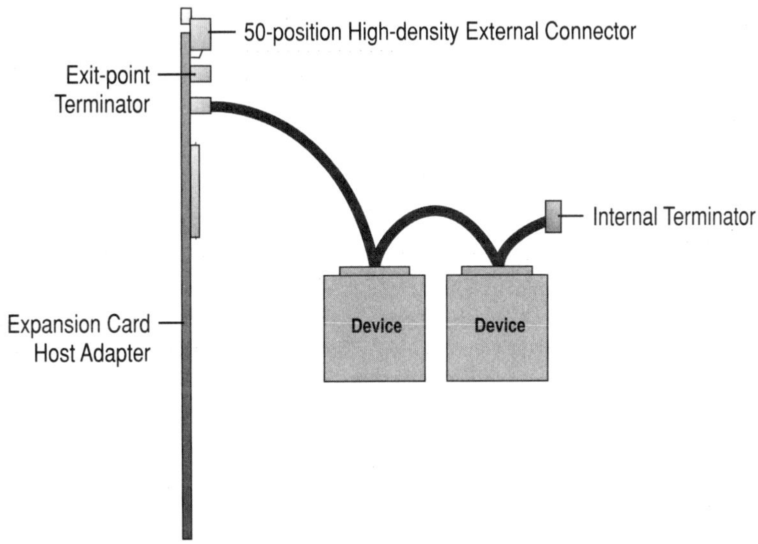


**Figure 7.2 Typical Plug and Play Internal Cabling**

The internal terminator must be as physically close as possible to the last peripheral on the cable. The distance shown in Figure 7.2 is exaggerated for clarity.

---

**Note** For the internal SCSI bus to comply with Plug and Play, no SCSI peripheral can terminate the bus. The terminator is placed at the end of the internal cable, and the other end is terminated on the host adapter.

---

The SCSI host adapter contains an exit-point terminator that can be disabled if an external peripheral is attached, moving the responsibility of termination to the end of the external cable. However, as long as no external peripheral is attached to the external connector, the exit-point terminator acts as one end of the cable.

## External Configuration

External SCSI peripherals are usually housed in a case, and connect to the system with a SCSI cable. An external SCSI peripheral that connects to the PC 95 must include several Plug and Play features that ensure proper cabling and termination of the SCSI bus.

External SCSI peripheral cases must have two 50-position, high-density, shielded device connectors, one of them SCSI-In and the other SCSI-Out. Both of the connectors must be clearly marked on the case. In addition, all external SCSI connectors must display the SCSI icon defined in SPI Annex F.

The SCSI bus cabling inside the peripheral case runs from the SCSI-In connector on the case to the SCSI peripheral; then from the peripheral to the SCSI-Out connector, as shown in Figure 7.3.

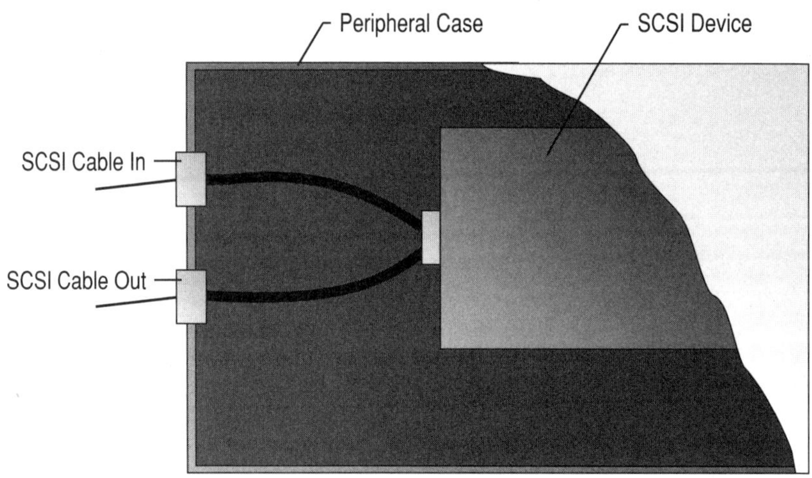


**Figure 7.3 Cabling Inside Peripheral Device Cases**

The cable from the external SCSI connector on the PC 95 connects to the SCSI-In connector on the first SCSI peripheral in the chain; a cable from the next SCSI peripheral in the chain connects to the SCSI-Out connector on the first SCSI peripheral, and so on. The last peripheral in the chain must be terminated.

For the external bus to comply with Plug and Play, no SCSI peripheral device can contain internal termination components unless those components are automatically switchable. In the absence of automatic termination, an external pluggable terminator must be connected to the last open device connector on the bus.

Figure 7.4 shows how an external terminator plugs into the chain of SCSI peripherals.

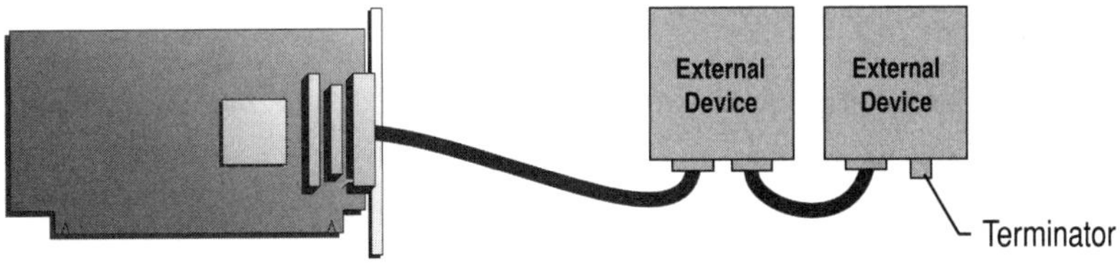


**Figure 7.4 SCSI External Peripheral Configuration**

Switchable termination automatically enables or disables when only one cable is connected to the SCSI peripheral. You can employ either mechanical or electrical means to detect whether only one cable is connected to the peripheral, or you can use a switchable terminator that is automatically enabled when the adapter detects that it is at one end of the internal or external SCSI bus.

### Combined Internal and External Configuration

In many instances, the SCSI bus consists of a combination of internal and external peripherals. The only requirement for SCSI peripherals is that they must not terminate the bus. However, to ensure that the user is able to connect these combinations of peripherals easily, the SCSI host adapter must contain some means of automatically enabling and disabling the exit-point terminator. For more information about the host adapter design, see Chapter 5, "System Devices."

## Termination

To comply with Plug and Play, all terminations in the SCSI bus must use regulated terminators (also known as active, SCSI-3 SPI, SCSI-2 alternative-2, or Boulay terminators). Regulated terminators provide better signal quality than do passive terminators.

Both the PC (either the host adapter or the motherboard) and the external SCSI peripherals should supply terminator power (TERMPWR) to the SCSI bus. (Exceptions may be necessary for PCMCIA host adapters and battery-operated peripherals. Neither of these may be capable of supplying the needed current, and the PCMCIA socket may also not be capable because of its limited number of pins.) All terminators on the host adapter and on the internal and external SCSI bus must be powered from the TERMPWR lines in the SCSI bus.

Devices that provide TERMPWR must also provide some means of current limiting. A positive-temperature-coefficient device or a circuit breaker must be designed into the circuit. These devices open during an overcurrent condition, and close after the condition ends.

# SCSI Peripheral Recommendations

You can implement the following recommendations in SCSI peripherals that connect to the PC 95:

- Provision of soft ejection in removable media, if used.
- Capability to properly execute the SCSI STOP UNIT and START UNIT commands. The drive should also be capable of properly spinning up when the system resumes.
- Inclusion of an icon on the PC end of the SCSI peripheral cable that matches an icon on the PC.

## Soft Ejection

As an option, you can make SCSI peripherals that use removable media, such as CD-ROM drives, able to eject media by software control.

For information about device drivers required to communicate between Windows 95 and the soft-eject control, see the *Microsoft Windows 95 Device Driver Reference,* supplied with the Windows 95 DDK. Windows 95 includes support for removable media, including lock, unlock, and eject.

## Power Management

The hardware in some existing SCSI peripherals cannot fully recover from a software-initiated *spin-down* without rebooting the system or cycling power. To properly support power management on SCSI drives, be sure to implement the STOP UNIT and START UNIT commands correctly. Correct implementation of these commands ensures that an APM 1.1 suspend and resume to the peripheral will function properly. As the number of new systems on the market that support the EPA's Energy Star program increases, the demand for this functionality will increase, even for desktop systems.

# ATA (IDE) Peripherals

The ATA (IDE) interface is one of the most widely used in the PC world. Originally intended only for hard drives, ATA (IDE) support is being extended to more and more device types and performance features.

# ATA (IDE) Peripheral Requirements

ATA (IDE) peripherals connected to the PC 95 need meet only a small number of requirements:

- Compliance with the hardware and software design guidelines of the current ATA specification
- Support of ATAPI in ATA (IDE) CD-ROM drives

## ATA Specification

All ATA (IDE) peripherals must meet the hardware and software design requirements listed in the current version of the *ATA (AT Attachment) 2* specification.

## ATAPI Support

CD-ROM drives attached to the PC 95 (and tape when an ATAPI standard is available) must support the hardware and protocols currently documented in the *ATA Packet Interface for CD-ROMs,* SFF-8020, Version 1.2.

To ensure peak performance of CD-ROM drives with Windows 95, you must include the following implementation details:

- Set the Signature after an ATA Read or ATA Identify command is received.
- Return CANNOT READ MEDIUM - INCOMPATIBLE FORMAT additional sense code - sense code qualifier when a READ is received on an audio track.
- Implement the SEEK command. The SEEK command is necessary for both overlapping seeks and audio support under Windows 95.
- Set the DSC bit when an ATAPI seek is complete, but do not change the drive select bit.

Windows 95 supports the Test_Unit_Ready command in the following manner:

```
CDB (0 0 0 0 0 0 0 0 0 0 0 0)
```

If the tray is open, or if no disk is in the drive, the sense data must return with a sense key of 2 and an ASC of 3A, medium_not_present.

Windows 95 supports the READ_CD command sector types mode 2 form 1, mode 2 form 2, mode 1 form 1, and mode 1 form 2 by issuing the following command:

```
BEh
0h
starting address
transfer length
0f8h
0
0
```

If CD-DA is implemented by the CD-ROM drive, Windows 95 issues the following command:

```
BEh
0h
start address
transfer length
0F0h
0
0
```

# ATA (IDE) Peripheral Recommendations

You can implement the following recommendations in an ATA (IDE) peripheral that connects to the PC 95:

- Provision of soft ejection in ATA (IDE) peripherals that use removable media.
- Support for larger capacity drives.
- Capability to properly execute the ATA STANDBY command. The drive must be able to spin up properly when the system resumes.
- Inclusion of an icon on the PC end of the ATA (IDE) peripheral cable that matches an icon on the PC.

## Soft Ejection

As an option, you can make ATA (IDE) peripherals that use removable media, such as CD-ROM drives, able to eject media by software control.

For information about device drivers required to communicate between Windows 95 and the soft-eject control, see the *Microsoft Windows 95 Device Driver Reference*, supplied with the Windows 95 DDK. Windows 95 includes support for removable media, including lock, unlock, and eject.

## Large Capacity Support

Currently, ATA (IDE) hard drive capacity is limited to less than 528 MB because of the structure of the system BIOS and the IDE interface. By extending the peripheral's firmware (and the system's Int 13 BIOS interface), you may expand the maximum capacity to support 8.4-GB drives.

## Power Management

The hardware in some existing ATA (IDE) peripherals cannot fully recover from a software-initiated spin-down without rebooting the system or cycling power. To properly support power management on ATA (IDE) drives, be sure to implement the ATA STANDBY command correctly. ATA (IDE) drives should also be able to spin up properly when power returns after a STANDBY command. As the number of new systems on the market that support the EPA's Energy Star program increases, the demand for this functionality will increase, even for desktop systems.

# Other Storage Peripherals

As has been noted in the previous sections, storage peripherals that attach to the SCSI bus and the ATA (IDE) bus should follow the requirements and recommendations for those buses. If you are designing a storage peripheral that attaches to a different standard bus (such as a parallel port), or are designing one that uses a proprietary bus, you should design them in such a way that they can take advantage of the Plug and Play interface with Windows 95. You should also consider designing the peripheral with power management capabilities built in.

To comply with Plug and Play, the proprietary adapter must be capable of identifying itself and its resources, and, at a minimum, be capable of disabling itself in the event of irreconcilable conflict. You must also supply Windows 95 with a device driver for the adapter and any peripheral that may be connected to the adapter. If more than one type of peripheral can be connected to the proprietary adapter, you must provide some means of differentiating the peripheral (or provide a single device driver that all the peripherals can use). After the peripheral has been identified, Windows 95 can use the information provided by the adapter to automatically load the device driver for the peripheral.

If you are designing peripherals that connect to an external port (such as a tape backup unit that attaches to the parallel port), you must follow the identification requirements for peripherals that attach to that particular type of port. For information about the identification requirements for external ports, see Chapter 5, "System Devices."

You should design some means of performing a software ejection of removable media into the hardware of tape, CD-ROM, and other types of drives that allow the user to insert and remove the storage media. Windows 95 includes support for removable media, including lock, unlock, and eject.

Storage peripherals should support the power management protocols given in the *Advanced Power Management (APM) BIOS Interface Specification*, Revision 1.1. Device drivers or option ROMs should contain the interface software to allow APM 1.1 to communicate with the peripheral's power management hardware. For more information about APM 1.1, see Chapter 8, "System BIOS Design." For more information about device driver control of peripheral power management, see the *Microsoft Windows 95 Device Driver Reference*, supplied with the Windows 95 DDK.

# Common Input Devices

There are many types of input devices for the PC. The three most common are the mouse, the keyboard, and the pen. By making input devices comply with Plug and Play, you will enable the user to plug or unplug them at any time, without turning the power off or manually reconfiguring the system.

To meet these requirements, some hardware changes are necessary to make input devices more rugged. You will also need to employ methods of identification that allow "hot insertion" with dynamic configuration.

## Mouse

The mouse has become popular because it has been the type of pointing device most commonly included in systems with graphical interfaces. Although the basic features of a mouse are well established, a mouse that attaches to a PC 95 must meet a specific minimum set of requirements.

### Mouse Requirements

A mouse for the PC 95 must meet these requirements, at a minimum:

- Connection to either a PS/2 port, a serial port, or an ACCESS.bus
- Ability to identify itself to the system
- Ability to be plugged in and unplugged from a fully powered PC 95 without resultant damage to either the mouse or the system

#### Mouse Interface

To comply with Plug and Play, the mouse design must meet the needs of the port to which it is connected. In some instances, such as with a PS/2-style mouse, no new hardware is required. Other interfaces require additional hardware to comply with Plug and Play.

### PS/2 Mouse

No hardware changes are required for a PS/2-style mouse interface. A PS/2 mouse must meet the interface requirements in the *Personal System/2 Specifications* published by IBM.

### Serial Mouse

You must make two modifications to the serial interface of a serial mouse to enable Plug and Play. You must connect the DTR pin to the DSR pin of the mouse connector to ensure that a Plug and Play serial port can detect that the mouse has been plugged in or unplugged. The mouse must also follow the *Plug and Play External COM Device Specification*, and return an appropriate device identifier. For more information about the serial mouse interface connection, see "Plug and Play Serial Mouse Requirements" later in this chapter.

### ACCESS.bus Mouse

You need not make any hardware changes to the mouse for an ACCESS.bus interface. The ACCESS.bus mouse must meet the interface requirements in the current version of the *ACCESS.bus Specifications*.

## Mouse Identification

For a mouse to comply with Plug and Play, it must be able to identify itself to the system. Several methods of identifying a mouse are possible, depending on the type of mouse interface used.

### PS/2 Mouse

On a PS/2-style port, the microcontroller sends a Send Identifier command (0F2h) to the mouse, which instructs it to send its 1-byte identifier. The mouse first returns an ACK (0FAh) to the microcontroller, and then sends the identification.

### Serial Mouse

After the system had detected a serial mouse, the identification process begins. The system detects the presence of the mouse by monitoring the DSR input of the serial port. When DSR=1, the system assumes a serial device is now connected to the port. The system then sets RTS=1. When the serial mouse detects that RTS=1, it begins sending its serial identification.

A serial mouse uses the RXD lead to provide the system with identification information. The serial data sent from the mouse is set to a fixed speed and format: start-stop asynchronous, 1200 bps, 9-bit frames consisting of one start bit, seven bits of data (least-significant bit first), no parity bit, and one stop bit.

The Plug and Play serial mouse uses the standard Plug and Play serial identification string. For more information about this identification string, see "Modems, Mice, and Other Serial Port Devices" later in this chapter.

Although a serial mouse uses the same identification strings as do other serial devices, the characters used to identify the mouse cannot use all of the ASCII bits. Because serial mice use bit 6 of the characters sent over the RXD lead to indicate the beginning of a motion report, the Plug and Play mouse identification strings must avoid using this bit. The ASCII identification strings must be offset by 20h, and lowercase characters must not be used.

For a complete description of the serial mouse identification strings, see the *Plug and Play External COM Device Specification.*

#### ACCESS.bus Mouse

For more information about the method for identifying any device attached to the ACCESS.bus, see the *ACCESS.bus Specifications*. For an ACCESS.bus mouse, the system uses the identification string that is sent to the system to assign an address for the mouse. The mouse stores the address information and is then able to send data to the system. The system also uses the identification string to load the appropriate device drivers.

### Hot-Plugging

Because users expect that a mouse can be plugged into a Plug and Play system at any time, you must implement some means of protecting the circuit so that hot-plugging will not cause damage to the mouse or the mouse port.

Neither the overcurrent circuit in the mouse nor the one in the system should require the user to open the case and replace parts if an overcurrent condition occurs. It is unacceptable, for example, to use a fuse that has to be replaced each time an overcurrent condition occurs. Instead, an overcurrent circuit should open the circuit when an overcurrent condition occurs and then automatically close the circuit when the overcurrent condition dissipates.

To meet the ACCESS.bus specifications, you must employ hardware to prevent damage to the mouse and the system.

## Mouse Recommendations

- The mouse for the PC 95 should be a PS/2-style mouse.
- The PC end of the mouse cable should include an icon that matches an icon on the PC.

# Keyboard

Keyboards are one of the most fundamental input devices on the PC 95. The keyboard is a serial device that is either connected to one of the ports on a microcontroller found on the motherboard (PS/2-style connection) or connected to the system through an ACCESS.bus. The PS/2 connector microcontroller (historically an 8042) controls both the keyboard and PS/2-style pointing devices, such as a mouse or a touch screen. (For the purposes of this guide, a "PS/2-style" keyboard refers to a keyboard that uses either the PS/2 connector or the standard AT keyboard connector.)

## Keyboard Requirements

A keyboard attached to a PC 95 must meet the following requirements:

- Connection to either a PS/2-style port or an ACCESS.bus port
- Ability to identify itself to the system
- Ability to be plugged in and unplugged from a fully powered PC 95 without resultant damage to the keyboard or the system

### Keyboard Identification

No changes need be made to the keyboard identification sequence of a PS/2-style keyboard. On a PS/2-style port, the microcontroller sends a Send Identifier command (0F2h) to the keyboard, which instructs it to send its 2-byte identifier. The keyboard first returns an ACK (0FAh) to the microcontroller, and then sends its 2-byte identification.

If you are designing a keyboard for the ACCESS.bus, the ACCESS.bus specification requires that the keyboard identify itself, and be capable of configuring various parameters. The system then uses the identification string sent by the device—in this instance, the keyboard—to assign an address for the device. The device stores the address information and is then able to send data to the system. The device also contains its capabilities in a string that is requested by the system. The system uses this information to load appropriate device drivers.

### Hot-Plugging

Because users expect that a keyboard can be connected or disconnected at any time, you must employ some type of overcurrent protection to protect the keyboard and the keyboard port.

Neither the overcurrent circuit in the keyboard nor the one in the system should require the user to open the case and replace parts. The overcurrent circuit should open the circuit when an overcurrent condition occurs and close the circuit when the overcurrent condition has dissipated.

To meet the ACCESS.bus specifications, you must employ hardware to prevent damage to the device and the system.

# Keyboard Recommendations

In addition to addressing the basic keyboard requirements, you can add extra functionality to a standard 101-key keyboard by including three new keys. Once added, these keys give the user a consistent mechanism for accessing functionality in Windows 95 and in individual applications. The three new keys are:

- Application key
- Right Windows key
- Left Windows key

You can also include an icon on the PC end of the keyboard cable that matches an icon on the PC.

## Application Key

When the user presses the unmodified Application key, the application brings up the Context menu (a pop-up menu) at the current selection, much as pressing the right mouse button does in some applications today. Pressing the Application key does not disturb the current mouse cursor position.

For compatibility with 101-key keyboards, the functionality of the Application key should map to existing keys—for example, the key combination SHIFT+F10 could map to the Application key functionality.

## Windows Keys

When the user presses either Windows key—Left or Right—the Start menu appears. Both keys can be used to modify other keys.

---

**Note** The operating system controls the functionality of the Windows keys. Only shell applications should implement these keys, and then only in such a way as to preserve and extend the keys' functionality in the Windows 95 shell.

---

## Scan Codes

Each of the three new keys will require new scan codes. Tables 7.4 through 7.10 describe the scan codes that should be provided with the new keys.

**Table 7.4 Scan Code Set 1: Base Case or SHIFT+NUM LOCK**

| New key | Scan code (make) | Scan code (break) |
|---|---|---|
| Left Windows key | 0xE0 0x5B | 0xE0 0xDB |
| Right Windows key | 0xE0 0x5C | 0xE0 0xDC |
| Application key | 0xE0 0x5D | 0xE0 0xDD |

**Table 7.5 Scan Code Set 1: Shift Case**

| New key | Scan code (make) | Scan code (break) |
|---|---|---|
| Left Windows key | 0xE0 0xAA 0xE0 0x5B | 0xE0 0xDB 0xE0 0x2A |
| Right Windows key | 0xE0 0xAA 0xE0 0x5C | 0xE0 0xDC 0xE0 0x2A |
| Application key | 0xE0 0xAA 0xE0 0x5D | 0xE0 0xDD 0xE0 0x2A |

**Table 7.6 Scan Code Set 1: NUM LOCK ON**

| New key | Scan code (make) | Scan code (break) |
|---|---|---|
| Left Windows key | 0xE0 0x2A 0xE0 0x5B | 0xE0 0xDB 0xE0 0xAA |
| Right Windows key | 0xE0 0x2A 0xE0 0x5C | 0xE0 0xDC 0xE0 0xAA |
| Application key | 0xE0 0x2A 0xE0 0x5D | 0xE0 0xDD 0xE0 0xAA |

**Table 7.7 Scan Code Set 2: Base Case or SHIFT+NUM LOCK**

| New key | Scan code (make) | Scan code (break) |
|---|---|---|
| Left Windows key | 0xE0 0x1F | 0xE0 0xF0 0x1F |
| Right Windows key | 0xE0 0x27 | 0xE0 0xF0 0x27 |
| Application key | 0xE0 0x2F | 0xE0 0xF0 0x2F |

**Table 7.8 Scan Code Set 2: Shift Case**

| New key | Scan code (make) | Scan code (break) |
|---|---|---|
| Left Windows key | 0xE0 0xF0 0x12 0x1F | 0xE0 0xF0 0x1F 0xE0 0x12 |
| Right Windows key | 0xE0 0xF0 0x12 0x27 | 0xE0 0xF0 0x27 0xE0 0x12 |
| Application key | 0xE0 0xF0 0x12 0x2F | 0xE0 0xF0 0x2F 0xE0 0x12 |

**Table 7.9 Scan Code Set 2: NUM LOCK ON**

| New key | Scan code (make) | Scan code (break) |
|---|---|---|
| Left Windows key | 0xE0 0x12 0xE0 0x1F | 0xE0 0xF0 0x1F 0xE0 0xF0 0x12 |
| Right Windows key | 0xE0 0x12 0xE0 0x27 | 0xE0 0xF0 0x27 0xE0 0xF0 0x12 |
| Application key | 0xE0 0x12 0xE0 0x2F | 0xE0 0xF0 0x2F 0xE0 0xF0 0x12 |

**Table 7.10 Scan Code Set 3**

| New key | Scan code (make) | Scan code (break) |
|---|---|---|
| Left Windows key | 0x8B | 0xF0 0x8B |
| Right Windows key | 0x8C | 0xF0 0x8C |
| Application key | 0x8D | 0xF0 0x8D |

## Recommended Key Locations

For 101- and 102-key keyboard designs, it is now possible to add the three new keys where they can be used easily as modifier keys—for example, on the bottom row adjacent to the SPACEBAR, near the existing CTRL, SHIFT, and ALT keys. The location of the new keys is up to the keyboard designer, however, and may vary between laptop and desktop configurations. Figure 7.5 shows one possible configuration:

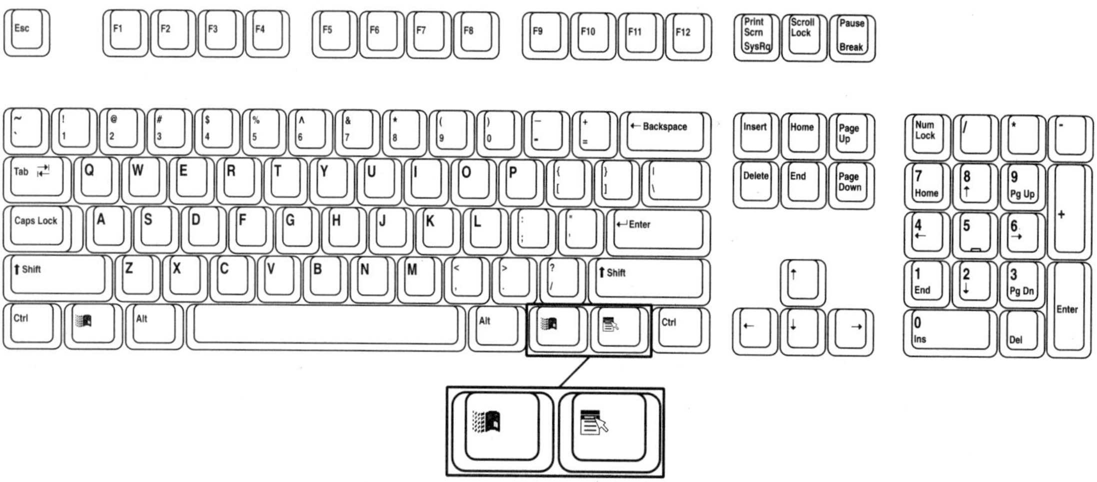


**Figure 7.5 A Keyboard with Three Additional Keys**

# Other Input Devices

In addition to the mouse and keyboard, many other types of input devices can be connected to the PC, including internal devices such as built-in trackballs and touch screens and external devices such as light pens, digitizers, joysticks, bar-code readers, scanners, and pen tablets. (For more information about pen tablets, see Chapter 4, "Mobile Hardware Designs.") Some of these devices are built in, some are connected through either a serial or parallel port, and others are connected to the PC using an expansion card.

Built-in devices (devices attached directly to a circuit designed on the PC motherboard, such as trackballs, in portable systems) must be capable of identifying themselves so the operating system can load the correct device drivers. Typically, the system BIOS handles this identification, because the built-in device is known to the system.

Devices attached to serial or parallel ports of a PC 95 must meet the requirements for those ports. For example, if a scanner is connected to the PC through a parallel port, it must meet the requirements listed under the heading "Printers and Other Devices Attached to Parallel Ports" later in this chapter.

If the input device uses a proprietary connection that requires the use of an expansion card to interpret the signals for the PC, it must meet two requirements. First, the expansion card must meet the Plug and Play requirements for the bus to which it is connected. For example, if the card connects to the ISA bus, it must meet the identification and configuration criteria in the *Plug and Play ISA Specification*. Second, hot-plugging of the device to the expansion card must not cause damage to either the device or the expansion card. The user must not be required to open the case of the PC to replace parts if an overcurrent condition has occurred.

# Modems, Mice, and Other Serial Port Devices

Many different types of devices attach to the serial port. Windows 95 supports high-speed serial devices with speeds up to 115.2K baud. The PC 95 contains a serial port driven by a 16550A UART (or the equivalent).

All serial devices have some requirements in common, but also have a few individual methods of communicating with the PC. For example, all serial devices use the same method to transmit their Plug and Play identification string to the system. But the methods of communicating data to and from the system differ, depending on the type of serial device. Serial mice and modems, in particular, use radically different approaches in communicating with the system. After the system receives the identification string from the serial device, it can determine which device drivers to load. These device drivers must allow the system to communicate with the serial device using the appropriate data transmission method.

# Serial Device Requirements

All serial peripherals that connect to the PC 95 must meet the requirements documented in the *Plug and Play External COM Device Specification*. Although not all serial peripherals must use the same method to communicate with the system, the following requirements for a serial peripheral are common to all serial devices:

- Must set DSR high to indicate they are ready to send their identification string.
- Must have the ability to identify themselves using the identification method described in the *Plug and Play External COM Device Specification*.
- Must report their identification string at 1200 baud. The data format used to send the identification string to the system must be compatible with a receiver set to a 9-bit frame (one start bit, seven data bits with the least-significant bit first, and one stop bit).

## Using DSR

The PC 95 uses the DSR line on the serial port to determine whether a device is attached to the port. When the PC is booted, the system sets DTR and RTS to 0 and waits approximately 200 ms. It then sets DTR to 1 and waits about 200 ms. At the end of this time, the system checks to see whether the DSR line is high, indicating that a serial device is attached to the serial port. The system responds by setting RTS high, and waits to receive the device identification string.

In some devices, such as a serial mouse, the DSR line can be held high by tying it directly to the DTR line. When the mouse is connected to the serial port on the PC, the power supplied through the DTR line also raises DSR high.

In other devices, such as modems, you may need to redesign the DSR line so it will no longer be used as a control line. For Plug and Play compatibility, DSR must stay high as long as the device is attached to the serial port.

## Serial Device Identification

The serial device must report its identification to the system using an identification string. The system can then use the identification string to load the appropriate device drivers. The identification string consists of 18 fields that identify the device, the class of device, and other compatible devices. Five of the fields are required by all serial devices; all others are optional. Table 7.11 describes the serial device identification string.

**Table 7.11 Serial Device ID String**

| Field name | Size | Required | Description |
|---|---|---|---|
| Other ID | <17 | No | Reserved for short, non–Plug and Play identifier (for example, 4Dh) |
| Begin PnP | 1 | Yes | Begin Plug and Play identifier (either ASCII 28h or 08h) |
| PnP rev | 2 | Yes | 2-byte (12-bit) Plug and Play revision code (see the *Plug and Play External COM Device Specification* for details) |
| EISA ID | 3 | Yes | EISA-determined unique manufacturers identifier |
| Product ID | 4 | Yes | Manufacturer-determined unique product identifier |
| Extend | 1 | No | \ - either ASCII 5Ch or 3Ch for a mouse[1] |
| Serial number | 8 | No | Optional device serial number |
| Extend | 1 | No | \ - either ASCII 5Ch or 3Ch for a mouse[1] |
| Class ID | <33 | No | Plug and Play class identifier |
| Extend | 1 | No | \ - either ASCII 5Ch or 3Ch for a mouse[1] |
| Driver ID | <41 | No | Compatible driver identifiers |
| Extend | 1 | No | \ - either ASCII 5Ch or 3Ch for a mouse[1] |
| User name | <41 | No | User-legible product description |
| Another ID | 1 | No | ; - either ASCII 1Bh or 3Bh |
| Checksum | 2 | Yes, if any option fields | 8-bit arithmetic checksum of all characters from Begin PnP to End PnP inclusive, exclusive of the checksum bytes themselves, represented as a two-character hexadecimal number |
| End PnP | 1 | Yes | ) - either ASCII 29h or 09h for a mouse |

1 Each of the character strings for an option field begins with the extend character, “\”. If you use any of the option fields, but do not want to use all of them, you must still add the extend character for all of the fields you skip.

2 No variable-length field can be more than 32 characters unless otherwise specified here. The length of the Plug and Play identifier, including all fields and delimiters, must not exceed 256 characters, to minimize delays during the boot process.

## Transmitting the Identification String

When a serial device is attached to the system or is turned on, it must send its identification string to the PC using a speed and format familiar to the operating system.

The serial device must set the data rate of the serial transmission to 1200 baud. After the system has received the serial identifier, the data rate can be changed to the normal rate for the serial device.

The system expects to receive the identification string in a data format compatible with a 9-bit frame. The serial device must set the format of the identification string to one of the following formats:

- 9-bit frame. One start bit, seven data bits, no parity, one stop bit
- 10-bit frame. One start bit, seven data bits, no parity, two stop bits
- 10-bit frame. One start bit, seven data bits, mark parity, one stop bit
- 10-bit frame. One start bit, eight data bits with most-significant bit set to 1, one stop bit

# Plug and Play Serial Mouse Requirements

The mouse must always echo DTR to DSR, both at power-up and whenever it is hot-plugged. The easiest way for a serial mouse to make its presence known on the system is to tie DSR to DTR. Whenever the system sets DTR high (1), DSR is also set high, and the system detects the presence of the mouse. This connection is shown in Figure 7.6.

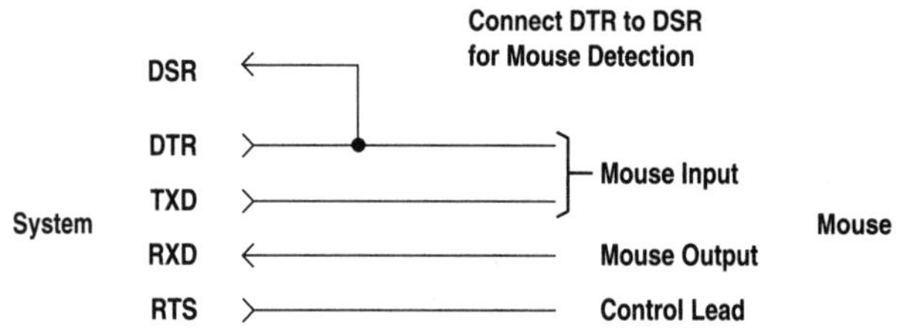


**Figure 7.6 Serial Mouse Connector**

The mouse must be capable of monitoring RTS. If RTS is low (0), the mouse must wait in an idle state. When RTS changes from low to high (0 to 1), the mouse must send its identification string. After the string is sent, normal mouse operations can begin. If RTS goes low, though, the mouse must wait in an idle state until RTS again goes high.

The identification string must be composed of characters that do not use bit 6 of the transmitted data on RXD. This bit is used by the mouse to indicate the beginning of a motion report to the system. In all instances, the identification string must be composed of characters in which bit 6 has been subtracted (for example, ASCII character 50h, "P," must be 30h for a serial mouse or compatible identification string). Lowercase characters must not be used.

A serial mouse (or serial mouse–compatible device) uses the following steps to identify itself and enable mouse operations:

1. Echo DTR to DSR. On power-up, the system sets DTR=1. The mouse echoes this to DSR.
2. If RTS=0, wait for RTS=1.
3. If RTS=1, send the identification string.
4. Begin mouse operations.
5. If RTS changes back to 0, return to step 2.

# Plug and Play Serial Modem Requirements

Serial modems must treat the DTR and RTS lines as special cases before and during the identification process, in spite of the modem commands that may attempt to condition the interpretation of the DTR or RTS line. These lines are the primary source the system uses to download the modem's serial identification string. After the identification string has been transmitted to the system and regular modem operation begins, the modem can use the relevant "AT" command settings to condition responses to DTR and RTS.

The modem must be capable of timing events after the system sets DTR high. If these events do not occur during the proper timing cycle, the modem must return to its idle state. After the system sets DTR high, the modem must monitor RTS to detect when the system sets it high. If RTS is set high before the first timing event expires (that is, before 150 ms), the modem must return to the idle state. If RTS is set high between the two events (that is, after 150 ms but before 250 ms), the modem must send its identification string to the system. If RTS is still low after 250 ms, the modem must return to the idle state.

A serial modem uses the following steps to identify itself and enable modem operations:

1. On power-up, set DSR=1.
2. Check for new commands, ringing, RTS, and DTR.
3. If an "AT" command is received, perform modem operation.
4. If ringing is detected, report the event at the default speed and continue modem operations.

5. If DTR=0 and RTS=0 (that is, the system is turned off or rebooting, or the peripheral is not connected to the PC) and the serial device is not executing a command, return to step 2.
6. If DTR=1, start T1 at 150 ms and T2 at 250 ms and check RTS.
7. If RTS=1 and T1 has not expired, quit and return to step 2.
8. If RTS=1 and T1 has expired but T2 has not expired, send the identification string and return to step 2.
9. If RTS=0 and T2 has expired, quit and return to step 2.

# Other Serial Device Requirements

With serial devices other than modems (that do not use DTR and RTS for special meanings), use the following steps to identify and enable peripheral operation:

1. On power-up, set DSR=1.
2. Check for new commands, external or internal events, RTS, and DTR.
3. If commands have been received from the system, execute those commands.
4. If an event occurs, process the event (for example, reports, actions, and so on).
5. If DTR=0 and RTS=0 (that is, the system is turned off or rebooting, or the peripheral is not connected to the PC) and the serial device is not executing a command, return to step 2.
6. If DTR=1, check to see if RTS=1.
7. If RTS=1, send the identification string and return to step 2.
8. If RTS=0, return to step 2.

# Serial Device Recommendations

In addition to the requirements documented here and in the *Plug and Play External COM Device Specification*, you can implement the following recommendations in serial devices for added capability:

- Capability for baud rates up to 115.2K baud to support the 16550A on motherboards or expansion bus serial cards
- Capability for slower baud rates to support older, non–Plug and Play systems
- Inclusion of an icon on the PC end of the serial device cable that matches an icon on the PC.

# Printers and Other Devices Attached to Parallel Ports

Printers and other devices attached to parallel ports should be capable of high-speed, bidirectional data transfers. The design criteria for parallel peripheral devices on a PC 95 closely follow those for the parallel ports described in Chapter 5, "System Devices." The requirements listed in this section enhance the capabilities of the parallel device, and maximize the speed of transfer of parallel data between the system and the peripheral.

## Parallel Device Requirements

A parallel device connected to the PC 95 must meet the following requirements:

- Compliant with IEEE P1284-I, at a minimum.
- Support of compatibility mode and nibble mode.
- Returns device identification string in nibble mode.
- Device identification strings composed only of ASCII values from 20h to 7Fh, inclusive.
- Capable of reporting the MANUFACTURER and MODEL portions of the device identifier (MFR, MDL).
- Static MANUFACTURER and MODEL key values for a specific unit. Static means that identifier values do not change for different hardware configurations. For example, adding memory modules to a PostScript® printer should not change the MODEL key value that is reported as part of the device identifier. If used, all COMPATIBLE and CLASS identifier key values must remain static for any device.
- Unique MANUFACTURER and MODEL key values from each manufacturer.
- Placement of labels on the cable between the device and the system, as described in the IEEE P1284 specification.

### IEEE P1284-I Compliance

A parallel device complies with IEEE P1284 if it meets a set of required criteria documented in the IEEE P1284 specification, *Standard Signaling Method for a Bi-directional Parallel Peripheral Interface for Personal Computers*. For a parallel device that connects to the PC 95, the minimum requirement is IEEE P1284 Level I compliance. Level I compliance implements the compatibility and nibble modes, as specified in IEEE P1284.

P1284-I compliance defines the mechanical and electrical specifications of the peripheral. A 1284-I–compliant peripheral uses the standard 36-pin 0.085 center-line connector found on existing peripherals, called a 1284-B connector in the specification. Figure 7.7 shows the 1284-I–compliant connector. In all cases, ensure that there is enough space between the connectors and the surrounding enclosure to allow for a mating connector, the connector shell, and the latch assembly.

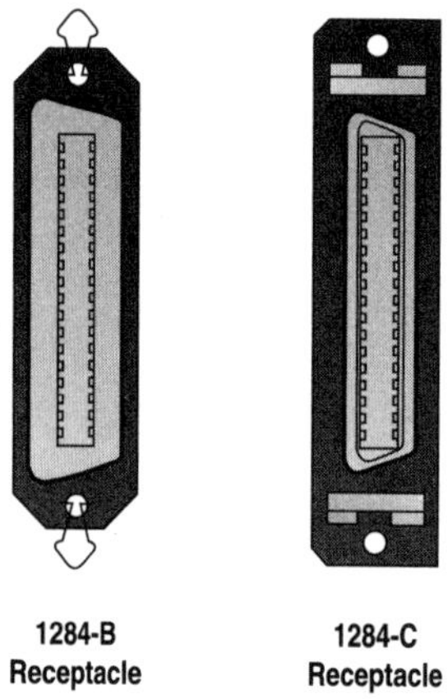


**Figure 7.7 1284-I– and 1284-II–Compliant Connectors**

For more information about the electrical specifications for P1284-I–compliant peripherals, see the IEEE P1284 specification.

## Mode Support

New peripherals that you design for the PC 95 must implement nibble mode and compatibility mode. Nibble mode provides a means of transferring the identification string from the peripheral to the system. Compatibility mode provides backward compatibility with non–Plug and Play systems that do not support more advanced modes.

## Parallel Device Identification Strings

A P1284 peripheral must contain a device identifier that is returned to the system. The system uses the device identifier to load the appropriate device drivers for the attached peripheral. For Plug and Play compatibility, the parallel device identification string must be returned to the system in nibble mode.

All characters in the device identification string must consist only of ASCII values from 20h to 7Fh.

The device identification string consists of a leading zero, a hexadecimal value that represents the length of the string, and then a set of fields, in ASCII, with a unique identification string. The string must contain the MANUFACTURER and MODEL keys, at a minimum. The keys are case sensitive and can be abbreviated to MFG and MDL. The device identifier is described more fully in the IEEE P1284 specification. For information about how the system determines the correct peripheral device driver, see the *Microsoft Windows 95 Device Driver Reference*, supplied with the Windows 95 DDK.

All MANUFACTURER and MODEL key values should remain static for a specific unit. Static means that identifier values do not change for different hardware configurations. For example, adding memory modules to a Postscript printer should not change the MODEL key value that is reported as part of the device identifier. If used, all CLASS and COMPATIBLE identifier key values must remain static for any device. In addition, all MANUFACTURER and MODEL key values must remain unique from each manufacturer.

### IEEE P1284 Cables

A cable assembly that meets all of the requirements of the IEEE P1284 specification must include a permanent and clear label with the phrase "IEEE Std 1284-19XX".

## Parallel Device Recommendations

In addition to the requirements already listed for a parallel device connected to the PC 95, you can implement the following recommendations for parallel devices:

- Support of an additional set of keys in the device identification string
- Compliance with IEEE P1284-II and support of ECP mode, for higher-speed parallel devices
- Inclusion of an icon on the PC end of the parallel device cable that matches an icon on the PC.

### Additional Keys

Devices attached to the PC parallel port should support an additional set of keys. These keys can be added to the device identification string, and provide the CLASS, DESCRIPTION, and COMPATIBLE ID keys of the device identifier. These keys are case sensitive and can be abbreviated as CLS, DES, and CID.

The CLASS key describes the type of parallel device. The CLASS key can contain the values PRINTER, MODEM, NET, HDC, PCMCIA, MEDIA, FDC, and PORTS. HDC refers to hard disk controller. MEDIA refers to any multimedia device. FDC refers to floppy disk drive controller.

The DESCRIPTION key is an ASCII string with a description of the device the manufacturer would like to have presented if a device driver is not found for the peripheral.

The COMPATIBLE identifier key can provide a value that exactly matches a peripheral name supported by a device driver shipped with Windows 95.

For more information, see the *Plug and Play Parallel Port Devices* specification.

### P1284-II Compliance

A 1284-II–compliant peripheral uses a new 36-pin 0.050 centerline connector, called a 1284-C connector. This connector is used on both the port and the peripheral device. Figure 7.6 shows the 1284-II–compliant connector. In all cases, ensure that there is enough space between the connectors and the surrounding enclosure to allow for a mating connector, the connector shell, and the latch assembly. The IEEE P1284 specification recommends a 1284-C connector for all new parallel ports and peripherals.

For more information about the electrical specifications for P1284-II–compliant peripherals, see the IEEE P1284 specification.

Peripheral devices that are capable of handling the high-speed data rate should support the protocols of the IEEE P1284 ECP mode.

## Additional Parallel Device Information

For information about device drivers for P1284 peripherals, see the *Microsoft Windows 95 Device Driver Reference*, supplied with the Windows 95 DDK.

# Peripheral Power Management

Power management is strongly recommended for peripherals attached to a PC 95. If you decide to implement power management in your peripheral design, you must supply a device driver that provides the power management interface to the hardware.

Two different types of device driver interfaces can be used. For Plug and Play device drivers, power management should be handled by detecting the appropriate CONFIG_TEST... and CONFIG_APM... messages from the configuration manager. For non–Plug and Play device drivers, power management can be handled by processing the WM_POWERBROADCAST messages.

For more information about device drivers for power management in peripherals, see the *Microsoft Windows 95 Device Driver Reference*, supplied with the Windows 95 DDK.

# Peripheral Cabling

Cables between the system and the peripheral can be confusing to the user. To ease the complexity of connecting cables, cables should be designed to prevent the user from mistakenly attaching the cable to an inappropriate connector.

# General Cable Requirements

Cables between peripherals (internal or external) and a PC 95 system must be either keyed or shaped in such a way that the cables cannot be plugged in incorrectly.

## General Cable Recommendations

Cables between internal peripherals and the system should be labeled to identify where to plug in the cables. External cables should contain an icon on the PC end of the cable that matches an icon near the proper connector on the PC case.

# Windows 95 Logo Peripheral Feature Set

Basic peripherals must have a minimum set of features for a system to qualify for the Windows 95 Logo. Table 7.12 through Table 7.16 summarize these peripheral features, which have been described throughout this chapter. In addition to the required features, you can include more advanced recommended hardware, which optimizes the system peripherals for Windows 95.

For a more complete explanation of each of these features, see the peripheral discussion in this chapter.

**Table 7.12 Monitor Requirements**

| Feature | Logo requirement | Recommendation |
|---|---|---|
| Color | N/A | Yes |
| VESA DDC1/2B | N/A | Yes |
| VESA ergonomic monitor timings | N/A | Yes |
| VESA DPMS | N/A | Yes |

**Table 7.13 SCSI Device**

| Feature | Logo requirement | Recommendation |
|---|---|---|
| Plug and Play SCSI specification | Yes | Yes |
| SCAM Level 1 ID | Yes | Level 2 |
| Automatic termination | Yes | Yes |
| 50-pin SCSI-2 connector | Yes | Yes |
| SCSI-2 | Yes | Yes |
| SCSI-3 | No | Yes |

**Table 7.14 Mouse**

| Feature | Logo requirement | Recommendation |
|---|---|---|
| PS/2 style | No | Yes |
| Plug and Play COM device identifier (for external serial mice) | Yes | Yes |

**Table 7.15 Modem**

| Feature | Logo requirement | Recommendation |
|---|---|---|
| Command set | TIA-602 (Hayes compatible) | TIA IS-131 (standard extensions) |
| Data modem | 9.6 Kps (V.32) | 28.8 Kps (V.34) |
| Protocol | V42/V42bis | V42/V42bis |
| Fax modem | 9.6 Kps (V.29) | 14.4 Kps (V.17) |
| Class | Class 1 (TIA-578) | Class 2 (TIA-592) with ECM and NSF |
| Voice | | IS-101 ('AT+V') |
| Voice coding | | GSM 6.10 or TrueSpeech I |
| Voice view | No | Yes |
| TDD (deaf communications) | No | V.18 and IS-131 |
| Plug and Play device identifier | Yes | Yes |
| Plug and Play COM specification (for external serial modems) | Yes | Yes |

**Table 7.16 Printer**

| Feature | Logo requirement | Recommendation |
|---|---|---|
| Plug and Play printer port device specification | Yes | Yes |
| Nibble Plug and Play identifier | Yes | Yes |
| MFG, CMD, MDL | Yes | Yes |
| CLS, DES, CID | No | Yes |
| ECP | No | Yes |

PART 3

# BIOS Design

BIOS design is an integral part of the PC 95. It is through the BIOS routines that a huge number of system functions are performed, from booting the system to power management. With Plug and Play, the BIOS is called on to support new functionality and to act as go-between for the operating system and the system hardware.

Chapter 8 discusses BIOS design for the system and focuses primarily on the impact of Plug and Play hardware on system BIOS design. This chapter also describes the system BIOS changes needed to support specific hardware recommendations for the PC 95.

Chapter 9 discusses option ROM design for expansion cards, with emphasis on the changes to ISA option ROMs for Plug and Play and for hardware recommendations for the PC 95.

CHAPTER 8

# System BIOS Design

Chapter 8

The only requirement for a Personal Computer for Microsoft® Windows™ 95 system BIOS is that it provide Plug and Play functions to the system. These functions enable the PC to configure the system board and boot devices before passing control of the configuration process to the operating system. A Plug and Play system BIOS is also able to notify the operating system about dynamic configuration events, such as docking a portable PC with a docking station.

The system BIOS should also support advanced power management (APM 1.1) in both portable and desktop systems. As power management becomes more critical because of the EPA's Energy Star initiative, demand for systems that conserve energy will increase. To meet this demand, Windows 95 provides extra power management functionality to systems that contain an APM 1.1 BIOS.

For more information about Plug and Play functions for the system BIOS, see the *Plug and Play BIOS Specification*. For more information about power management functions, see the *Advanced Power Management (APM) BIOS Interface Specification*, Revision 1.1.

This chapter concentrates on system BIOS implementation details of Plug and Play and power management for the PC 95. This chapter also gives an overview of how the Plug and Play system BIOS interacts with Windows 95, and how the operating system and applications use the Plug and Play functions of the system BIOS. The system BIOS implementation of power management described in this chapter concentrates on enhancements provided by Windows 95, and how the system BIOS can interact fully with the operating system and applications.

# Plug and Play System BIOS

The PC 95 must contain a Plug and Play system BIOS. A system BIOS that does not conform to the *Plug and Play BIOS Specification*, Version 1.0a, is not considered a Plug and Play BIOS for the PC 95. Therefore, a system BIOS that contains only extensions to support Plug and Play ISA cards will not qualify. For more information about the Plug and Play functions for the system BIOS in a PC 95, see the *Plug and Play BIOS Specification*.

To ensure that the user is able to make optimal use of Plug and Play, the BIOS capabilities must be tightly integrated with the Plug and Play operating system.

A Plug and Play BIOS must configure the motherboard and boot devices (at a minimum) before giving control of the configuration process to the operating system. The BIOS configuration process involves initializing the motherboard devices (PIC, DMA controller, system display adapter, FDC, and so on), as well as isolating and initializing Plug and Play expansion cards required to boot the PC. A Plug and Play BIOS must also maintain a list of motherboard device configuration information, and communicate the information to the operating system after the POST process has finished.

When incorporating Plug and Play functionality in mobile computers, you must ensure that the Plug and Play BIOS is able to notify the Plug and Play operating system of dynamic configuration events, such as the insertion of a notebook computer into its docking station. A Plug and Play BIOS provides a mechanism for a Plug and Play operating system to reconfigure the system without requiring the user to turn the computer system off. The Plug and Play BIOS then notifies applications and drivers about the new system configuration. For software-controlled devices, the Plug and Play BIOS can give the operating system early warning to prevent errors and data loss when the drive is removed.

# System BIOS as Motherboard Enumerator

A system motherboard is made up of a number of devices. Devices such as the PIC, DMA controller, and keyboard controller are found on all motherboards, and are generally considered static because their resources have been firmly established for years and are well known. In more modern motherboards, some devices, such as FDCs and HDCs, parallel and serial ports, and display adapters, have been designed directly on the motherboard, freeing more space in the expansion bus. Although these devices also have resources that are well established, other considerations make it necessary that these resources be more flexible than are the static devices.

The system BIOS must act as a motherboard enumerator for all of these devices. It is the responsibility of the system BIOS to identify all of these devices on the motherboard, configure them so there are no conflicts in their resources, and store the information for later use. The system BIOS must also be able to enumerate any expansion cards that may contain Plug and Play devices used during the boot process. For example, if a display adapter is contained on an ISA bus expansion card, the system BIOS must be able to isolate, identify, configure, and disable (in cases of resource conflicts) the Plug and Play ISA card before it can use the display adapter as the output device. The system BIOS must also be able to identify any bus that exists on the motherboard that is not otherwise enumerated.

Each device and bus that the system BIOS enumerates is added to a system device configuration list. This list contains a device node for each device and bus. The device node structure includes information that identifies the device and the system resources used by that device. After the boot process has finished and control has been turned over to the operating system, Windows 95 uses the Plug and Play system BIOS functions to retrieve the system device configuration list, and uses it to construct the portion of the hardware tree that contains everything enumerated by the system BIOS.

If the motherboard contains an ISA bus, the system BIOS must contain an ISA bus device node or Windows 95 will not load the ISA enumerator. If the motherboard contains a PCI bus with a bridge to an ISA bus, however, the PCI bus will report the ISA device node. In this case, the system BIOS should not list an ISA bus device node, or the ISA enumerator will be loaded twice, wasting system RAM.

Every device and bus on the motherboard must have a unique device identifier that distinguishes it from every other device. This identifier is usually a standard EISA identifier that the system BIOS uses to construct the device node in the system device configuration list. Many motherboard devices and buses, and non–Plug and Play expansion card devices, do not have a standard EISA identifier. To make it possible to identify the devices that do not have a standard EISA identifier, an EISA prefix of "PNP" has been reserved. For information about reserved device identifiers and the devices to which they are assigned, see Appendix B.

## Enabling Boot Devices Through Bus Bridges

On some systems, more than one type of expansion bus is located on the motherboard. For example, many systems contain a PCI bus and an ISA bus on the same board. In many cases, the motherboard buses are connected by a bus bridge.

If a bus bridge is used on the motherboard, the system BIOS must be capable of enabling both buses. If a boot device is on the bus on the other side of the bridge, the bridge must be capable of passing the proper signals and commands through the bus bridge, and the system BIOS must be capable of enabling any devices that are required during the boot sequence. For example, if the motherboard contains a PCI bus and a PCI bridge to an ISA bus, the system BIOS must be capable of performing the Plug and Play isolation, identification, and configuration sequence on the ISA cards through the PCI bridge, and be capable of using any boot device that is found on any of the ISA cards.

# The Boot Process

The system BIOS begins to boot by performing the POST process. You must add several new Plug and Play functions to the system BIOS to identify and configure the new Plug and Play hardware that is a part of the PC 95. This section discusses the POST process to show how the new functions interact with the hardware and Plug and Play option ROMs.

# Plug and Play BIOS POST

A Plug and Play system BIOS should perform the following steps during the POST process:

1. At the beginning of the POST process, the system BIOS should disable any configurable devices on the system that it is aware of. This includes Plug and Play ISA boot devices that come up active when power is turned on (as a default for systems with a non–Plug and Play system BIOS).
2. If the motherboard contains an ISA bus, isolate the Plug and Play ISA cards and assign a CSN to each. No ISA devices should be activated at this time. Determine which, if any, of the ISA devices are boot devices.
3. The system BIOS should now determine the static devices on the system and their resources, and construct an initial resource map. If any of the devices on the ISA bus contain static resources, assign these resources to the initial resource map. Alternately, a resource map can be constructed from a previous working configuration that has been saved (for example, in NVRAM). Note that this saved configuration can contain both static and configurable devices, which will be loaded into the resource map in its entirety at this time.
4. The input and output device (generally, the keyboard and display subsystem) should now be selected and enabled. Static devices, such as a non–Plug and Play display adapter, always take precedence over configurable devices, because the resources of the static devices cannot be reallocated or disabled. If no static device exists, enable the configurable device. If the configurable device is Plug and Play compatible, initialize the option ROM (if present).
5. An ISA ROM scan now occurs starting at C0000h and continuing through EFFFFh. The scan checks each 2K boundary for an AAh followed by a 55h, indicating that an option ROM exists at that address. Plug and Play option ROMs are disabled while the ROM scan takes place, unless the ROM is located on the input or output device.
6. Use the option ROM initialization procedure if a Plug and Play device has been selected as the IPL device. If Int 19h, the system bootstrap loader, has been captured by an option ROM, the system BIOS must recapture it if the primary IPL device is either a Plug and Play ISA device or a device known to the system BIOS, such as an ATA (IDE) host adapter on the motherboard. This ensures system BIOS control of the bootstrap sequence.
7. Enable as few ISA cards and other configurable devices as possible under the resource allocation scheme being used (to ensure maximum flexibility for Windows 95). If a static resource allocation scheme is used, the resources for all ISA cards and other configurable devices will be allocated using the information obtained in the last working configuration. If a dynamic resource allocation scheme is used, only the bootable Plug and Play ISA cards are enabled, their resources are configured in a conflict-free configuration, and their option ROMs are initialized.

8. The Int 19h bootstrap loader now begins. If for some reason the operating system does not load, restore the Int 19h vector to the last ISA option ROM that captured it and execute the Int 19h bootstrap loader again.
9. After the operating system successfully loads, it takes control of the system resources and uses the run-time services of the system BIOS to determine the current allocation of system resources. Any Plug and Play devices that have not been configured and enabled by the BIOS can then be configured by either the Plug and Play operating system or by appropriate system applications.

To ensure that Windows 95 has maximum flexibility in setting up the devices on the PC, the system BIOS should activate only the devices and buses on the motherboard and boot devices (either on the motherboard or on expansion cards). Any device that Windows 95 finds to be active will not have its resources reassigned, nor will Windows 95 disable that device if a conflicting device is found in the system.

## Option ROMs

Option ROMs are generally found on expansion cards that are required for the system boot process. (Because there may be exceptions to this rule on ISA cards, a Plug and Play option ROM expansion header can contain the static resource information vector. For more information, see the *Plug and Play BIOS Specification.*

During the boot process, option ROMs are used to initialize the boot devices on expansion cards. The system BIOS performs a ROM scan during the POST process between addresses C0000h and EFFFFh on every 2K boundary for a 55AA header to determine if the system contains any option ROMs. If the header is found, a checksum is performed to confirm the presence of the option ROM. The system BIOS then performs a jump to offset 03h in the 2K segment in which the header was found to begin initializing the option ROM.

For more information about option ROMs and the initialization process of expansion card boot devices, see Chapter 9, "Option ROM Design."

# Plug and Play BIOS Detection

After the system BIOS gives the operating system control of the PC, Windows 95 performs an installation check to determine if the system BIOS supports Plug and Play. Windows 95 scans between F0000h and FFFFFh at every 16-byte boundary for the ASCII string $PnP. If the string is found, the operating system performs a checksum operation to ensure that the system BIOS is compatible with Plug and Play. If it is, Windows 95 begins loading the system configuration for the motherboard devices. For more information about the structure of the installation check, see the *Plug and Play BIOS Specification*.

# Power Management with APM 1.1

Power management can involve many parts of the PC 95. Motherboard devices, expansion cards, and peripherals can all be designed to provide low-power modes controlled by software; both desktop and mobile systems benefit from power management. The Energy Star program created by the EPA is one impetus behind the drive to incorporate power management in all PCs. Although power management is not a requirement for the PC 95, it is highly recommended.

A system BIOS, whether in a desktop system or a mobile system, should provide power management capabilities by supporting the *Advanced Power Management (APM) BIOS Interface Specification*, Revision 1.1. APM 1.1 provides calls for battery level detect, suspend and resume, and other power management functions. Windows 95 fully supports the conventions described in APM 1.1.

The BIOS should retain power management policy for all devices it knows about, such as motherboard display adapters, processor states, and so on. On an APM 1.1 system, Windows 95 may issue some Set Device Power State calls to those individual devices, in particular, the display class, but the BIOS must set timers, save and restore the device state, and otherwise provide power management features for these devices.

For more information about specific methods of implementing power management in the system BIOS, see the APM 1.1 specification. The following sections discuss some techniques and additional power management details that enhance the interaction of the system BIOS and Windows 95.

## Battery Status

A battery status indicator is very important to the user of a portable system. This indicator visually verifies the remaining battery power, and the time available to continue running applications before a suspend occurs.

The system BIOS should be able to supply battery status information to the operating system using the APM 1.1 Get Power Status (0Ah) call. At a minimum, the Get Power Status call should return the High, Low, Critical, or Charging Battery status. Although this is the minimal acceptable amount of information, Remaining Battery Life (percentage of charge) and Remaining Battery Life (time units) are preferred for more accuracy. If the system BIOS returns both the percentage of charge and the time units remaining, Windows 95 displays the approximate time left on the current charge.

# Suspend and Resume

The APM 1.1 specification describes three types of suspend requests: a user suspend, a system suspend, and a critical suspend. Windows 95 interprets these different types of requests as follows:

- A user-initiated suspend allows applications to present choices to the user while the suspend process proceeds.
- A system-initiated suspend usually occurs after a preset time has elapsed during which no activity has taken place, with the assumption that no one is available to answer questions.
- A critical suspend occurs only in an emergency, such as when loss of battery power is imminent.

A system BIOS that supports APM 1.1 must be able to notify the appropriate drivers of each of these power management events.

System BIOS designers who incorporate APM 1.1 in their BIOS should ensure that suspends originating in the operating system work properly. Otherwise, user suspends through the operating system are impossible, which limits the capabilities of the power management functions in Windows 95.

A critical suspend should occur only as an emergency shutdown procedure. (It has sometimes been used as the system's only notification that the battery is almost out of power.) When the critical suspend notification is sent, the system must comply immediately, without taking time to prepare any running applications or drivers. When this type of critical suspend occurs, some parts of the system may not be able to resume, such as open network files. To circumvent this problem, you must enable the system to detect when battery power is running low. When the system BIOS detects that the battery has only a few minutes of power left, it should send a system suspend request notification. This should allow the system time to prepare applications and drivers before the system BIOS sends a critical suspend request notification. However, if the system is still busy processing the suspend request and battery power loss is imminent, the system BIOS can send a critical suspend request notification to interrupt the normal suspend, and force the system to suspend immediately.

A system BIOS that implements APM 1.1 must allow the operating system to reject either user-initiated or system-initiated suspends. Windows 95 uses the Set Power State calls to indicate that it is busy or is processing a request. It then either rejects the request or sends the appropriate call to set the power state to the requested level. If the system reaches a critical battery condition during this "busy" state, the system BIOS should post a critical suspend so Windows 95 will comply immediately. (Critical suspends must be used only in true critical power situations, not as a means to defeat ordinary suspend processing.)

Occasionally, the system BIOS may detect some device activity (such as DMA transfers) after the operating system has accepted a suspend request. Typically, the system BIOS would independently decide to cancel the suspend request by sending a resume notification. However, when the BIOS posts a resume notification, the operating system begins to notify all drivers to reinitialize their hardware and resume normal operation, which can be a lengthy process. To speed up the process, Windows 95 includes a shortcut that allows the BIOS to retry suspends the BIOS has canceled temporarily because of device activity or other short-term causes. When the system BIOS posts a second suspend request, Windows 95 immediately attempts another Set Power State call. The order of events for this process is as follows:

1. The system BIOS requests the suspend.
2. The operating system processes the request (shutting down the network, closing applications, and so on).
3. The operating system calls Set Power State to suspend.
4. The system BIOS decides to temporarily cancel the request for some reason, but will retry shortly.
5. The system BIOS returns from the Set Power State call and posts another suspend request instead of a resume notification.
6. The operating system immediately recalls Set Power State.

This process of posting more than one suspend request without intervening resume notifications allows the DMA transfer to finish while the rest of the system remains in a ready-to-suspend state. The system BIOS, however, must determine when to "give up" the repeated suspend attempts and stop (or send a resume notification), because Windows 95 will continue to process all of the suspend requests sent to it.

If the system BIOS is not able to return the power state of a particular device when Get Power State is called with the device identifier, it should return error code 9, Unknown Device ID. This method should be used for devices that are incapable of power management, or for devices that cannot report their power management status.

## APM and Docking Systems

A system with an APM 1.1 BIOS allows devices to suspend and resume in a more orderly fashion. By providing a mechanism for communication of suspend and resume requests between the system BIOS, the operating system, and applications, APM 1.1 includes the operating system in the warm docking and undocking process. With this capability, the operating system can delay or possibly reject an undocking request because of (for example) open files that may be lost when a network connection is severed.

A warm undocking event in which APM 1.1 participates should occur using the following general process:

1. The docking station decides that it is time to undock based on an event generated by the user (who pushes the eject button) or by the operating system.
2. The system BIOS calls the operating system to inform it that an undocking event has been initiated.
3. The operating system queries all devices marked as being on the docking station for which it has a device node. If no devices object to the undocking event, the operating system informs the system BIOS that it is OK to undock.
4. At this point, the BIOS switches to its APM 1.1 side and performs a Suspend Request notification.
5. The operating system then queries applications and drivers to determine whether they are ready to suspend. Devices that were originally configured by the operating system are suspended through a cooperative effort between it and the hardware device drivers. If no applications or drivers object to the suspend, the operating system informs the system BIOS that it is OK to suspend.
6. The system BIOS suspends all devices and components of which it is aware. It then tells the ejection mechanism to eject the portable system.
7. The system BIOS performs a Normal Resume System notification that informs the operating system to reinitialize the hardware and resume normal operation.
8. The system BIOS reports that the undocking event has finished.
9. Certain device nodes will send a message to the operating system that they failed to resume (because the hardware for these device nodes is located on the docking station), so the operating system configuration manager will reenumerate all devices on the portable system to discover which have changed. Device drivers for devices that are no longer present will be unloaded. If a new device has been added to the system, the appropriate drivers will be loaded.

A docking event works in much the same way, except that in most cases, devices are added to the system when the docking occurs. When the devices are reenumerated, the operating system loads device drivers for any added device.

# Display Power Management Support

Power management support is recommended for desktop systems and required for mobile systems. To properly provide power management support for monitors and display panels, some means of controlling the power management signaling must be included, either in the system BIOS or in the display BIOS ROM.

A PC 95 should contain either the display power management calls given in the *VESA BIOS Extensions/Power Management (VBE/PM) Standard* or the APM 1.1 device 01FF support described in the *Advanced Power Management (APM) BIOS Interface Specification*, Revision 1.1.

For more information about power management support for display adapter option ROMs, see Chapter 9, "Option BIOS Design."

# Plug and Play System BIOS Functions

This section describes the Plug and Play system BIOS functions that Windows 95 uses. For more information about the new Plug and Play functions for the system BIOS, see the *Plug and Play BIOS Specification.*

All of the BIOS functions listed in the *Plug and Play BIOS Specification* must be supported in the system ROM. Any functions that are not used must return the FUNCTION_NOT_SUPPORTED error code.

# Function Requirements

The system BIOS in a PC 95 must provide the following:

- Accurate information about motherboard devices (Plug and Play BIOS Functions 0h and 1h)
- Motherboard device configuration, if BIOS-configurable resources are present (Plug and Play BIOS Function 2h)
- Power management control of individual devices known to the system BIOS (Function 0Bh), if the system BIOS utilizes APM 1.1
- Dynamic event management (Functions 3, 4, and 5) on systems that dock and undock with a docking station

## Motherboard Device Information

Windows 95 retrieves information about the motherboard devices by calling Function 0 and Function 1 in the system BIOS.

Function 0 returns the maximum number of device nodes for motherboard devices that the system BIOS found during the POST process. (On docking systems with the portable system docked, this number would include both the devices on the portable system and in the docking station.) It also returns the size of the largest device node the system BIOS found. (On docking systems, it is the largest device found either on the portable system or in the docking station.) Windows 95 uses these parameters to determine the amount of available memory that must be used to retrieve and store all of the information about the devices nodes.

Windows 95 uses Function 1 to copy the information about a particular device node into a memory buffer, where it is used to construct the hardware tree for motherboard devices. This function also allows Windows 95 to request a device node that shows how the device was configured during the boot process or how the device will be configured in the next boot process.

# Configuring Motherboard Devices

Windows 95 can change the configuration of devices that the system BIOS has enumerated by calling Function 2 on the system BIOS. However, Windows 95 generally does not reconfigure any device that the system BIOS has already configured. This includes boot devices on the ISA bus, and Bus0 devices (main PCI bus) or boot devices located on the other side of a bus bridge.

Nevertheless, flexibility with Windows 95 is enhanced when the system BIOS leaves nonboot devices (ISA and PCI) unconfigured, because Windows 95 can reconfigure them when necessary to avoid conflicts. However, other operating systems that currently do not offer dynamic reconfiguration will require the system BIOS to configure all devices. Windows 95 cannot determine if a real-mode driver has been hooked into a card-resource combination before Windows 95 was loaded.

One solution to this problem is to create a system BIOS switch in the BIOS setup routine to select which behavior the BIOS uses. This switch would have three options: Configure All, Auto Configure, and Minimum Configure.

Configure All would cause the system BIOS to enumerate all of the devices known to it, including devices on the motherboard, boot devices on the ISA bus, and PCI devices (using the PCI emulator). This configuration would be used with non–Plug and Play operating systems, with systems that contain devices using real-mode drivers, and on systems that multiboot between Plug and Play and non–Plug and Play operating systems.

Auto Configure would perform a Configure All the first time the system is booted. When Windows 95 boots for the first time, the system BIOS cannot know until after it has finished loading that it is a Plug and Play system. After Windows 95 has loaded, it sends the PNP_OS_ACTIVE message to the system BIOS. The system BIOS in turn sets the BIOS switch to Minimum Configure for its devices from that point on. For non–Plug and Play operating systems that do not send the message PNP_OS_ACTIVE, the system BIOS would continue to perform the configurable functions, while maintaining the Auto Configure switch setting.

Minimum Configure would cause the system BIOS to enumerate only the minimum number of devices required to boot. (This is the configuration used by Windows 95 after its first boot.) This configuration could also be set manually. This method can only be used by Plug and Play systems, and with systems that do not use any real-mode drivers.

You, the system BIOS designer, must add this functionality to your BIOS setup routine. Windows 95 supports the PNP_OS_ACTIVE message to allow the system BIOS to set the BIOS switch appropriately.

## Plug and Play Power Management Support

A Plug and Play system BIOS that supports power management must be able to provide a list of power-managed devices on the motherboard to whomever calls the system BIOS, usually the operating system or a device driver. Function 0Bh provides the APM 1.1 (or greater) portion of the system BIOS with a method of communicating to the caller the device identifiers of all devices on the motherboard that are capable of power management. The device identifier for a power-managed device is the same EISA identifier that identifies the device during the system BIOS enumeration.

This is the only power management function in the Plug and Play portion of the system BIOS. All other power management functions are provided by the APM 1.1 support in the system BIOS.

## Docking System Support

A Plug and Play BIOS is the heart of any Windows 95 docking system, and is critical for effective docking support. Windows 95 uses the event notification interface documented in the *Plug and Play BIOS Specification* to manipulate docking and undocking events. BIOS Functions 3, 4, and 5 provide enough event notification for the system BIOS and Windows 95 to perform appropriate actions during docking and undocking events.

Function 3, Get Event, returns a message to the caller that identifies the type of event that occurred on the system. Windows 95 typically uses the BIOS.386 to process these events, and polls roughly twice a second. (Windows 95 checks the control word in the BIOS Plug and Play header structure to determine which type of event notification method the system BIOS uses, either polling or interrupt driven. Windows 95 supports both polling and interrupts as notification methods.) When an event occurs, the caller of this function receives a message describing the event. One of six possible messages is returned:

- ABOUT_TO_CHANGE_CONFIG (0001h) warns that the system is about to be docked or undocked. This message mandates a response through Function 4, Send Message. The two appropriate responses are OK and ABORT. For an example of how these messages are exchanged and acted upon, see the undocking scenarios in Appendix E, "Docking System Scenarios."
- DOCK_CHANGED (0002h) indicates that the system has just been warm-docked or undocked.
- SYSTEM_DEVICE_CHANGED (0003h) indicates that a device has been added to or removed from the system. Note that this may be relevant to any Plug and Play system, not only to docking systems.
- CONFIG_CHANGE_FAILED (0004h) indicates that a docking or undocking sequence was canceled.
- UNKNOWN_SYSTEM_EVENT (FFFFh) indicates that an event has occurred, but the system BIOS doesn't know what type of event it was.
- OEM_DEFINED_EVENTS (8xxxh) is reserved for OEM-specific events. The standard BIOS.386 that ships with Windows 95 ignores these events.

Function 4, Send Message, provides a mechanism for the operating system to respond to system BIOS messages and to initiate docking events in software. If the system BIOS does not support one of the specified messages, this function must return MESSAGE_NOT_SUPPORTED. The messages that Windows 95 sends to the system BIOS relating to docking are:

- OK approves an ABOUT_TO_CHANGE_CONFIG message that the Plug and Play system BIOS sent.
- ABORT discontinues a configuration change when the Plug and Play system BIOS sent an ABOUT_TO_CHANGE_CONFIG message.
- UNDOCK_DEFAULT_ACTION instructs the Plug and Play system BIOS to undock the portable PC in any state that it deems appropriate.
- OEM_DEFINED_MESSAGES gives OEMs the opportunity to define messages specific to their system implementation.

The operating system uses Function 5, Get Docking Station Information, to retrieve the docking identifier and serial number. Windows 95 uses this information to determine the capabilities of the docking system of the docked and undocked configuration states. This function uses three fields:

- The docking station identifier allows Windows 95 to differentiate between the types of docking stations and port replicators to which the portable system can be connected. (For a description of the different strategies that OEMs can take regarding the implementation of docking identifiers and serial numbers, see the information about Plug and Play system BIOS Function 5.)
- The serial number is not required, but it allows the system to differentiate between two docking stations of the same type.
- The Capabilities field defines the system's docking capabilities, including whether the system supports cold, warm, or hot docking, and whether it is VCR style or surprise style. With this information, Windows 95 can decide on the correct undocking command in its system menu. Although Windows 95 supports all of these docking capabilities, the PC 95 must use warm or hot docking and a VCR style or locking mechanism—that is, not surprise style. For more information, see Chapter 4, "Mobile Hardware Designs." If the system supports docking but cannot determine the docking station capabilities, this function returns UNABLE_TO_DETERMINE_DOCK_CAPABILITIES. This function returns FUNCTION_NOT_SUPPORTED if the system does not support docking.

As part of Function 5, Get Docking Station Information, the system BIOS must return a docking station identifier and, optionally, a serial number. (This number distinguishes between docking states, and potentially between two different docks.) Windows 95 uses the combined identifier and number (known as the *dock serial identifier*) when it boots up, and after a warm docking or undocking event, to determine which configuration to use.

There is some leeway in how unique dock serial identifiers must be. The more unique they are, the better the user experience will be. But incorporating more unique serial identifiers may increase manufacturing costs. You can choose from three basic levels of uniqueness:

- One dock serial identifier for all docking stations is the minimum acceptable solution. This solution requires no extra work or cost, because any Plug and Play system BIOS can distinguish between the docked and undocked states to answer the Get Docking Station Information Plug and Play BIOS function. This solution will suffice for customers who have only one docking station.

- One dock serial identifier for each type of docking product sold. This would involve, for example, one identifier for undocked, one for a port replicator, and one for a docking station, if those were the two docking options you offered. This solution increases convenience for a customer who has a docking station at the office and a port replicator at home.
- One dock serial identifier for each product type and one serial number. This ensures that Windows 95 can distinguish between any two docking states the system may be in. This solution may add significant cost to the docks, depending on how it is implemented. Another potential problem with this approach is that a user who uses only Plug and Play hardware would be forced to create different hardware profiles for each dock used, even if different hardware profiles were otherwise unnecessary.

# Function Recommendations

In real-world scenarios, most systems will contain a mix of Plug and Play and non–Plug and Play expansion cards. Many non–Plug and Play ISA cards have no means of identifying the resources that they require, unless the person who installs the board can manually store them somewhere. Other boards can report their resource requirements, although the resources are static. Some non–Plug and Play ISA cards can configure their resources to more than one location using a configuration routine supplied with the card.

The *Plug and Play BIOS Specification* defines functions that allow the operating system to store static resource information for non–Plug and Play ISA cards in nonvolatile storage. The system BIOS can then use this information during the next POST process to identify the resources around which it must configure other Plug and Play devices.

The following capabilities allow the system BIOS to keep information on non–Plug and Play ISA cards in a nonvolatile location:

- Store and retrieve a complete list of all system resources used by all non–Plug and Play ISA devices on the PC (Plug and Play BIOS Functions 9h and 0Ah)
- Get, read, and write *legacy* ISA device information using the ESCD format (Plug and Play BIOS Functions 41h, 42h, and 43h)

Function 40h, Get Plug and Play ISA Configuration Structure, is not used by the initial version of Windows 95, but should be included for compatibility with other operating systems.

## List of All System Resources

This method involves storing a list of the system resources previously used by all non–Plug and Play ISA devices in some form of nonvolatile storage. The system BIOS can use this information during the enumeration process to avoid the resources required by the non–Plug and Play ISA devices, and configure other device resources around the fixed resources. This method only stores information about the resources used, and therefore requires less storage space.

You may sometimes need to add new hardware to the motherboard to provide adequate nonvolatile storage space to store the information provided by these functions.

The system BIOS should provide Function 9h, Set Statically Allocated Resource Information, to allow the system software—usually the operating system—to store the non–Plug and Play device configuration. The system software communicates this information to the system BIOS in the format of resource data type functions (as described in the *Plug and Play ISA Specification* and Appendix A of this guide). The system BIOS can use whatever proprietary method you choose to store this information in nonvolatile storage.

Function 0Ah, Get Statically Allocated Resource Information, should return the device configuration of the non–Plug and Play ISA devices on the system. This information should be returned as a block using the format of the resource data type functions.

Windows 95 uses Functions 9h and 0Ah to store and retrieve information about non–Plug and Play ISA cards. It is strongly recommended that you provide these functions in the system BIOS for any systems that contain an ISA bus capability.

## List of Device Information

This method stores information about all non–Plug and Play ISA devices and the resources these devices can use. The information describes which device is using what particular resources. The system BIOS can use this information in systems that do not have a Plug and Play operating system.

Because of the amount of information provided by these functions, you may need to add new hardware to the motherboard to create adequate nonvolatile storage space for the information.

Function 41h should return the size of the ESCD information. For more information about this format, see the *Extended System Configuration Data Specification.*

Function 42h reads the ESCD information stored in nonvolatile storage.

Function 43h writes data in ESCD format to the nonvolatile storage.

# 32-Bit and 16-Bit Stack

Because a caller of a BIOS function may consist of 32-bit code, the BIOS must always be prepared for a 32-bit stack. While the stack itself might be 32 bit, the contents of the stack (the integers, the pointers, and the return address) are always 16 bit.

A 32-bit caller to a BIOS function has to do a lot of work to convert all of its parameters to 16-bit values. All the data values are 16-bit integers; all 32-bit flat pointers have been converted (for example, using the selector manipulation functions in Windows 95) into 16-bit selector:offsets; and the return address has been converted from a flat 32-bit value into a 16-bit selector:offset pair. Therefore, the 16-bit BIOS function can put selectors into ES and offsets into BX and refer to ES:[BX] without problems, and can do a simple RETF when it has finished.

But because the caller is 32 bit, one thing the caller cannot do is convert the entire stack to 16 bit. The offset of any stack reference must be 32 bit (ESP, EBP) and not 16 bit (SP, BP). Therefore, when the BIOS code takes a parameter off the stack, it must look like this:

```
MOV AX,[EBP+10]
```

When the BIOS code refers to a local variable, it must look like this:

```
AND [EBP-20],0007
```

When it is popping values off the stack (because it called a_cdecl function), it must use this:

```
ADD ESP,4
```

It must not use this:

```
ADD SP,4        :::WRONG
```

Any access to the stack in a BIOS function must use 32-bit registers even though the stack's contents (and internal pointers, internal integers, and so on) are 16 bit.

The following sample entry code will work both in real mode and protected mode, regardless of whether the stack is 16 bit or 32 bit:

```
     push eax
     mov  ax, ss
     lar  eax, ax
     test eax, 400000h
     pop  eax
     push ebp
     jz   16BitStack
     mov  ebp, esp
Entry:
     ...

16BitStack:
     movzx     ebp, sp
     jmp  Entry
```

The entry code is a function header that checks whether the stack is 16 bit or 32 bit, using the LAR instruction. If it is 32 bit, it does the usual MOV EBP,ESP. If the stack is 16 bit, it performs a MOVZX EBP,SP. At this point, regardless of whether the stack was 16 bit or 32 bit, the code can refer to [EBP+n] or [EBP−m] and it will always point to the expected location on the stack.

If the BIOS wrote pure 16-bit code with 16-bit stack references, the BIOS would function acceptably for 16-bit operating systems. However, if the caller were 32 bit, the ESP would be a value such as 0x12345678. The BIOS code would then look for its parameters at SS:SP (SS:0x5678) and would either generate incorrect results or simply page fault.

# Assigning LPT1

Centronics-style parallel ports typically use three contiguous I/O ports in memory (for example, 378h, 379h, 37Ah). Windows 95 uses the base I/O port address stored in the BIOS data area (BDA) at 40:08h as the assigned address for LPT1. Windows 95 will map the first parallel port in the BDA as LPT1, the second as LPT2, and the third as LPT3. The system BIOS therefore determines the mapping of a parallel port's physical port addresses to LPT1, LPT2, and LPT3 by how these slots in the BDA are populated.

The BDA is an area of RAM, beginning at 40:00h, in which the system BIOS stores specific hardware information. The beginning of the BDA contains the base I/O port addresses for the four COM ports. Following the COM ports are four addresses, beginning at 40:08h, that contain the base I/O port addresses for the LPT ports. Each address contains a word of storage that points to the base address of the given port.

Some EPP parallel port implementations require eight contiguous I/O ports—for example, 378h through 37Fh. Because VGA devices use I/O port 3C0h, an EPP parallel port cannot use 3BCh—one of the standard legacy printer-port base addresses—as a base address, because it will conflict with the standard VGA register I/O port at 3C0h.

For those ports that cannot use 3BCh as LPT1 (in most cases, for parallel ports that use EPP mode and have an I/O port conflict), the system BIOS can put 378h or 278h in 40:08h, and it will become LPT1 for Windows 95. Alternatively, you can activate the EPP port as LPT2 in the BDA, mapped at 378h. Finally, you should disable the availability of EPP transfer modes if the printer port is enabled at base address 3BCh.

# Int 13h Extensions

The Plug and Play system BIOS should support the current Int 13h BIOS functions for compatibility with existing non–Plug and Play systems. For enhanced disk drive support, the system BIOS should also support the Int 13h extensions described in the *IBM BIOS Technical Reference Manual.*

The system BIOS should also support Int 13h BIOS extensions that provide support for ATA (IDE) drives with capacities greater than 528 MB and that allow more than two ATA (IDE) drives to be run on the system. See one possible set of Int 13h extensions for this purpose in the *Enhanced Disk Drive Specification*, published by Phoenix Technologies Ltd.

# Motherboard Device Node Layout

Every device on the motherboard of a PC 95 contains a device node that describes the device and all of the resources allocated for that device. Device nodes for both static devices and Plug and Play devices are included in a structure called the configuration list. Although devices that are connected through a motherboard bus are not included in the device node layout, the auto-configuration ports used for isolating and assigning a CSN for an ISA bus expansion card will be included.

The following example shows one type of motherboard device node layout. Note that the PS/2 mouse port and keyboard port have their own device node. Although both the mouse port and the keyboard port are attached to the same physical controller, their resources must be reported separately, just as multifunction devices must report each of their device resources separately.

```
    :
    :
    :
#define IRQ_DESC_WITHOUT_FLAGS    0x22     /* IRQ resource descriptor without flags */
#define IRQ_DESC_WITH_FLAGS       0x23     /* IRQ resource descriptor with flags */
#define DMA_DESC                  0x2A     /* DMA resource descriptor */
#define DF_START                  0x30     /* dependent function start identifier */
#define DF_START_WITH_PRIORITY    0x31     /* dependent function start identifier with priority byte */
#define DF_END               0x38     /* dependent function end identifier */
#define IOPORT_DESC          0x47     /* I/O port resource descriptor */
#define IOPORT_FIXED_DESC         0x4B     /* fixed-location I/O port descriptor */
#define END_TAG                   0x79     /* end tag - end of resource descriptors */
#define SUBOPTIMAL_CONFIGURATION  0x02     /* priority byte - suboptimal configuration */
#define 32_BIT_FIXED_MEMORY       0x86     /* 32-bit fixed-memory descriptor */
    :
    :
struct DEV_NODE         /* Programmable interrupt controller */
    {
    Node size,                         /* size of this device node */
    0,                                 /* device node number */
    0000D041h,                         /* PNP0000-AT interrupt controller device ID */
    08,00,01,                          /* ISA PIC */
    0000000000000011b,                 /* device attributes - device is static/cannot be disabled */
    IOPORT_FIXED_DESC,                 /* fixed-location I/O port descriptor */
    0020h,                             /* base address */
    02h,                               /* range length */
    IOPORT_FIXED_DESC,                 /* fixed-location I/O port descriptor */
    00A0h,                             /* base address */
    02h,                               /* range length */
    IRQ_DESC_WITHOUT_FLAGS,            /* IRQ resource descriptor without flags */
    00000100b,                         /* IRQ 2 is used */
    00000000b,                         /* IRQ 8-15 not used */
    END_TAG,                           /* end tag for allocated resource configuration */
    00h,                               /* checksum for allocated resource configuration block */
    END_TAG,                           /* end tag for possible resource info. */
    00h,                               /* checksum for possible resource info. */
    END_TAG,                           /* end tag for compatible device IDs */
    00h                                /* checksum for compatible device IDs info. */
    };

struct DEV_NODE         /* DMA controller */
    {
    Node size,                         /* size of this device node */
    1,                                 /* device node number */
    0002D041h,                         /* PNP0200 DMA controller device ID */
    08,01,01,                          /* ISA DMA controller */
    0000000000000011b,                 /* device attributes - device static/cannot be disabled */
    IOPORT_FIXED_DESC,                 /* fixed-location I/O port descriptor */
    0000h,                             /* base address */
```

```
    10h,                             /* range length */
    IOPORT_FIXED_DESC,               /* fixed-location I/O port descriptor */
    0081h,                           /* base address */
    03h,                             /* range length */
    IOPORT_FIXED_DESC,               /* fixed-location I/O port descriptor */
    0087h,                           /* base address */
    01h,                             /* range length */
    IOPORT_FIXED_DESC,               /* fixed-location I/O port descriptor */
    0089h,                           /* base address */
    03h,                             /* range length */
    IOPORT_FIXED_DESC,               /* fixed-location I/O port descriptor */
    008Fh,                           /* base address */
    03h,                             /* range length */
    IOPORT_FIXED_DESC,               /* fixed-location I/O port descriptor */
    00C0h,                           /* base address */
    20h,                             /* range length */
    END_TAG,                         /* end tag for allocated resource info. */
    00h,                             /* checksum for allocated resource info. */
    END_TAG,                         /* end tag for possible resource info. */
    00h,                             /* checksum for possible resource info. */
    END_TAG,                         /* end tag for compatible device IDs */
    00h                              /* checksum for compatible device IDs info. */
    };

struct DEV_NODE         /* System timer */
    {
    Node size,                       /* size of this device node */
    2,                               /* device node number */
    0001D041h,                       /* PNP0100 - AT timer device ID */
    08,02,01,                        /* system timer */
    0000000000000011b,               /* device attributes - device static/cannot be disabled */
    IOPORT_FIXED_DESC,               /* fixed-location I/O port descriptor */
    0040h,                           /* base address */
    04h,                             /* range length */
    IRQ_DESC_WITHOUT_FLAGS,          /* IRQ resource descriptor without flags */
    00000001b,                       /* IRQ 0 is used */
    00000000b,                       /* IRQ 8-15 not used */
    END_TAG,                         /* end tag for allocated resource info. */
    00h,                             /* checksum for allocated resource info. */
    END_TAG,                         /* end tag for possible resource info. */
    00h,                             /* checksum for possible resource info. */
    END_TAG,                         /* end tag for compatible device IDs */
    00h                              /* checksum for compatible device IDs info. */
    };
```

```
struct DEV_NODE          /* Real-time clock */
    {
    Node size,                          /* size of this device node */
    3,                                  /* device node number */
    000BD041,                           /* PNP0B00 - AT real-time clock device ID */
    08,03,01,                           /* ISA-compatible RTC */
    0000000000000011b,                  /* device attributes - device static/cannot be disabled */
    IOPORT_FIXED_DESC,                  /* fixed-location I/O port descriptor */
    0070h,                              /* base address */
    02h,                                /* range length */
    IRQ_DESC_WITHOUT_FLAGS,             /* IRQ resource descriptor without flags */
    00000000b,                          /* IRQ 0-7 not used */
    00000001b,                          /* IRQ 8 used */
    END_TAG,                            /* end tag for allocated resource info. */
    00h,                                /* checksum for allocated resource info. */
    END_TAG,                            /* end tag for possible resource info. */
    00h,                                /* checksum for possible resource info. */
    END_TAG,                            /* end tag for compatible device IDs */
    00h                                 /* checksum for compatible device IDs info. */
    };

struct DEV_NODE          /* PC speaker */
    {
    Node size,                          /* size of this device node */
    4,                                  /* device node number */
    0008D041,                           /* PNP0800 - PC speaker device ID */
    08,80,00,                           /* other system peripheral */
    0000000000000011b,                  /* device attributes - device static/cannot be disabled */
    IOPORT_FIXED_DESC,                  /* fixed-location I/O port descriptor */
    0061h,                              /* base address */
    01h,                                /* range length */
    END_TAG,                            /* end tag for allocated resource info. */
    00h,                                /* checksum for allocated resource info. */
    END_TAG,                            /* end tag for possible resource info. */
    00h,                                /* checksum for possible resource info. */
    END_TAG,                            /* end tag for compatible device IDs */
    00h                                 /* checksum for compatible device IDs info. */
    };

struct DEV_NODE          /* Math coprocessor */
    {
    Node size,                          /* size of this device node */
    5,                                  /* device node number */
    040CD041,                           /* PNP0C04 - math coprocessor device ID */
    08,80,00,                           /* other system peripheral */
    0000000000000011b,                  /* device attributes - device static/cannot be disabled */
    IOPORT_FIXED_DESC,                  /* fixed-location I/O port descriptor */
    00F0h,                              /* base address */
    10h,                                /* range length */
```

```
    IRQ_DESC_WITHOUT_FLAGS,          /* IRQ resource descriptor without flags */
    00000000b,                       /* IRQ 0-7 not used */
    00100000b,                       /* IRQ 13 used */
    END_TAG,                         /* end tag for allocated resource info. */
    00h,                             /* checksum for allocated resource info. */
    END_TAG,                         /* end tag for possible resource info. */
    00h,                             /* checksum for possible resource info. */
    END_TAG,                         /* end tag for compatible device IDs */
    00h                              /* checksum for compatible device IDs info. */
    };


struct DEV_NODE         /* Keyboard controller */
    {
    Node size,                       /* size of this device node */
    6,                               /* device node number */
    0303D041,                        /* PNP0303 - IBM enhanced keyboard device ID */
    09,00,00,                        /* keyboard controller */
    0000000000001011b,               /* device attributes - device static/cannot be */
                                     /* ...disabled/primary input device */
    IOPORT_FIXED_DESC,               /* fixed-location I/O port descriptor */
    0060h,                           /* base address */
    01h,                             /* range length */
    IOPORT_FIXED_DESC,               /* fixed-location I/O port descriptor */
    0064h,                           /* base address */
    01h,                             /* range length */
    IRQ_DESC_WITHOUT_FLAGS,          /* IRQ resource descriptor without flags */
    00000010b,                       /* IRQ 1 used */
    00000000b,                       /* IRQ 8-15 not used */
    END_TAG,                         /* end tag for allocated resource info. */
    00h,                             /* checksum for allocated resource info. */
    END_TAG,                         /* end tag for possible resource info. */
    00h,                             /* checksum for possible resource info. */
    END_TAG,                         /* end tag for compatible device IDs */
    00h                              /* checksum for compatible device IDs info. */
    };

struct DEV_NODE         /* PS/2 mouse port */
    {
    Node size,                       /* size of this device node */
    7,                               /* device node number */
    130FD041,                        /* PNP0F13 - Microsoft PS/2 mouse device ID */
    09,02,00,                        /* mouse controller */
    0000000000000011b,               /* device attributes - device static/cannot be */
                                     /* ...disabled */
    IRQ_DESC_WITHOUT_FLAGS,          /* IRQ resource descriptor without flags */
    00000000b,                       /* IRQ 0-7 not used */
    00010000b,                       /* IRQ 12 used */
    END_TAG,                         /* end tag for allocated resource info. */
```

```
    00h,                            /* checksum for allocated resource info. */
    END_TAG,                        /* end tag for possible resource info. */
    00h,                            /* checksum for possible resource info. */
    END_TAG,                        /* end tag for compatible device IDs */
    00h                             /* checksum for compatible device IDs info. */
    };

struct DEV_NODE         /* Parallel interface */
    {
    Node size,                      /* size of this device node */
    8,                              /* device node number */
    0104D041,                       /* PNP0401 - ECP 1.? printer port device ID */
    07,01,00,                       /* AT-compatible parallel port */
    0000000000000000b,              /* device attributes - device supports dynamic.. */
                                    /* ...configurability, can be disabled */

    /* Allocated block, device configured as LPT1=IRQ7, I/O ports 3BCh-3BFh */
    IRQ_DESC_WITHOUT_FLAGS,         /* IRQ resource descriptor without flags */
    10000000b,                      /* IRQ 7 is used */
    00000000b,                      /* IRQ 8-15 not used */
    IOPORT_FIXED_DESC,              /* fixed-location I/O port descriptor */
    03BCh,                          /* base address */
    4,                              /* four contiguous ports */
    END_TAG,                        /* end tag for allocated resource info. */
    00h,                            /* checksum for allocated resource info. */

    /* Possible resource settings */
    /* LPT1 resource allocation */
    DF_START,                       /* dependent function start (LPT1=IRQ7... */
                                    /* ...I/O port 3BCh) */
    IRQ_DESC_WITHOUT_FLAGS,         /* IRQ resource descriptor without flags */
    10000000b,                      /* IRQ 7 is used */
    00000000b,                      /* IRQ 8-15 not used */
    IOPORT_FIXED_DESC,              /* fixed-location I/O port descriptor */
    03BCh,                          /* base address */
    4,                              /* four contiguous ports */

    /* LPT1 resource allocation without IRQ*/
    DF_START,                       /* dependent function start (LPT1=I/O port 3BCh) */
    IRQ_DESC_WITHOUT_FLAGS,         /* IRQ resource descriptor without flags */
    00000000b,                      /* no IRQ is used */
    00000000b,                      /* no IRQ is used */
    IOPORT_FIXED_DESC,              /* fixed-location I/O port descriptor */
    03BCh,                          /* base address */
    4,                              /* four contiguous ports */
```

```
/* LPT2 resource allocation */
    DF_START,                          /* dependent function start (LPT2=IRQ7,... */
                                       /* ...I/O port 378h) */
    IRQ_DESC_WITHOUT_FLAGS,            /* IRQ resource descriptor without flags */
    10000000b,                         /* IRQ 7 is used */
    00000000b,                         /* IRQ 8-15 not used */
    IOPORT_FIXED_DESC,                 /* fixed-location I/O port descriptor */
    0378h,                             /* base address */
    4,                                 /* four contiguous ports */

    /* LPT2 resource allocation without IRQ*/
    DF_START,                          /* dependent function start (LPT2=I/O port 378h) */
    IRQ_DESC_WITHOUT_FLAGS,            /* IRQ resource descriptor without flags */
    00000000b,                         /* no IRQ is used */
    00000000b,                         /* no IRQ is used */
    IOPORT_FIXED_DESC,                 /* fixed-location I/O port descriptor */
    0378h,                             /* base address */
    4,                                 /* four contiguous ports */

    /* LPT3 resource allocation */
    DF_START,                          /* dependent function start (LPT3=IRQ5,...*/
                                       /*... I/O port 278h) */
    IRQ_DESC_WITHOUT_FLAGS,            /* IRQ resource descriptor without flags */
    00100000b,                         /* IRQ 5 used */
    00000000b,                         /* IRQ 8-15 not used */
    IOPORT_FIXED_DESC,                 /* fixed-location I/O port descriptor */
    0278h,                             /* base address */
    4,                                 /* four contiguous ports */

    /* LPT3 resource allocation without IRQ*/
    DF_START,                          /* dependent function start (LPT3=I/O port 278h) */
    IRQ_DESC_WITHOUT_FLAGS,            /* IRQ resource descriptor without flags */
    00000000b,                         /* no IRQ is used */
    00000000b,                         /* no IRQ is used */
    IOPORT_FIXED_DESC,                 /* fixed-location I/O port descriptor */
    0278h,                             /* base address */
    4,                                 /* four contiguous ports */

    /* The following resource descriptor specifies a suboptimal resource allocation */
    /* LPTx resource allocation - any I/O port with IRQ 5 or 7 */
    DF_START_WITH_PRIORITY,            /* dependent function start with priority byte */
    SUBOPTIMAL_CONFIGURATION,          /* suboptimal - functional configuration, not optimal */
                                       /* LPTx=IRQ5 or 7 and start I/O port 100h-3FFh */
    IRQ_DESC_WITHOUT_FLAGS,            /* IRQ resource descriptor without flags */
    10100000b,                         /* IRQ 5 or 7 used */
    00000000b,                         /* IRQ 8-15 not used */
```

```
    IOPORT_DESC,                      /* I/O ports descriptor */
    00000001b,                        /* resource attributes */
    0100h,                            /* minimum base address */
    03FCh,                            /* maximum base address */
    4,                                /* alignment/increment of 4 bytes */
    4,                                /* four contiguous ports */

    /* The following resource descriptor specifies a suboptimal resource allocation */
    /* LPTx resource allocation - any I/O port, no IRQ */
    DF_START_WITH_PRIORITY,           /* dependent function start with priority byte */
    SUBOPTIMAL_CONFIGURATION,         /* suboptimal - functional configuration, not optimal */      /*
LPTx=start I/O port 100h-3FFh */
    IRQ_DESC_WITHOUT_FLAGS,           /* IRQ resource descriptor without flags */
    00000000b,                        /* no IRQ is used */
    00000000b,                        /* no IRQ is used */
    IOPORT_DESC,                      /* I/O ports descriptor */
    00000001b,                        /* resource attributes */
    0100h,                            /* minimum base address */
    03FCh,                            /* maximum base address */
    4,                                /* alignment/increment of 4 bytes */
    4,                                /* four contiguous ports */

    DF_END,                           /* dependent function end */
    END_TAG,                          /* end tag for possible resource info. */
    00h,                              /* checksum for possible resource info. */
    END_TAG,                          /* end tag - no compatible device ID  */
    00h
    };

struct DEV_NODE        /* VGA adapter */
    {
    Node size,                        /* size of this device node */
    9,                                /* device node number */
    0009D041,                         /* PNP0900 - generic VGA adapter device ID */
    03,00,00,                         /* generic VGA display controller */
    0000000000000111b,                /* device attributes - device static/cannot be disabled... */
                                      /* .../primary output device */
    32_BIT_FIXED_MEMORY,              /* 32-bit fixed-location memory descriptor */
    0009h,                            /* length of resource */
    00001011,                         /* 16-bit memory/supports range length/read-cacheable */
                                      /* ...write-through/writable */
    000A0000h,                        /* range base address */
    00020000h,                        /* range length */
    32_BIT_FIXED_MEMORY,              /* 32-bit fixed-location memory descriptor */
    0009h,                            /* length of resource */
    01001010,                         /* ROM/16-bit memory/supports range length/read- */
                                      /* ...-cacheable, write-through/nonwritable */
    000C0000h,                        /* range base address */
    00008000h,                        /* range length */
```

```
    IOPORT_FIXED_DESC,               /* fixed-location I/O port descriptor */
    03B4h,                           /* base address */
    02h,                             /* range length */
    IOPORT_FIXED_DESC,               /* fixed-location I/O port descriptor */
    03BAh,                           /* base address */
    01h,                             /* range length */
    IOPORT_FIXED_DESC,               /* fixed-location I/O port descriptor */
    03C0h,                           /* base address */
    10h,                             /* range length */
    IOPORT_FIXED_DESC,               /* fixed-location I/O port descriptor */
    03D0h,                           /* base address */
    10h,                             /* range length */
    END_TAG,                         /* end tag for allocated resource info. */
    00h,                             /* checksum for allocated resource info. */
    END_TAG,                         /* end tag for possible resource info. */
    00h,                             /* checksum for possible resource info. */
    END_TAG,                         /* end tag for compatible device IDs */
    00h                              /* checksum for compatible device IDs info. */
    };

struct DEV_NODE        /* IDE controller */
    {
    Node size,                       /* size of this device node */
    10,                              /* device node number */
    0006D041,                        /* PNP0600 - AT real-time clock device ID */
    01,01,00,                        /* generic IDE controller */
    0000000000010011b,               /* device attributes - device static/cannot be disabled... */
                                     /* /IPL device */
    IOPORT_FIXED_DESC,               /* fixed-location I/O port descriptor */
    01F0h,                           /* base address */
    08h,                             /* range length */
    IOPORT_FIXED_DESC,               /* fixed-location I/O port descriptor */
    03F6h,                           /* base address */
    01h,                             /* range length */
    IRQ_DESC_WITHOUT_FLAGS,          /* IRQ resource descriptor without flags */
    00000000b,                       /* IRQ 0-7 not used */
    01000000b,                       /* IRQ 14 used */
    END_TAG,                         /* end tag for allocated resource info. */
    00h,                             /* checksum for allocated resource info. */
    END_TAG,                         /* end tag for possible resource info. */
    00h,                             /* checksum for possible resource info. */
    END_TAG,                         /* end tag for compatible device IDs */
    00h                              /* checksum for compatible device IDs info. */
    };
```

```
struct DEV_NODE         /* Floppy controller */
    {
    Node size,                          /* size of this device node */
    11,                                 /* device node number */
    0007D041,                           /* PNP0700 - floppy controller device ID */
    01,02,00,                           /* generic floppy controller */
    0000000000010011b,                  /* device attributes - device static/cannot be disabled */
                                        /* ...IPL device */
    IOPORT_FIXED_DESC,                  /* fixed-location I/O port descriptor */
    03F2h,                              /* base address */
    01h,                                /* range length */
    IOPORT_FIXED_DESC,                  /* fixed-location I/O port descriptor */
    03F4h,                              /* base address */
    02h,                                /* range length */
    IOPORT_FIXED_DESC,                  /* fixed-location I/O port descriptor */
    03F7h,                              /* base address */
    01h,                                /* range length */
    IRQ_DESC_WITHOUT_FLAGS,             /* IRQ resource descriptor without flags */
    01000000b,                          /* IRQ 6 used */
    00000000b,                          /* IRQ 8-15 not used */
    DMA_DESC,                           /* DMA resource descriptor */
    04h,                                /* DMA channel 2 is used */
    01h,                                /* 8- and 16-bit transfer type preference */
    END_TAG,                            /* end tag for allocated resource info. */
    00h,                                /* checksum for allocated resource info. */
    END_TAG,                            /* end tag for possible resource info. */
    00h,                                /* checksum for possible resource info. */
    END_TAG,                            /* end tag for compatible device IDs */
    00h                                 /* checksum for compatible device IDs info. */
    };

struct DEV_NODE         /* PCMCIA controller */
    {
    Node size,                          /* size of this device node */
    12,                                 /* device node number */
    000ED041,                           /* PNP0E00 - PCMCIA controller device ID */
    06,05,00,                           /* PCMCIA bridge */
    0000000000000000b,                  /* device attributes - device supports dynamic... */
                                        /* ...configurability, can be disabled */

    /* Allocated block, device configured to IRQ9, I/O port 03E0h */
    IRQ_DESC_WITHOUT_FLAGS,             /* IRQ resource descriptor without flags */
    00000000b,                          /* IRQ 0-7 not used */
    00000010b,                          /* IRQ 9 used */
    IOPORT_FIXED_DESC,                  /* fixed-location I/O port descriptor */
    03E0h,                              /* base address */
    2,                                  /* two contiguous ports */
    END_TAG,                            /* end tag for allocated resource info. */
    00h,                                /* checksum for allocated resource info. */
```

```
    /* Possible resource settings - IRQ 3,4,5,7,9,10,11,12,or 14; I/O port 03E0h or 03E2h */
    IRQ_DESC_WITHOUT_FLAGS,          /* IRQ resource descriptor without flags */
    10111000b,                       /* IRQ 3,4,5, or 7 can be used, or... */
    01011110b,                       /* IRQ 9,10,11,12 or 14 can be used */
    IOPORT_DESC,                     /* I/O ports descriptor */
    00000001b,                       /* resource attributes */
    03E0h,                           /* minimum base address */
    03E2h,                           /* maximum base address */
    2,                               /* alignment/increment of 2 */
    2,                               /* two contiguous ports */
    END_TAG,                         /* end tag for possible resource info. */
    00h,                             /* checksum for possible resource info. */
    END_TAG,                         /* end tag for compatible device IDs */
    00h                              /* checksum for compatible device IDs info. */
    };

struct DEV_NODE         /* PCMCIA controller on the docking station */
    {
    Node size,                       /* size of this device node */
    13,                              /* device node number */
    000ED041,                        /* PNP0E00 - PCMCIA controller device ID */
    06,06,00,                        /* PCMCIA controller */
    0000000000100000b,               /* device attributes - docking station device,... */
                                     /* ...device supports dynamic... */
                                     /* ...configurability, can be disabled */

    /* Allocated block, device configured to IRQ9, I/O port 03E0h */
    IRQ_DESC_WITHOUT_FLAGS,          /* IRQ resource descriptor without flags */
    00000000b,                       /* IRQ 0-7 not used */
    00000010b,                       /* IRQ 9 used */
    IOPORT_FIXED_DESC,               /* fixed-location I/O port descriptor */
    03E0h,                           /* base address */
    2,                               /* two contiguous ports */
    END_TAG,                         /* end tag for allocated resource info. */
    00h,                             /* checksum for allocated resource info. */
```

```
    /* Possible resource settings - IRQ 3,4,5,7,9,10,11,12,or 14; I/O port 03E0h or 03E2h */
    IRQ_DESC_WITHOUT_FLAGS,             /* IRQ resource descriptor without flags */
    10111000b,                          /* IRQ 3,4,5, or 7 can be used, or... */
    01011110b,                          /* IRQ 9,10,11,12 or 14 can be used */
    IOPORT_DESC,                        /* I/O ports descriptor */
    00000001b,                          /* resource attributes */
    03E0h,                              /* minimum base address */
    03E2h,                              /* maximum base address */
    2,                                  /* alignment/increment of 2 */
    2,                                  /* two contiguous ports */
    END_TAG,                            /* end tag for possible resource info. */
    00h,                                /* checksum for possible resource info. */
    END_TAG,                            /* end tag for compatible device IDs */
    00h                                 /* checksum for compatible device IDs info. */
};

struct DEV_NODE         /* ISA bus on docking station */
    {
    Node size,                          /* size of this device node */
    14,                                 /* device node number */
    000AD041,                           /* PNP0A00 - ISA bus device ID */
    06,01,00,                           /* ISA bus */
    0000000000100011b,                  /* device attributes - docking station device,... */
                                        /*...and cannot be disabled or configured */
    END_TAG,                            /* end tag - uses no resources */
    00h,                                /* checksum for allocated resource info. */
    END_TAG,                            /* end tag - no possible resources */
    00h,                                /* checksum for possible resource info. */
    END_TAG,                            /* end tag - no compatible device IDs */
    00h                                 /* checksum for compatible device IDs info. */
    };
```

CHAPTER 9

# Option ROM Design

By adding Plug and Play functions to option ROMs contained on system expansion cards, the Plug and Play system BIOS in a Personal Computer for Microsoft® Windows™ 95 can better identify and select the primary boot devices. By giving more control of the boot process to the system BIOS, a Plug and Play option ROM provides the system BIOS with the ability to manage boot devices without conflict.

This chapter primarily emphasizes option ROM control of Plug and Play hardware, but also discusses other option ROM routines pertinent to the PC 95, such as display adapter option ROM power management of monitors.

# Plug and Play Option ROMs

Boot devices are unique among most system devices in that they must provide the primary input, primary output, and IPL device to boot the system. It is important that the capabilities of these types of devices are identified before the boot process begins.

The primary input, primary output, and IPL device are most often the keyboard, display subsystem (display adapter and monitor), and hard disk (or floppy disk). If the boot device is located on an expansion card, the system BIOS must be capable of identifying these devices. If any of these expansion card devices require the hardware to be initialized before the system boots, an option ROM can be added that contains the necessary procedures.

For information about how to add Plug and Play capabilities to an option ROM, see the *Plug and Play BIOS Specification*. The specification discusses the Plug and Play expansion header, the interaction between the system BIOS and the option ROM, and the boot process.

Option ROMs can be found on expansion cards for a variety of buses. However, not all boot devices on every type of bus must have the Plug and Play expansion header added to the option ROM. In general, only ISA cards and VL-bus cards will use the Plug and Play expansion header (the VL-bus uses the Plug and Play expansion header because the VL-bus uses the ISA Plug and Play conventions for identifying and configuring devices). Micro Channel cards may use the header on rare occasions, but it and other expansion buses generally do not need the Plug and Play option ROM header because the identification and ability to control boot devices is already contained in the option ROM structure documented in their specifications.

Most ISA Plug and Play option ROMs will probably include code that allows a PC with a non–Plug and Play system BIOS to boot successfully (for compatibility with existing PCs). Because these non–Plug and Play systems exist, the option ROM code will, in most cases, contain a default resource configuration that older systems can use. Although this default configuration is necessary for a system with a non–Plug and Play system BIOS, the option BIOS must still be capable of working with the card's resources in any valid reconfiguration. This allows a Plug and Play operating system or a Plug and Play card configuration utility (on non–Plug and Play systems) to reconfigure the device's resources.

In most cases, option ROMs are located on cards used as boot devices in the system. However, Plug and Play option ROMs can be used to supply the Plug and Play expansion header to devices other than boot devices, enabling them to initialize both devices on the card and peripherals attached to the card, when the system boots.

# Plug and Play Option ROM Design

To design an option ROM with Plug and Play capabilities, follow the requirements documented in the *Plug and Play BIOS Specification*. Some of the points described in the specification are emphasized here:

- A Plug and Play option ROM must not hook Int 9h, Int 10h, Int 13h, Int 18h, or Int 19h until the system BIOS calls the boot connection vector contained in the Plug and Play expansion header.
- A Plug and Play option ROM must be capable of determining whether the system BIOS complies with Plug and Play. If the system ROM is not Plug and Play compliant, the option ROM should immediately initialize the card and hook the proper interrupt as though it were a non–Plug and Play option ROM. This will allow the expansion card to be used in systems that are not Plug and Play compatible.
- Although the Plug and Play option ROM can use the run-time functions of the system BIOS, these functions are not available until after the POST process has completed and Int 19 has been called.

## Hooking Interrupts

Boot devices on ISA cards generally "hook" interrupts to add device-specific code during the boot process by placing the address of the option BIOS routines in the interrupt vector table. From then on, any software interrupts that call that part of the interrupt vector table will jump to the address specified during option ROM initialization.

During a non–Plug and Play boot process, the interrupts are hooked while the option ROM is initializing the board. The option ROM immediately takes charge of the address in the interrupt vector table and becomes the de facto boot device.

This presents a problem for the Plug and Play boot process. In a Plug and Play system, the system BIOS must be capable of determining which devices it wants to use as boot devices. If, for example, more than one display adapter is available in the system, the system BIOS must choose one of the two, and disable the other. If both devices have already hooked Int 10 (the system BIOS cannot know which one hooked it last and now has control of the interrupt vector address), a serious error may occur, ultimately hanging the system.

To prevent this type of conflict from occurring in a Plug and Play system, the option ROM routine must ensure that Int 9, Int 10, Int 13, Int 18, and Int 19 are not hooked until the Plug and Play system BIOS calls the boot connection vector in the selected option ROM expansion header. The system BIOS chooses the device it will use in the boot process by calling the selected device's option ROM boot connection vector, while ignoring the other device. The system BIOS passes a set of parameters to the boot connection vector that describe what vectors can be hooked by the device and provide the CSN and Read Data Port address (if the expansion card is connected to the ISA bus).

If the Plug and Play option ROM determines that the system BIOS is not Plug and Play compliant, it must perform a non–Plug and Play initialization.

## Non–Plug and Play Initialization

An expansion card with a Plug and Play option ROM can be used in a PC that does not have a Plug and Play system BIOS. In this case, the expansion card will not be isolated or assigned a CSN, and the system BIOS will expect the expansion card to be active and contain fixed resources.

The Plug and Play option ROM should contain code that enables it to determine whether the system BIOS is Plug and Play compliant, and to act accordingly. During the POST process, the option ROM determines the compatibility of the system BIOS by examining register information passed to the option ROM's initialization routine. If the information provided by the system BIOS does not conform to a valid Plug and Play installation check register, the option ROM can proceed under the assumption that the system does not contain a Plug and Play system BIOS.

If the system BIOS is not Plug and Play compliant, the option ROM code must branch to a set of routines that imitate a non–Plug and Play option ROM initialization sequence. The option ROM should hook the interrupt vector using a default configuration.

## System BIOS Run-Time Functions

The Plug and Play system BIOS run-time functions can be used by the Plug and Play option ROMs, but are not available until after the POST process has completed and Int 19 has been called. Option ROM routines should not try to use these run-time functions until that time because the results may be unpredictable.

# Display Adapter Option ROM

A display adapter can either be located directly on the motherboard, or can be added as an expansion card device. For a display adapter located on the motherboard, the contents of the option ROM can either be located in a separate ROM, or can be built in as part of the system BIOS. If the display adapter is on an expansion card, the option ROM must also be located there.

You must implement all of the Plug and Play capabilities previously mentioned in this chapter for display adapter option ROMs. You can also add several new features to enhance the option ROM's interaction with the display monitor during the boot process.

Display adapter option ROMs must implement the monitor power management BIOS extensions documented in the *VESA BIOS Extensions/Power Management (VBE/PM) Standard*. This standard documents a set of functions that software can call to control the power management features of a VESA DPMS–compliant monitor. These BIOS extensions are accessed through Int 10.

Another feature the display adapter option ROM should support is the data display channel documented in VESA's *Display Data Channel* standard. This standard defines functions that support a data channel between the display adapter and a DDC-compliant monitor. The display adapter uses this channel to determine the identity of the monitor and its characteristics. In most cases, this information can be used to load appropriate drivers. When more than one display adapter is connected to the PC, DDC might also be useful in determining which display adapter is actually driving a monitor. (The system BIOS could query the DDC-compatible display adapter to determine whether the adapter is receiving an EDID data string from a DDC-compatible monitor, and then boot from that adapter.) The option ROM functions to support the display data channel are documented in the *VESA BIOS Extensions/Display Data Channel* standard.

# SCSI Adapter Option ROM

Most IPL devices used on the PC 95 consist of either an ATA (IDE) interface, a SCSI bus, or a combination of the two. If an attached SCSI peripheral is to be used as a boot device, you may need to make firmware enhancements to the option ROMs to support Plug and Play functions and to meet some hardware requirements and recommendations.

A SCSI host-adapter option ROM may need a variety of different functions. If the SCSI bus is attached to a PC that contains an ATA (IDE) adapter, the system ROM will force the primary master device on the IDE interface to be the boot device for the system. If, however, there is no ATA (IDE) adapter on the PC, and the system is depending on a SCSI device to be the IPL device, the SCSI host-adapter option ROM must be capable of handling sufficient functions to properly boot each time the system is reset or power is cycled.

SCSI devices must be capable of recovering from a software-initiated spin-down that occurs during low-power management. To properly support power management in a SCSI peripheral, you must ensure that the STOP UNIT and START UNIT commands are properly implemented. Correct implementation of these commands ensures the proper functioning of an APM 1.1 suspend and resume for the peripheral.

A SCSI host adapter SCAM master must ensure that the same SCSI identifier is assigned to the SCSI devices on the system each time the system is reset or power is cycled. If the SCAM master has no nonvolatile source for storing this information, the option ROM should contain a SCAM identifier assignment algorithm, which ensures that the same SCSI peripheral is always used as the boot device. This algorithm is documented in the *Plug and Play SCSI Specification.*

Option ROMs must be capable of reporting to the system BIOS the device identifiers that the SCSI protocol chip has set. The SCSI protocol chip sets the identification number using SCAM.

Plug and Play SCSI host adapters that support bus-mastering must support virtual DMA services (VDS) in the host-adapter option ROM. VDS solves the problem of mapping linear addresses (segment:offset) into physical addresses. VDS is not applicable to host adapters that do not use bus-mastering. For information about how to obtain the *Virtual DMA Service (DMA)* document, see Appendix D, "References."

Host-adapter option ROMs (or the system BIOS) must also support the Int 13h BIOS extensions, as documented in the *IBM BIOS Technical Reference Manual.* The host-adapter option ROM must also support the current Int 13h functions for backward compatibility with non–Plug and Play systems.

PART 4

# Appendixes

Appendix A contains large and small resource data types used by ISA cards for Plug and Play identification.

Appendix B supplies general device information that may be needed when designing hardware for Microsoft® Windows™ 95. It also provides a list of device identifiers for motherboard devices and buses, as well as some non – Plug and Play expansion cards.

Appendix C contains a glossary of terms and phrases used throughout the guide, as well as terms and phrases that describe various aspects of Plug and Play and the PC 95.

Appendix D lists source references for the material included in this guide.

Appendix E contains docking station scenarios that describe the sequence of events that occur during docking and undocking events.

APPENDIX A

# Resource Data Type Functions

Plug and Play resource data type functions describe the resource requirements of an ISA expansion card, along with the programmability available on the card and the interdependencies. The system uses these functions to identify and configure the properties contained on the card. Because of limited space to store some of these functions, two types are defined: small and large. For more information about Plug and Play ISA expansion cards, see Chapter 6, "Plug and Play Cards and Buses."

# Small Resource Data Type

Each small resource data type is preceded by the Small Resource Data Type tag. The tag describes which resource data type is being tagged, and its length. The resource data described by this tag can be 2 to 8 bytes in size. Table A.1 contains the format of the Small Resource Data Type tag and the resource data that is described by the tag.

**Table A.1 Small Resource Data Type Tag Definitions**

| Offset | Field |
|---|---|
| Byte 0 | Tag bit[7]: Type = 0<br>Tag bits[6:3]: Small item value<br>Tag bits[2:0]: Length = *n* bytes |
| Bytes 1 to *n* | Resource Data Type Information |

Byte 0 contains the tag information. Bit 7, when set to 0, means the tag is a Small Resource Data Type tag. Bits[6:3] contain a value that describes the item name for this tag. Small resource item names and their corresponding values are described in Table A.2. Bits[2:0] indicate the length, in bytes, of the item information.

Bytes 1 through *n* contain the resource data information.

**Table A.2 Small Resource Items**

| Small item name | Value |
|---|---|
| Plug and Play version number | 1h |
| Logical device ID | 2h |
| Compatible device ID | 3h |
| IRQ format | 4h |
| DMA format | 5h |
| Start-dependent function | 6h |
| End-dependent function | 7h |
| I/O port descriptor | 8h |
| Fixed-location I/O port descriptor | 9h |

**Table A.2 Small Resource Items (*continued*)**

| Small item name | Value |
|---|---|
| Reserved | 0Ah–0Dh |
| Vendor defined | 0Eh |
| End tag | 0Fh |

The following paragraphs contain the resource data information. Note that the tables described in these paragraphs also contain the tag information in byte 0.

# Plug and Play Version Number

The Plug and Play version number, shown in Table A.3, identifies the version of the Plug and Play specification with which this card is compatible. A vendor-specific version number is included and can be used by a device driver to verify the version of the card.

**Table A.3 Plug and Play Version number**

| Offset | Field name |
|---|---|
| Byte 0 | Value = 00001010b (Type = 0, Small item name = 1h, Length = 2) |
| Byte 1 | Plug and Play Version Number (in packed BCD format, major bits[7:4], minor bits[3:0]) Example: version 1.0 = 10h, version 2.3 = 23h, version 2.91 = 29h |
| Byte 2 | Vendor-Specific Version Number |

# Logical Device Identifier

The logical device identifier, shown in Table A.4, provides a means of uniquely identifying multiple logical devices on a single physical board. The format of the logical device identifier is identical to the Vendor Identifier field described in Chapter 6, "Plug and Play Cards and Buses." This identifier consists of:

- Bits[16:00]. Three-character compressed ASCII EISA identifier.
- Compressed ASCII is defined as 5 bits per character, "00001" = "A" ... "11010" = "Z".
- Bits[31:16]. Manufacturer-specific device code. The vendor must select the unique values for this field.

This identifier can be used to select a device driver for the device. It also contains information about supported optional commands. Bit 0 of the Flags field indicates the device should be activated by the BIOS at boot time if the system includes a Plug and Play BIOS. Nonbooting, single-function devices must not include the logical device identifier.

**Table A.4 Logical Device ID**

| Offset | Field name |
|---|---|
| Byte 0 | Value = 000101xxb (Type = 0, Small item name = 2h, Length = [5 or 6]). |
| Byte 1 | Logical Device ID, bits[7:0]. |
| Byte 2 | Logical Device ID, bits[15:8]. |
| Byte 3 | Logical Device ID, bits[23:16]. |
| Byte 4 | Logical Device ID, bits[31:24]. |
| Byte 5 | Flags:<br>Bit[0], if set, indicates that this logical device is capable of participating in the boot process. Cards that power up active must have this bit set. However, if this bit is set, the card may or may not power up active.<br>Bits[7:1], if set, indicate commands supported per logical device for registers in the range of 31h to 37h, respectively. |
| Byte 6 | Flags:<br>Bits[7:0], if set, indicate commands supported per logical device for registers in the range of 38h to 3Fh, respectively. |

# Compatible Device Identifier

The compatible device identifier, shown in Table A.5, provides the identifiers of other devices with which this logical device is compatible. The system uses this information to load compatible device drivers, if necessary. Each logical device can have several compatible device identifiers. The system can use the order of these device identifiers as a criterion to determine which driver to search for and load first.

**Table A.5 Compatible Device ID**

| Offset | Field name |
|---|---|
| Byte 0 | Value = 00011100b (Type = 0, Small item name = 3h, Length = 4) |
| Byte 1 | Compatible Device ID, bits[7:0] |
| Byte 2 | Compatible Device ID, bits[15:8] |
| Byte 3 | Compatible Device ID, bits[23:16] |
| Byte 4 | Compatible Device ID, bits[31:24] |

The compatible device identifier can be used if you have added functionality to a new device, but that device is completely compatible with an older device. The old device, for example, could have contained a logical identifier of ABCD0000h. The new device has a logical identifier of ABCD0001h. For this device, you could include the compatible device identifier of ABCD0000h. In this case, the driver for ABCD0001h is loaded, if it can be located. If the driver cannot be found, the driver for device ABCD0000h is loaded for the device.

For information about device identifiers for standard buses and devices, see Appendix B, "Device Information."

# IRQ Format

The IRQ resource structure, shown in Table A.6, indicates that the logical device uses an interrupt level and supplies a mask with bits set to indicate the levels implemented in this device. Because there are 16 possible interrupt levels for a standard ISA implementation, a 2-byte field is used. The IRQ resource structure is repeated for each separate interrupt level required for the logical device.

**Table A.6 IRQ Format**

| Offset | Field name |
|---|---|
| Byte 0 | Value = 0010001xb (Type = 0, Small item name = 4h, Length = [2 or 3]). |
| Byte 1 | IRQ Mask, bits[7:0]. Bit[0] represents IRQ0, bit[1] IRQ1, and so on. (Bit 2 is reserved and cannot be used.) |
| Byte 2 | IRQ Mask, bits[15:8]. Bit[0] represents IRQ8, bit[1] IRQ2(9), and so on. |
| Byte 3 | IRQ Information. Each bit, when set, indicates that this device is capable of driving a certain type of interrupt. (Optional — if not included, assume ISA-compatible, edge sensitive, high true interrupts.)<br><br>Bits[7:4] Reserved and must be written as 0.<br>Bit[3] Low true, level sensitive.<br>Bit[2] High true, level sensitive.<br>Bit[1] Low true, edge sensitive.<br>Bit[0] High true, edge sensitive. (Must be supported for ISA compatibility.) |

**Note** Low, true, level-sensitive interrupts can be electrically shared. Only IRQs that exist on the ISA bus connectors are valid.

# DMA Format

The DMA resource structure, shown in Table A.7, indicates that the logical device uses a DMA channel and supplies a mask with bits set to indicate the channels implemented in this device. The DMA resource structure is repeated for each separate channel required.

**Table A.7 DMA Format**

| Offset | Field name |
|---|---|
| Byte 0 | Value = 00101010b (Type = 0, Small item name = 5h, Length = 2). |
| Byte 1 | DMA Channel Mask, bits[7:0]. Bit[0] is channel 0. |
| Byte 2 | Bit[7] Reserved and must be written as 0.<br>Bits[6:5] DMA channel speed supported.<br>Status<br>00 Indicates compatibility mode.<br>01 Indicates Type A DMA as described in the EISA specification.<br>10 Indicates Type B DMA.<br>11 Indicates Type F.<br>Bit[4] DMA word mode.<br>Status<br>0 DMA may not execute in count-by-word mode.<br>1 DMA may execute in count-by-word mode.<br>Bit[3] DMA byte-mode status.<br>Status<br>0 DMA may not execute in count-by-byte mode.<br>1 DMA may execute in count-by-byte mode.<br>Bit[2] Logical device bus-master status.<br>Status<br>0 Logical device is not a bus master.<br>1 Logical device is a bus master.<br>Bits[1:0] DMA transfer type preference.<br>Status<br>00 8 bit only.<br>01 8 bit and 16 bit.<br>10 16 bit only.<br>11 Reserved. |

# Dependent Functions

Each logical device requires a set of resources. These resources may have interdependencies that must be expressed to allow arbitration software to make resource allocation decisions about the logical device. Dependent functions express these interdependencies, and because these functions must be grouped together, there is a Start-Dependent Functions field and an End-Dependent Functions field. For more information about the use of dependent functions, see "Resource Data and Dependent Function Examples" later in this appendix.

Start-Dependent Function fields can be of the length 0 or 1 bytes. The extra byte optionally denotes priority for the resource group following the Start-Dependent Function tag. If the extra byte is not included, the dependent-function priority is "acceptable." The Start-Dependent Function field is described in Table A.8. If the length in byte 0 of the Start-Dependent Function field is set to 1, the priority byte is included. The priorities set by this byte are described in Table A.9.

The end-dependent function is described in Table A.10.

**Table A.8 Start-Dependent Functions**

| Offset | Field name |
|---|---|
| Byte 0 | Value = 0011000xb (Type = 0, Small item name = 6h, Length = [0 or 1]) |

**Table A.9 Priority Byte Description**

| Value | Definition |
|---|---|
| 0 | Best configuration—Best possible configuration. |
| 1 | Acceptable configuration—Lower priority but acceptable configuration. |
| 2 | Suboptimal configuration—Functional configuration but not optimal. |
| 3–255 | Reserved. |

**Table A.10 End-Dependent Functions**

| Offset | Field name |
|---|---|
| Byte 0 | Value = 00111000b (Type = 0, Small item name = 7h, Length = 0) |

The priority of configuration options can be explicitly set to one of three priority levels:

- Priority 0—Highest
- Priority 1—Middle
- Priority 2—Lowest

Each priority level can contain more than one set of configurations. Within priority levels, Microsoft® Windows™ 95 will process the resource requests in the order the data is stored. So if a printer port reports three priority 0 configurations, corresponding to the standard LPT assignments, Windows 95 starts with the first data resource configuration listed. If this conflicts with existing resources already allocated (if the LPT port already exists), Windows 95 moves to the next resource request in the list. This allows sublevel priorities to be ordered by rank.

If no priority byte is specified, Windows 95 still processes the functions in the order the data is stored.

# I/O Port Descriptor

There are two types of descriptors for I/O ranges. The first descriptor, shown in Table A.11, is a full-function descriptor for programmable ISA cards. The second descriptor, shown in Table A.12, is a minimal fixed-location descriptor for old ISA cards with fixed I/O requirements that use a 10-bit ISA address decode. The first descriptor can also describe fixed I/O requirements for ISA cards that require a 16-bit address decode. This is accomplished by setting the range minimum base address and range maximum base address to the same fixed I/O value.

**Table A.11 Full-Function I/O Port Descriptor**

| Offset | Field name | Definition |
|---|---|---|
| Byte 0 | I/O Port Description | Value = 01000111b (Type = 0, Small item name = 8h, Length = 7). |
| Byte 1 | Information | Bits[7:1] are reserved and must be zero.<br>Bit[0], if set, indicates that the logical device decodes the full 16-bit ISA address. If bit[0] is not set, this indicates that the logical device decodes only ISA address bits[9:0]. |
| Byte 2 | Range Minimum Base Address, bits[7:0] | Address bits[7:0] of the minimum base I/O address for which the card can be configured. |
| Byte 3 | Range Minimum Base Address, bits[15:8] | Address bits[15:8] of the minimum base I/O address for which the card can be configured. |
| Byte 4 | Range Maximum Base Address, bits[7:0] | Address bits[7:0] of the maximum base I/O address for which the card can be configured. |
| Byte 5 | Range Maximum Base Address, bits[15:8] | Address bits[15:8] of the maximum base I/O address for which the card can be configured. |
| Byte 6 | Base Alignment | Alignment for minimum base address, increment in 1-byte blocks. Valid values are greater than 0. |
| Byte 7 | Range Length | The number of contiguous I/O ports requested. |

**Table A.12 Fixed-Location I/O Port Descriptor**

| Offset | Field name | Definition |
|---|---|---|
| Byte 0 | Fixed-Location I/O Port Descriptor | Value = 01001011b (Type = 0, Small item name = 9h, Length = 3). |
| Byte 1 | Range Base Address, bits[7:0] | Address bits[7:0] of the base I/O address for which the card can be configured. This descriptor assumes a 10-bit ISA address decode. |
| Byte 2 | Range Base Address, bits[9:8] | Address bits[9:8] of the base I/O address for which the card can be configured. This descriptor assumes a 10-bit ISA address decode. |
| Byte 3 | Range Length | The number of contiguous I/O ports requested. |

# Vendor Defined

The vendor-defined resource data type, shown in Table A.13, is reserved for use by the vendor.

**Table A.13 Vendor-Defined Resource Data Type**

| Offset | Field name |
|---|---|
| Byte 0 | Value = 01110xxxb (Type = 0, Small item name = Eh, Length = [1–7]) |
| Byte 1 to 7 | Vendor Defined |

# End Tag

The End tag, shown in Table A.14, identifies the end of the resource data. (If the checksum field is zero, resource data is treated as if the checksum were correct, and configuration proceeds normally.)

**Table A.14 End Tag**

| Offset | Field name |
|---|---|
| Byte 0 | Value = 01111001b (Type = 0, Small item name = Fh, Length = 1). |
| Byte 1 | Checksum covering all resource data after the serial identifier. This checksum is generated such that adding it to the sum of all the data bytes produces a zero sum. |

# Large Resource Data Type

The Large Resource Data Type tag, shown in Table A-15, allows larger amounts of data to be included in the resource data structure. The tag includes a 16-bit length field that allows up to 64K of data.

Byte 0 contains the tag information. Bit 7, when set to 1, indicates that the tag is a Large Resource Data Type tag. Bits[6:0] contain the value that describes the item name for this tag. Large resource item names and their corresponding values are described in Table A.16.

Bytes 1 and 2 contain the length of the resource data for the item.

Bytes 3 through *n* contain the resource data information.

**Table A.15 Large Resource Data Type Tag Bit Definitions**

| Offset | Field name |
|---|---|
| Byte 0 | Value = 1xxxxxxxb (Type = 1, Large item name = xxxxxxx) |
| Byte 1 | Length of Data Items, bits[7:0] |
| Byte 2 | Length of Data Items, bits[15:8] |
| Bytes 3 to *n* | Actual Data Items |

**Table A.16 Large Resource Item Names**

| Large item name | Value |
|---|---|
| Memory range descriptor | 1h |
| Identification string (ANSI) | 2h |
| Identification string (Unicode) | 3h |
| Vendor defined | 4h |
| 32-bit memory range descriptor | 5h |
| 32-bit fixed-location memory range descriptor | 6h |
| Reserved | 7h–7Fh |

# Memory Range Descriptor

The memory range descriptor is described in Table A.17.

**Table A.17 Memory Range Descriptor**

| Size | Field name | Definition |
|---|---|---|
| Byte | Memory Range Descriptor | Value = 10000001b (Type = 1, Large item name = 1). |
| Byte | Length, bits[7:0] | Value = 00001001b (9). |
| Byte | Length, bits[15:8] | Value = 00000000b. |
| Byte | Information | This field provides extra information about this memory.<br>Bit[7] Reserved.<br>Bit[6] Memory is an expansion ROM.<br>Bit[5] Memory is shadowable.<br>Bits[4:3] Memory control.<br>Status<br>00 8-bit memory only.<br>01 16-bit memory only.<br>10 8-bit and 16-bit memory supported.<br>11 Reserved.<br>Bit[2] Support type.<br>Status<br>1 Decode supports high address.<br>0 Decode supports extent.<br>Bit[1] Cache support type.<br>Status<br>1 Read-cacheable, write-through.<br>0 Noncacheable.<br>Bit[0] Write status.<br>Status<br>1 Writable.<br>0 Nonwritable (ROM). |
| Byte | Range Minimum Base Address, bits[7:0] | Address bits[15:8] of the minimum base memory address for which the card can be configured. See note below for bits[7:0]. |
| Byte | Range Minimum Base Address, bits[15:8] | Address bits[23:16] of the minimum base memory address for which the card can be configured. |
| Byte | Range Maximum Base Address, bits[7:0] | Address bits[15:8] of the maximum base memory address for which the card can be configured. |
| Byte | Range Maximum Base Address, bits[15:8] | Address bits[23:16] of the maximum base memory address for which the card can be configured. |

**Table A.17 Memory Range Descriptor (*continued*)**

| Size | Field name | Definition |
|---|---|---|
| Byte | Base Alignment, bits[7:0] | This field contains the lower eight bits of the base alignment. The Base Alignment field provides the increment for the minimum base address (0000h = 64K). |
| Byte | Base Alignment, bits[15:8] | This field contains the upper eight bits of the base alignment. The Base Alignment field provides the increment for the minimum base address (0000h = 64K). |
| Byte | Range Length, bits[7:0] | This field contains the lower eight bits of the memory range length. The Range Length field provides the length of the memory range in 256-byte blocks. |
| Byte | Range Length, bits[15:8] | This field contains the upper eight bits of the memory range length. The Range Length field provides the length of the memory range in 256-byte blocks. |

Notes: Address bits[7:0] of memory base addresses are assumed to be 0.

A memory range descriptor can be used to describe a fixed-memory address by setting the range minimum base address and the range maximum base address to the same value.

# ANSI Identification String

The identification string, whose format is described in Table A.18, is 8-bit ANSI. Because the length of the string is defined in the structure, the string must not be zero terminated. Display software must ensure that the proper termination is added to the string so a termination byte must not be stored in the card's nonvolatile storage. Every Plug and Play ISA card is required to have an identification string. Each logical device may optionally have an identification string.

**Table A.18 ANSI Identification String**

| Size | Field name | Definition |
|---|---|---|
| Byte | Identification String | Value = 10000010b (Type = 1, Large item name = 2) |
| Byte | Length, bits[7:0] | Lower eight bits of identification string length |
| Byte | Length, bits[15:8] | Upper eight bits of identification string length |
| N * bytes | Identification String | Device description as an ANSI string |

# Unicode Identification String

Table A.19 contains the format of the Unicode identification string.

**Table A.19 Unicode Identification String**

| Size | Field name | Definition |
|---|---|---|
| Byte | Identification String | Value = 10000011b (Type = 1, Large item name = 3) |
| Byte | Length, bits[7:0] | Lower eight bits of length of string plus four |
| Byte | Length, bits[15:8] | Upper eight bits of length of string plus four |
| Byte | Country Identifier, bits[7:0] | Not defined in version 1.0a of the Plug and Play specification |
| Byte | Country Identifier, bits[15:8] | Not defined in version 1.0a of the Plug and Play specification |
| N * bytes | Identification String | Device description characters |

# Vendor Defined

The vendor-defined resource data type, shown in Table A.20, is reserved for use by the vendor.

**Table A.20 Vendor Defined**

| Size | Field name | Definition |
|---|---|---|
| Byte | Vendor Defined | Value = 10000100b (Type = 1, Large item name = 4) |
| Byte | Length, bits[7:0] | Lower eight bits of vendor-defined data |
| Byte | Length, bits[15:8] | Upper eight bits of vendor-defined data |
| N * bytes | Vendor Defined | Vendor-defined data bytes |

# 32-Bit Memory Range Descriptor

The 32-bit memory range descriptor is described in Table A.21.

**Table A.21 32-bit Memory Range Descriptor**

| Size | Field name | Definition |
|---|---|---|
| Byte | Memory Range Descriptor | Value = 10000101b (Type = 1, Large item name = 5). |
| Byte | Length, bits[7:0] | Value = 00010001b (17). |
| Byte | Length, bits[15:8] | Value = 00000000b. |
| Byte | Information | This field provides extra information about this memory.<br>Bit[7] Reserved.<br>Bit[6] Memory is an expansion ROM.<br>Bit[5] Memory is shadowable.<br>Bits[4:3] Memory control.<br>Status<br>00 8-bit memory only.<br>01 16-bit memory only.<br>10 8-bit and 16-bit memory supported.<br>11 32-bit memory only.<br>Bit[2] Support type.<br>Status<br>1 Decode supports high address.<br>0 Decode supports range length.<br>Bit[1] Cache support type.<br>Status<br>1 Read-cacheable, write-through.<br>0 Noncacheable.<br>Bit[0] Write status.<br>Status<br>1 Writable.<br>0 Nonwritable (ROM). |
| Byte | Range Minimum Base Address, bits[7:0] | Address bits[7:0] of the minimum base memory address for which the card can be configured. |
| Byte | Range Minimum Base Address, bits[15:8] | Address bits[15:8] of the minimum base memory address for which the card can be configured. |
| Byte | Range Minimum Base Address, bits[23:16] | Address bits[23:16] of the minimum base memory address for which the card can be configured. |
| Byte | Range Minimum Base Address, bits[31:24] | Address bits[31:24] of the minimum base memory address for which the card can be configured. |

**Table A.21 32-bit Memory Range Descriptor (*continued*)**

| Size | Field name | Definition |
|---|---|---|
| Byte | Range Maximum Base Address, bits[7:0] | Address bits[7:0] of the maximum base memory address for which the card can be configured. |
| Byte | Range Maximum Base Address, bits[15:8] | Address bits[15:8] of the maximum base memory address for which the card can be configured. |
| Byte | Range Maximum Base Address, bits[23:16] | Address bits[23:16] of the maximum base memory address for which the card can be configured. |
| Byte | Range Maximum Base Address, bits[31:24] | Address bits[31:24] of the maximum base memory address for which the card can be configured. |
| Byte | Base Alignment, bits[7:0] | This field contains bits[7:0] of the base alignment. The Base Alignment field provides the increment for the minimum base address. |
| Byte | Base Alignment, bits[15:8] | This field contains bits[15:8] of the base alignment. The Base Alignment field provides the increment for the minimum base address. |
| Byte | Base Alignment, bits[23:16] | This field contains bits[23:16] of the base alignment. The Base Alignment field provides the increment for the minimum base address. |
| Byte | Base Alignment, bits[31:24] | This field contains bits[31:24] of the base alignment. The Base Alignment field provides the increment for the minimum base address. |
| Byte | Range Length, bits[7:0] | This field contains bits[7:0] of the memory range length. The Range Length field provides the length of the memory range in 1-byte blocks. |
| Byte | Range Length, bits[15:8] | This field contains bits[15:8] of the memory range length. The Range Length field provides the length of the memory range in 1-byte blocks. |
| Byte | Range Length, bits[23:16] | This field contains bits[23:16] of the memory range length. The Range Length field provides the length of the memory range in 1-byte blocks. |
| Byte | Range Length, bits[31:24] | This field contains bits[31:24] of the memory range length. The Range Length field provides the length of the memory range in 1-byte blocks. |

# 32-Bit Fixed-Location Memory Range Descriptor

The 32-bit fixed-location memory range descriptor is described in Table A.22.

**Table A.22 32-Bit Fixed-Location Memory Range Descriptor**

| Size | Field name | Definition |
|---|---|---|
| Byte | Memory Range Descriptor | Value = 10000110b (Type = 1, Large item name = 6). |
| Byte | Length, bits[7:0] | Value = 00001001b (17). |
| Byte | Length, bits[15:8] | Value = 00000000b. |
| Byte | Information | This field provides extra information about this memory.<br>Bit[7] Reserved.<br>Bit[6] Memory is an expansion ROM.<br>Bit[5] Memory is shadowable.<br>Bits[4:3] Memory control.<br>Status<br>00 8-bit memory only.<br>01 16-bit memory only.<br>10 8-bit and 16-bit memory supported.<br>11 32-bit memory only.<br>Bit[2] Support type.<br>Status<br>1 Decode supports high address.<br>0 Decode supports range length.<br>Bit[1] Cache support type.<br>Status<br>1 Read-cacheable, write-through.<br>0 Noncacheable.<br>Bit[0] Write status.<br>Status<br>1 Writable.<br>0 Nonwritable (ROM). |
| Byte | Range Base Address, bits[7:0] | Address bits[7:0] of the base memory address for which the card can be configured. |
| Byte | Range Base Address, bits[15:8] | Address bits[15:8] of the base memory address for which the card can be configured. |

**Table A.22 32-Bit Fixed-Location Memory Range Descriptor** *(continued)*

| Size | Field name | Definition |
|---|---|---|
| Byte | Range Base Address, bits [23:16] | Address bits[23:16] of the base memory address for which the card can be configured. |
| Byte | Range Base Address, bits[31:24] | Address bits[31:24] of the base memory address for which the card can be configured. |
| Byte | Range Length, bits[7:0] | This field contains bits[7:0] of the memory range length. The Range Length field provides the length of the memory range in 1-byte blocks. |
| Byte | Range Length, bits[15:8] | This field contains bits[15:8] of the memory range length. The Range Length field provides the length of the memory range in 1-byte blocks. |
| Byte | Range Length, bits[23:16] | This field contains bits[23:16] of the memory range length. The Range Length field provides the length of the memory range in 1-byte blocks. |
| Byte | Range Length, bits[31:24] | This field contains bits[31:24] of the memory range length. The Range Length field provides the length of the memory range in 1-byte blocks. |

# Resource Data and Dependent Function Examples

Resource data describes a Plug and Play card to system software. Resource information for a Plug and Play card must include a Plug and Play version number and an identification string. Each logical device on an ISA card must specify a logical identifier and a list of all the Plug and Play resources the logical device needs to use. The list of resources must completely describe the configurability of the logical device.

Shown here are several examples of how to encode card resource data.

**Note** Dependent functions cannot be nested. Each Start DF tag identifies the beginning of a dependent function, which is simply a set of interdependent resource descriptors, optionally with an assigned priority, that must be allocated together. The End DF tag indicates that the last of these dependent functions has been reached. No accommodation is made for "nesting" relationships.

## Example 1

The first example is a simple card, such as a parallel printer card, with a limited amount of configurability. This example card needs four consecutive I/O ports at a base address of 378h, 278h, or 3BCh. This device also needs one interrupt, which can be IRQ5 or IRQ7. The choice of the IRQ is completely independent from the choice of I/O port. The resource data for this card would be:

```
TAG Plug and Play version number
TAG Identification string
TAG Logical device ID
TAG IRQ format (MASK IRQ5, IRQ7)
TAG Start DF (Length 0)
    TAG I/O format (Length 4, Min Base 0x0378, Max Base 0x0378)
TAG Start DF (Length 0)
    TAG I/O format (Length 4, Min Base 0x0278, Max Base 0x0278)
TAG Start DF (Length 0)
    TAG I/O format (Length 4, Min Base 0x03BC, Max Base 0x03BC)
TAG End DF
TAG END tag
```

## Example 2

Dependent functions can be used to express relationships between resources that are interdependent. For example, consider a card that can be configured to use I/O port 300h and IRQ5 or I/O port 310h and IRQ7. This device has the following resource structure:

```
TAG Plug and Play version number
TAG Identification string
TAG Logical device ID
TAG Start DF (Length 0)
    TAG I/O format (Length 4, Min Base 0x0300, Max Base 0x0300)
    TAG IRQ format (MASK IRQ 5)
TAG Start DF (Length 0)
    TAG I/O format (Length 4, Min Base 0x0310, Max Base 0x0310)
    TAG IRQ format (MASK IRQ 7)
TAG End DF
TAG END tag
```

## Example 3

Dependent functions can also express the priority of configuration options (see the explanation of priority of resource allocations earlier in this appendix). For example, consider a card that performs DMA using a memory buffer, if memory space is available. Alternatively, the card uses a DMA channel, if no memory resources are available. This example card needs 16 consecutive I/O ports that can be located anywhere in the range of 300h to 3F0h. The card needs one interrupt that can be either IRQ5, 7, 10, 11, or 12. The card needs a 128K memory window. If that is not available, it can use a 64K memory window. If that is not available, it will run using a DMA channel. It supports DMA channels 5, 6, and 7. This device has the following resource data structure:

```
TAG Plug and Play version number
TAG Identification string
TAG Logical device ID
TAG I/O format (Length 16, Min Base 0x0300, Max Base 0x03F0)
TAG IRQ format (MASK IRQ 5,7,10,11,12)
TAG Start DF (Length 1) (Priority 0)
    TAG Memory format (Length = 128K, Min Base 0x0C0000, Max Base
        0x0E0000)
    TAG DMA format (MASK no DMA channel)
TAG Start DF (Length 1) (Priority 1)
    TAG Memory format (Length = 64K, Min Base 0x0C0000, Max Base
        0x0E0000)
    TAG DMA format (MASK no DMA channel)
TAG Start DF (Length 1) (Priority 2)
    TAG Memory format (Length = 0, Min Base 0x0C0000, Max Base
        0x0E0000)
    TAG DMA format (MASK 5,6,7)
TAG End DF
TAG END tag
```

## Example 4

The following example shows an illegal use of dependent functions. The structure below includes two END DF tags, which is not allowed.

```
TAG Plug and Play version number
TAG Identification string
TAG Logical device ID
TAG IRQ format (MASK IRQ 5,IRQ7)
TAG Start DF (Length 0)
    TAG I/O format (Length 4, Min Base 0x0378, Max Base 0x0378)
TAG Start DF (Length 0)
    TAG I/O format (Length 4, Min Base 0x0278, Max Base 0x0278)
TAG Start DF (Length 0)
    TAG I/O format (Length 4, Min Base 0x03BC, Max Base 0x03BC)
TAG End DF
TAG Start DF (Length 1 - Priority 1)
    TAG DMA format (MASK no DMA channel)
TAG Start DF (Length 1 - Priority 2)
    TAG DMA format (MASK 5,6,7)
TAG End DF
TAG END tag
```

The correct structure is:

```
TAG Plug and Play version number
TAG Identification string
TAG Logical device ID
TAG IRQ format (MASK IRQ 5,IRQ7)
TAG Start DF (Length 0)
    TAG I/O format (Length 4, Min Base 0x0378, Max Base 0x0378)
    TAG DMA format (MASK no DMA channel)
TAG Start DF (Length 0)
    TAG I/O format (Length 4, Min Base 0x0278, Max Base 0x0278)
    TAG DMA format (MASK no DMA channel)
TAG Start DF (Length 0)
    TAG I/O format (Length 4, Min Base 0x03BC, Max Base 0x03BC)
    TAG DMA format (MASK no DMA channel)
TAG Start DF (Length 1 - Priority 2)
    TAG I/O format (Length 4, Min Base 0x0378, Max Base 0x0378)
    TAG DMA format (MASK 5,6,7)
TAG Start DF (Length 1 - Priority 2)
    TAG I/O format (Length 4, Min Base 0x0278, Max Base 0x0278)
    TAG DMA format (MASK 5,6,7)
TAG Start DF (Length 1 - Priority 2)
    TAG I/O format (Length 4, Min Base 0x03BC, Max Base 0x03BC)
    TAG DMA format (MASK 5,6,7)
TAG End DF
TAG END tag
```

APPENDIX B

Appendix B

# Device Identifiers

Every device and bus on the motherboard must have a unique device identifier that distinguishes it from every other device. Many motherboard devices and buses, and non–Plug and Play expansion card devices, do not have a standard EISA identifier. To identify various devices that do not have the standard EISA identifier, an EISA prefix of "PNP" has been reserved for Microsoft. Tables B.1 through B.16 list the currently assigned EISA PNP device identifiers.

---

**Note** The current list of PNP device identifiers is available for downloading from the CompuServe PLUGPLAY forum. You should also review the example motherboard device identifier structure in Chapter 8, "System BIOS Design."

---

PNP device identifiers enable existing legacy devices to report their resource requirements to a Plug and Play operating system. These identifiers are useful only if the operating system itself contains drivers that can use the hardware. Microsoft® Windows™ 95 uses a device identifier to map a hardware device to its corresponding .INF driver information file, and therefore to its drivers. If the PNP identifier is not assigned by Microsoft, Windows 95 will not recognize it.

All new Plug and Play ISA, EISA, and VL-bus cards must provide their own, vendor-specific device identifier, .INF file, and device driver. These cards do not use a PNP prefix; they use the vendor's unique EISA device identifier. Using an undefined number may cause conflicts. To obtain a standard EISA device identifier, contact BCPR Services, Inc. (See Appendix D, "References," for more information.)

It may seem ironic that the PNP device identifier is used for non–Plug and Play devices, but these device identifiers allow the non–Plug and Play devices to operate with new Plug and Play devices and operating systems.

**Table B.1 Interrupt Controllers**

| Description | EISA device ID |
|---|---|
| AT interrupt controller | PNP0000 |
| EISA interrupt controller | PNP0001 |
| Micro Channel interrupt controller | PNP0002 |
| APIC | PNP0003 |
| Cyrix SLiC MP interrupt controller | PNP0004 |

**Table B.2 Timers**

| Description | EISA device ID |
|---|---|
| AT timer | PNP0100 |
| EISA timer | PNP0101 |
| Micro Channel timer | PNP0102 |

**Table B.3 DMA**

| Description | EISA device ID |
|---|---|
| AT DMA controller | PNP0200 |
| EISA DMA controller | PNP0201 |
| Micro Channel DMA controller | PNP0202 |

**Table B.4 Keyboards**

| Description | EISA device ID |
|---|---|
| IBM PC/XT™ keyboard controller (83-key) | PNP0300 |
| IBM PC/AT keyboard controller (86-key) | PNP0301 |
| IBM PC/XT keyboard controller (84-key) | PNP0302 |
| IBM Enhanced keyboard (101/102-key) | PNP0303 |
| Olivetti® keyboard (83-key) | PNP0304 |
| Olivetti keyboard (102-key) | PNP0305 |
| Olivetti keyboard (86-key) | PNP0306 |
| Microsoft Windows keyboard | PNP0307 |
| General Input Device Emulation Interface (GIDEI) legacy | PNP0308 |
| Olivetti keyboard (A101/102 key) | PNP0309 |
| AT&T® 302 keyboard | PNP030A |
| PS/2 port (for PS/2 Mouse) | PNP0313 |

**Table B.5 Parallel Devices**

| Description | EISA device ID |
|---|---|
| Standard LPT printer port | PNP0400 |
| ECP printer port | PNP0401 |

**Table B.6 Serial Devices**

| Description | EISA device ID |
|---|---|
| Standard PC COM port | PNP0500 |
| 16550A-compatible COM port | PNP0501 |

**Table B.7 Disk Controllers**

| Description | EISA device ID |
|---|---|
| Generic ESDI/IDE/ATA–compatible hard disk controller | PNP0600 |
| Plus Hardcard II | PNP0601 |
| Plus Hardcard IIXL/EZ | PNP0602 |
| PC standard floppy disk controller | PNP0700 |

**Table B.8 Display Adapters**

| Description | EISA device ID |
|---|---|
| VGA compatible | PNP0900 |
| Video Seven™ VRAM/VRAM II/1024i | PNP0901 |
| 8514/A compatible | PNP0902 |
| Trident VGA | PNP0903 |
| Cirrus Logic laptop VGA | PNP0904 |
| Cirrus Logic VGA | PNP0905 |
| Tseng ET4000 | PNP0906 |
| Western Digital® VGA | PNP0907 |
| Western Digital laptop VGA | PNP0908 |
| S3 Inc. 911/924 | PNP0909 |
| ATI™ Ultra Pro/Plus (Mach 32) | PNP090A |
| ATI Ultra (Mach 8) | PNP090B |
| XGA® compatible | PNP090C |
| ATI VGA Wonder | PNP090D |
| Weitek® P9000 graphics adapter | PNP090E |
| Oak Technology VGA | PNP090F |
| COMPAQ® QVision® | PNP0910 |
| XGA/2 | PNP0911 |
| Tseng Labs W32/W32i/W32p | PNP0912 |

**Table B.8 Display Adapters (*continued*)**

| Description | EISA device ID |
|---|---|
| S3 Inc. 801/928/964 | PNP0913 |
| COMPAQ Advanced VGA (AVGA) | PNP0914 |
| ATI Ultra Pro Turbo (Mach 64) | PNP0915 |
| Chips & Technologies Super VGA | PNP0930 |
| Chips & Technologies Accelerator | PNP0931 |
| NCR® 77c22e Super VGA | PNP0940 |
| NCR 77c32blt | PNP0941 |

**Table B.9 Expansion Buses**

| Description | EISA device ID |
|---|---|
| ISA bus | PNP0A00 |
| EISA bus | PNP0A01 |
| Micro Channel bus | PNP0A02 |
| PCI bus | PNP0A03 |
| VESA/VL-bus | PNP0A04 |

**Table B.10 Real-Time Clock, Motherboard Devices**

| Description | EISA device ID |
|---|---|
| AT-style speaker sound | PNP0800 |
| AT real-time clock | PNP0B00 |
| Plug and Play BIOS (only created by the ROOT enumerator) | PNP0C00 |
| Motherboard | PNP0C01 |
| General ID for reserving private resources required by Plug and Play motherboard registers (not specific to a particular device) | PNP0C02 |
| Plug and Play BIOS event notification interrupt | PNP0C03 |
| Math coprocessor | PNP0C04 |

**Table B.11 PCMCIA Controller Chip Sets**

| Description | EISA device ID |
|---|---|
| Intel 82365–compatible PCMCIA controller | PNP0E00 |
| Cirrus Logic CL-PD6720 PCMCIA controller | PNP0E01 |
| VLSI BL82C146 PCMCIA controller | PNP0E02 |

**Table B.12 Mouse**

| Description | EISA device ID |
|---|---|
| Microsoft® Bus Mouse | PNP0F00 |
| Microsoft® Serial Mouse | PNP0F01 |
| Microsoft® InPort™ Mouse | PNP0F02 |
| Microsoft® PS/2™ Mouse | PNP0F03 |
| Mouse Systems™ Mouse | PNP0F04 |
| Mouse Systems 3-Button Mouse (COM2) | PNP0F05 |
| Genius Mouse (COM1) | PNP0F06 |
| Genius Mouse (COM2) | PNP0F07 |
| Logitech™ Serial Mouse | PNP0F08 |
| Microsoft® BallPoint™ Serial Mouse | PNP0F09 |
| Microsoft® Plug and Play Mouse | PNP0F0A |
| Microsoft® Plug and Play BallPoint Mouse | PNP0F0B |
| Microsoft-compatible Serial Mouse | PNP0F0C |
| Microsoft-compatible InPort Mouse | PNP0F0D |
| Microsoft-compatible PS/2 Mouse | PNP0F0E |
| Microsoft-compatible Serial BallPoint Mouse | PNP0F0F |
| Texas Instruments® Quick Port Mouse | PNP0F10 |
| Microsoft-compatible Bus Mouse | PNP0F11 |
| Logitech PS/2 Mouse | PNP0F12 |
| PS/2 Mouse Port | PNP0F13 [1] |

[1]The system BIOS should report PS/2 port, not which type of mouse is connected to that port.

**Table B.13 Modems**

| Description | EISA device ID |
|---|---|
| Legacy modems[1] | PNPC000 to PNPDFFF |

[1] Although legacy modems will use EISA device identifiers from PNPC000 the PNPDFFF, the actual identifiers have not been determined as of this printing. Before designing any hardware using this information, download a copy of the current EISA device identifiers for legacy modems from CompuServe. Type "go plugplay" and retrieve the file DEVIDS.ZIP.

**Table B.14 Network Adapters**

| Description | EISA device ID |
|---|---|
| Novell®/Anthem NE3200 | PNP8001 |
| COMPAQ NE3200 | PNP8004 |
| Intel EtherExpress™/32 | PNP8006 |
| HP® Ethertwist® EISA LAN Adapter/32 (HP27248A) | PNP8008 |
| Ungermann-Bass NIUps or NIUps/EOTP | PNP8065 |
| DEC™ (DE211) EtherWorks MC/TP | PNP8072 |
| DEC (DE212) EtherWorks MC/TP_BNC | PNP8073 |
| HP MC LAN Adapter/16 TP (PC27246) | PNP8074 |
| DCA 10 MB MCA | PNP8078 |
| IBM Token Ring® | PNP80C9 |
| IBM Token Ring II® | PNP80CA |
| IBM Token Ring II/Short | PNP80CB |
| IBM Token Ring 4/16 MB | PNP80CC |
| Novell/Anthem NE1000 | PNP80D3 |
| Novell/Anthem NE2000 | PNP80D4 |
| NE1000 compatible | PNP80D5 |
| NE2000 compatible | PNP80D6 |
| Novell/Anthem NE1500T | PNP80D7 |
| Novell/Anthem NE2100 | PNP80D8 |
| SMC® ARCNETPC | PNP80DD |
| SMC ARCNET PC100, PC200 | PNP80DE |
| SMC ARCNET PC110, PC210, PC250 | PNP80DF |
| SMC ARCNET PC130/E | PNP80E0 |
| SMC ARCNET PC120, PC220, PC260 | PNP80E1 |
| SMC ARCNET PC270/E | PNP80E2 |
| SMC ARCNET PC600W, PC650W | PNP80E5 |
| DEC DEPCA | PNP80E7 |
| DEC (DE100) EtherWorks LC | PNP80E8 |
| DEC (DE200) EtherWorks Turbo | PNP80E9 |
| DEC (DE101) EtherWorks LC/TP | PNP80EA |
| DEC (DE201) EtherWorks Turbo/TP | PNP80EB |
| DEC (DE202) EtherWorks Turbo/TP_BNC | PNP80EC |
| DEC (DE102) EtherWorks LC/TP_BNC | PNP80ED |

**Table B.14 Network Adapters (*continued*)**

| Description | EISA device ID |
|---|---|
| DEC EE101 (built-in) | PNP80EE |
| DECpc 433 WS (built-in) | PNP80EF |
| 3Com® EtherLink Plus® | PNP80F1 |
| 3Com EtherLink II® or IITP® (8 bit or 16 bit) | PNP80F3 |
| 3Com TokenLink® | PNP80F4 |
| 3Com EtherLink® 16 | PNP80F6 |
| 3Com EtherLink III® | PNP80F7 |
| Thomas-Conrad™ TC6045 | PNP80FB |
| Thomas-Conrad TC6042 | PNP80FC |
| Thomas-Conrad TC6142 | PNP80FD |
| Thomas-Conrad TC6145 | PNP80FE |
| Thomas-Conrad TC6242 | PNP80FF |
| Thomas-Conrad TC6245 | PNP8100 |
| DCA 10 MB | PNP8105 |
| DCA 10 MB Fiber Optic | PNP8106 |
| DCA 10 MB Twisted Pair | PNP8107 |
| Racal® NI6510 | PNP8113 |
| Ungermann-Bass NIUpc | PNP811C |
| Ungermann-Bass NIUpc/EOTP | PNP8120 |
| SMC StarCard Plus (WD/8003S) | PNP8123 |
| SMC StarCard Plus with on-board hub (WD/8003SH) | PNP8124 |
| SMC EtherCard Plus (WD/8003E) | PNP8125 |
| SMC EtherCard Plus with boot ROM socket (WD/8003EBT) | PNP8126 |
| SMC EtherCard Plus with boot ROM socket (WD/8003EB) | PNP8127 |
| SMC EtherCard Plus TP (WD/8003WT) | PNP8128 |
| SMC EtherCard Plus 16 with boot ROM socket (WD/8013EBT) | PNP812A |
| Intel EtherExpress™ 16 or 16TP | PNP812D |
| Intel TokenExpress™ 16/4 | PNP812F |
| Intel TokenExpress MCA 16/4 | PNP8130 |
| Intel EtherExpress 16 (MCA) | PNP8132 |
| Artisoft® AE-1 | PNP8137 |
| Artisoft AE-2 or AE-3 | PNP8138 |
| Amplicard AC 210/XT | PNP8141 |
| Amplicard AC 210/AT | PNP8142 |

**Table B.14 Network Adapters (*continued*)**

| Description | EISA device ID |
|---|---|
| Everex™ SpeedLink™ /PC16 (EV2027) | PNP814B |
| HP PC LAN Adapter/8 TP (HP27245) | PNP8155 |
| HP PC LAN Adapter/16 TP (HP27247A) | PNP8156 |
| HP PC LAN Adapter/8 TL (HP27250) | PNP8157 |
| HP PC LAN Adapter/16 TP Plus (HP27247B) | PNP8158 |
| HP PC LAN Adapter/16 TL Plus (HP27252) | PNP8159 |
| National Semiconductor® Ethernode *16AT | PNP815F |
| National Semiconductor AT/LANTIC Ethernode 16-AT3 | PNP8160 |
| NCR® Token-Ring 4 MB ISA | PNP816A |
| NCR Token-Ring 16/4 MB ISA | PNP816D |
| Olicom™ 16/4 Token-Ring Adapter | PNP8191 |
| SMC EtherCard Plus Elite (WD/8003EP) | PNP81C3 |
| SMC EtherCard Plus 10T (WD/8003W) | PNP81C4 |
| SMC EtherCard Plus Elite 16 (WD/8013EP) | PNP81C5 |
| SMC EtherCard Plus Elite 16T (WD/8013W) | PNP81C6 |
| SMC EtherCard Plus Elite 16 Combo (WD/8013EW or 8013EWC) | PNP81C7 |
| Pure Data™ PDI9025-32 (Token Ring) | PNP81E4 |
| Pure Data PDI508+ (ARCNET) | PNP81E6 |
| Pure Data PDI516+ (ARCNET) | PNP81E7 |
| Proteon™ Token Ring (P1390) | PNP81EB |
| Proteon Token Ring (P1392) | PNP81EC |
| Proteon ISA Token Ring (1340) | PNP81ED |
| Proteon ISA Token Ring (1342) | PNP81EE |
| Proteon ISA Token Ring (1346) | PNP81EF |
| Proteon ISA Token Ring (1347) | PNP81F0 |
| Cabletron™ E2000 Series DNI | PNP81FF |
| Cabletron E2100 Series DNI | PNP8200 |
| Zenith Data Systems™ Z-Note | PNP8209 |
| Zenith Data Systems NE2000 compatible | PNP820A |
| Xircom Pocket Ethernet II | PNP8213 |
| Xircom Pocket Ethernet I | PNP8214 |
| RadiSys™ EXM-10 | PNP821D |
| SMC 3000 Series | PNP8227 |

**Table B.14 Network Adapters (*continued*)**

| Description | EISA device ID |
|---|---|
| Intel '595-based Ethernet | PNP8228A |
| TI2000-style Token Ring | PNP8228B |
| Advanced Micro Devices AM2100/AM1500T | PNP8231 |
| Tulip® NCC-16 | PNP8263 |
| Exos® 105 | PNP8277 |
| IBM PCMCIA-NIC | PNP82BD |
| DEC Ethernet (all types) | PNP8321 |
| SMC EtherCard (all types except 8013/A) | PNP8323 |
| ARCNET Compatible | PNP8324 |
| Thomas-Conrad (all ARCNET types) | PNP8326 |
| IBM Token Ring (all types) | PNP8327 |
| Remote Network Access Driver | PNP8385 |
| RNA Point-to-point Protocol Driver | PNP8387 |

**Table B.15 SCSI and Proprietary CD Adapters**

| Description | EISA device ID |
|---|---|
| Adaptec™ 154x–compatible SCSI controller | PNPA000 |
| Adaptec 174x–compatible SCSI controller | PNPA001 |
| Future Domain™ 16-700–compatible controller | PNPA002 |
| Panasonic® proprietary CD-ROM adapter (SBPro/SB16) | PNPA003 |
| Trantor™ 128 SCSI controller | PNPA01B |
| Trantor T160 SCSI controller | PNPA01D |
| Trantor T338 Parallel SCSI controller | PNPA01E |
| Trantor T348 Parallel SCSI controller | PNPA01F |
| Trantor Media Vision™ SCSI controller | PNPA020 |
| Always IN-2000 SCSI controller | PNPA022 |
| SONY® proprietary CD-ROM controller | PNPA02B |
| Trantor T13b 8-bit SCSI controller | PNPA02D |
| Trantor T358 Parallel SCSI controller | PNPA02F |

**Table B.16 Sound, Video-Capture, and Multimedia Adapters**

| Description | EISA device ID |
|---|---|
| Sound Blaster 1.5–compatible sound device | PNPB000 |
| Sound Blaster 2.0–compatible sound device | PNPB001 |
| Sound Blaster Pro–compatible sound device | PNPB002 |
| Thunderboard-compatible sound device | PNPB004 |
| Adlib®-compatible FM synthesizer device | PNPB005 |
| MPU401 compatible | PNPB006 |
| Microsoft Windows Sound System–compatible sound device | PNPB007 |
| COMPAQ Waveform audio device | PNPB008 |
| New Plug and Play Microsoft Sound System device | PNPB0009 |
| Motion Video Device (MCI) | PNPB010 |
| MIDI Sequencer Device (MCI) | PNPB011 |
| Wave Audio Device (MCI) | PNPB012 |
| VISCA VCR Device (MCI) | PNPB013 |
| Pioneer® LaserDisk Device (MCI) | PNPB014 |
| CD Audio Device (MCI) | PNPB015 |
| Yamaha® OPL3–compatible FM synthesizer device | PNPB020 |
| Joystick/game port | PNPB02F |

APPENDIX C

Appendix C

# Glossary

This glossary contains definitions of terms and phrases printed in italic throughout this guide. Also included are additional terms and phrases important to the PC 95 that are found in various industry standard specifications and the Plug and Play specifications published by Microsoft®.

Among the definitions in this appendix, some words and acronyms also appear in italics. This indicates that the definition for that term is also found in the glossary.

## A

### ACCESS.bus

A four-pin serial bus that connects a local computer with a low-speed I/O device such as a keyboard, a mouse, and so on.

### Advanced port replicator

A *port replicator* that provides some extra functionality not available in the portable system. This makes it possible to offload onto an optional attachment *devices* that add weight and hinder portability.

### Advanced power management

(1) A software interface (defined by Microsoft and Intel) between hardware-specific power management software (such as that located in a system BIOS) and an operating system power management driver. Advanced power management supplies one or more layers of software that can reduce the power consumption of power-manageable hardware in a computer system.

(2) The specification that documents the software interface—that is, an abridgment of the *Advanced Power Management (APM) BIOS Interface Specification* title.

### APM

See *advanced power management.*

### Arbitrator

A software module in Windows 95 that handles the allocation of hardware *resources* among *devices*.

### ASIC

Acronym for application-specific integrated circuit.

### ATA

Acronym for *AT Attachment*, formerly known as, and used interchangeably with, Integrated Drive Electronics.

### ATAPI

See *AT Attachment Packet Interface*.

### AT Attachment

An integrated bus generally used between host processors and disk drives.

### AT Attachment Packet Interface

A hardware and software specification that documents the interface between a host computer and CD-ROM drives using the *AT Attachment* (ATA) bus.

# B

### Bus enumerator

A bus device driver that detects *devices* located on a specific bus and loads information on these devices into the *hardware tree*.

# C

### Card select number

The handle created by the system BIOS or the operating system through the *isolation* process, and assigned to each *Plug and Play* card on the ISA bus as a unique identifier.

### Children

Any number of *devices* attached to a system bus that must be enumerated by a *bus enumerator*.

### Cold docking

A method of removing or installing a mobile system in a *docking station*, in which the computer must be completely shut down (power off) before it can be docked or undocked.

### Compatibility mode

See *printer port compatibility mode*.

### Configurable resources

A group of *resources*, such as IRQ signals, DMA channels, I/O port addresses, and memory addresses, available on a *device* from which the *configuration manager* can choose one of each to represent the resources of the device, and thus avoid *resource conflicts* with other devices. See also *static resources*.

### Configuration manager

The *Plug and Play* system component that drives the process of locating *devices*, setting up their nodes in the *hardware tree*, and running the resource allocation/deallocation process.

### Conflict

See *resource conflict*.

### CSN

See *card select number*.

## D

### DCI

See *Display Control Interface*.

### DDC

See *display data channel*.

### Device

Any circuit that performs a specific function, such as a parallel port.

### Device ID

A *device* identification string, in many cases beginning with a three-letter standard EISA identifier, that distinguishes every logical device and bus from all others on the system.

### Device node

A data structure that contains the unique characteristics of each logical *device* and bus on the system. This structure consists of the device identifier, a list of *resources* required by the logical device or bus, a list of resources allocated to the logical device or bus, and, in the case of a bus, a list of *children* associated with the device node. Commonly referred to as a devnode.

### DIB

Acronym for device-independent bitmap.

### DIB engine

A dynamic-link library (DLL) provided by Microsoft. Minidrivers call the functions in this library to perform bitmap operations, manage graphics objects, manage color palettes, and draw lines, curves, filled shapes, and text. Display drivers written for display adapters that do not allow direct access to the frame buffer can also use the DIB engine to perform memory-bitmap operations.

### Digital signal processor

An integrated circuit designed for high-speed data manipulations, used in audio, communications, image manipulation, and other data-acquisition and data-control applications.

### Direct memory access

A method of moving data from a device to memory (or vice versa) without the help of the microprocessor. The motherboard uses a DMA controller to handle a fixed number of "channels," each of which may be used by only one *device* at a time.

### Display Control Interface

A driver-level software interface that provides access to display *devices*. DCI provides a device-independent way for Windows subsystem software such as 3-D graphics packages, games interface packages, or digital video codecs to access display device–dependent features.

### Display data channel

A communications channel between a monitor and the display adapter to which it is connected. This channel provides a method for the monitor to convey its identity to the display adapter.

### Display power management signaling

A standard method by which the display adapter signals the monitor to enter into a defined set of power management states. This method is defined in VESA's *Display Power Management Signaling (DPMS)* standard.

### DL-VxD

See *Dynamic Load Virtual "anything" Driver.*

### DMA

See *direct memory access.*

### Dock serial identifier

An identification method used by Windows 95 that involves combining the *docking station* location identifier and the serial number returned by the system BIOS Function 5, Get Docking Station Information. Windows 95 uses the dock serial identifier during the boot process, and after a *warm docking* or undocking event, to determine whether to use the docked or undocked configuration.

### Docking station

A base unit into which a user can insert a mobile system to provide additional hardware functionality and expansion.

### DPMS

See *display power management signaling*.

### DSP

See *digital signal processor*.

### Dynamic detection

The process by which a system can detect that a new *device* has been added or removed from the PC. This process allows the operating system and applications to immediately begin using the added devices or stop using the removed devices without rebooting the system.

### Dynamic Load Virtual "anything" Driver

A type of VxD that can be dynamically loaded or unloaded after the system starts. DL-VxDs are the best type of driver for *devices* in docking systems that employ *warm docking* or *hot docking* because Windows 95 does not have to be rebooted after the portable system is docked or undocked. This type of driver can also receive messages from Windows 95, which means that if a device is going to be removed during a warm undocking event, it can be consulted first.

## E

### ECP

See *Extended Capabilities Port*.

### EDID

See *Extended Display Identification*.

### EISA

See *Extended Industry Standard Architecture* bus.

### Energy Star

Abridgment of EPA Energy Star computers. A program initiated by the U.S. Environment Protection Agency and computer manufacturers documenting standards of power management designed to reduce the electricity load of computer systems in the commercial sector. Computers that meet the requirements of the Energy Star program qualify for the Energy Star logo.

### Enhanced Parallel Port

An asynchronous, 8-bit-wide parallel channel controlled by the computer, as defined by the IEEE P1284 standard.

### Enumeration

The process by which logical *devices* and buses, and their available resources, are identified. The logical devices and buses can be enumerated by the system BIOS, the operating system, or device drivers.

### Enumerator

A *Plug and Play* system component that takes responsibility for detecting logical child *devices* and reports the existence of those devices to the *configuration manager* during startup. Enumerators can also take responsibility for setting up their *children*.

### EPP

See *Enhanced Parallel Port*.

### Exit-point terminator

A SCSI bus terminator that resides at the conjunction of the internal and external connectors on the host adapter. This terminator can be automatically turned on or off depending on the configuration of the SCSI bus. If an internal and external drive are connected to the bus, the exit-point terminator is disabled. For all other configurations, the terminator is enabled. The exit-point terminator can be enabled or disabled either mechanically or through a software interface.

### Expansion bus

A group of address, data, and control lines that provide a buffered interface to *devices* located either on the *motherboard* or on cards that are plugged into expansion connectors. Common expansion buses included on the motherboard are the ISA, EISA, *Micro Channel*, *PCMCIA*, *VL-bus*, and PCI buses.

### Expansion card

A card that connects to an *expansion bus* that contains one or more *devices*.

### Expansion ROM

See *option ROM*.

### Extended Capabilities Port

An asynchronous, 8-bit-wide parallel channel defined by IEEE P1284 that provides PC-to-peripheral and peripheral-to-PC data transfers.

### Extended Display Identification

A data structure containing information about the identity and capabilities of a monitor that supports VESA's *Display Data Channel* standard.

### Extended Industry Standard Architecture bus

A 32-bit PC *expansion bus* designed as a superset of the Industry Standard Architecture (ISA) bus. This bus was designed to expand the speed and data width of the PC expansion bus, while still supporting older ISA cards.

# F

### FDC

Acronym for floppy disk drive controller.

# H

### Hardware Compatibility Tests

A suite of tests that verify hardware and device driver operation under a specific operating environment. These tests exercise the combination of a *device*, a software driver, and an operating system under controlled conditions, to verify that all three components are operating properly.

### Hardware tree

A collection of hierarchical *device node*s that describe the *devices* and buses on the PC. The main data structure in the *Plug and Play* framework of Windows 95. The hardware tree is an in-memory tree of all existing *device nodes* that represent logical devices currently on the system. The hardware tree on a purely Plug and Play system is completely dynamic and is populated every time the PC boots. The hardware tree can also be changed without booting if certain devices are added or removed from the system. The hardware tree reflects existing logical devices and *resources*, resource requirements (including interdependencies), and current resource allocation.

### HCT

See *Hardware Compatibility Tests*.

### Hot docking

A method of removing or installing a mobile system in a *docking station*, with which the user can dock or undock while the computer is running at full power.

### Hot-plugging

The capability of connecting or disconnecting a peripheral to the PC without turning off the peripheral or the PC. Neither the peripheral nor the PC can be permanently damaged during hot-plugging. The user need not intervene for the peripheral and the PC to recover fully. Hot-plugging does not necessarily indicate that the peripheral can be dynamically detected. See also *dynamic detection*.

# I

### IHV

Acronym for independent hardware vendor.

### Industry Standard Architecture bus

An 8-bit, and later a 16-bit, *expansion bus* that provides a buffered interface from *devices* on *expansion cards* to the PC internal bus. The most common expansion bus found on PC-compatible *motherboards*.

### .INF file

A file typically provided on a disk with an adapter that provides SETUP with the information required to set up that *device*, such as a list of valid logical configurations for that device, the names of driver files associated with the device, and so on.

### Initial program load

A device used by the system BIOS during the boot process to load an operating system into memory.

### Initiation key

A sequence of hexadecimal writes to the ADDRESS port on the ISA bus used as a key to enable the *Plug and Play* logic on all ISA cards in the system (including boot devices). The sequence consists of 32 known hexadecimal values supplied by the system software that are compared with the hexadecimal values generated by an initiation key *linear feedback shift register*. The initiation key sequence occurs after any system reset, whether it is a hardware or software reset. If the proper series of I/O writes is detected, the ISA Plug and Play auto-configuration ports are enabled and the actual configuration sequence can begin.

### Integrated devices

Any *devices*, such as parallel ports, display adapters, and so on, that are designed on the *motherboard* rather than on an *expansion card*.

### Integrated pointing device

Any pointing *device*, such as a mouse, that is mechanically integrated into the case of a mobile computer.

### Interrupt request

A method by which a *device* can request to be serviced by the device's software driver. The *motherboard* uses a programmable interrupt controller (PIC) to monitor the priority of the requests from all devices. When a request occurs, the microprocessor suspends the current operation and gives control to the device driver associated with the interrupt number issued. The lower the number, for example, IRQ3, the higher the priority of the interrupt. Many devices only support raising requests of specific numbers.

### IPL

See *initial program load.*

### IrDA

Acronym for Infrared Data Association.

### IRQ

See *interrupt request.*

### ISA

See *Industry Standard Architecture.*

### Isolation

The process by which cards on an ISA bus are distinguished from one another after power is applied to the system, or the system is reset.

## L

### Legacy

A colloquial description usually referring to older devices or systems that are not *Plug and Play* compatible.

### LFSR

See *linear feedback shift register.*

### Linear feedback shift register

A function used on a *Plug and Play* ISA *expansion card* that generates an *initiation key* and provides a checksum verification of serial data that is read during the ISA *isolation* sequence.

### Local bus

Generally refers to a system bus that is directly connected to the microprocessor on a *motherboard*. Local bus is used colloquially to refer to motherboard buses located closer to the microprocessor than are ordinary *expansion buses* (that is, with less buffering), which are therefore capable of greater throughput. The PCI bus and *VL-bus* are often referred to as local buses.

# M

### Micro Channel architecture

A high-performance, 32-bit bus structure developed by IBM and implemented in the PS/2-series computers.

### Motherboard

The primary circuit board in a computer system that contains most of the basic components of the system. Also referred to as system board and planar.

### MPEG

Acronym for Motion Picture Experts Group, used when referring to one of several standard video-compression schemes.

# N

### NDIS

Acronym for *Network Driver Interface Specification.*

### Network Driver Interface Specification

An interface for network card drivers. It provides transport independence for network card vendors because all transport drivers call the NDIS interface to access network cards.

### Nibble mode

An asynchronous, peripheral-to-host channel defined in the IEEE P1284 standard. This mode provides a channel for the peripheral to send data to the host, which is commonly used as a means of identifying the peripheral.

# O

### OEM

Acronym for original equipment manufacturer, used in this guide primarily to refer to PC systems manufacturers.

### Option ROM

An optional read-only memory found on PC bus *expansion cards*. This ROM usually contains additional firmware required to properly boot the peripheral connected to the expansion card, for instance, a hard drive. Also referred to as an expansion ROM.

# P

### Packed-pixel frame buffer

A portion of the display memory that holds the contents of a single screen image with screen bits stored in a single plane, with each pixel on the screen having a set of two or more corresponding bits that define the pixel color.

### Parent

A *device node* located on the *hardware tree* that is capable of having one or more *children* (typically a system bus of some sort).

### PC 95

A PC specifically designed to incorporate all aspects of the *Plug and Play* initiative (hardware, BIOS, and *device* drivers), which includes additional hardware enhancements optimized for Windows 95.

### PCI

See *Peripheral Component Interconnect*.

### PCMCIA

Although this acronym makes up the name of the Personal Computer Memory Card International Association, it is generally used to refer to a type of *expansion card* documented in the PCMCIA standards.

### Peripheral Component Interconnect

A high-performance 32-bit or 64-bit bus designed to be used with *devices* that have high bandwidth requirements, such as the display subsystem.

### PIC

Acronym for programmable interrupt controller.

### Planar

See *motherboard.*

### Plug and Play

A design philosophy and a set of specifications that describe hardware and software changes to the PC and its peripherals that automatically identify and arbitrate *resource* requirements among all *devices* and buses on the system.

### PnP

See *Plug and Play.*

### Port replicator

Low-cost *docking station* substitute, intended to provide convenient, one-step connection to multiple desktop *devices.*

### POST

See *power-on self test.*

### Power-on self test

A procedure of the system BIOS that identifies, tests, and configures the PC in preparation for loading the operating system.

### Printer port compatibility mode

An asynchronous, host-to-peripheral parallel port channel defined in the IEEE P1284 standard. This mode is compatible with existing peripherals that attach to the Centronics-style PC parallel port.

## R

### RAMDAC

See *random access memory digital-to-analog converter.*

### Random access memory digital-to-analog converter

A chip built into some VGA and SVGA display adapters that translates the digital representation of a pixel into the analog information needed by the monitor to display it. The presence of a RAMDAC chip generally enhances overall display performance.

### Redbook audio

The data format standard for conventional audio CDs used in home and automotive stereo systems.

### Registry

The tree-structured hierarchical database in which general system hardware and software settings are to be stored. The registry is intended to supersede use of separate .INI files, over time.

### Resource arbitrator

A set of functions used by the *configuration manager* to arbitrate and allocate *resources* on the PC.

### Resource conflict

The result of more than one *device* sharing the same, nonsharable *resource*. Conflicts may cause the device to be partially functional or nonfunctional, or may cause the PC to malfunction completely.

### Resource data type function

A function that describes the *resource* requirements of an *ISA expansion card*, along with the programmability available on the card and its interdependencies.

### Resources

A general term that refers to *interrupt request* (IRQ) signals, *direct memory access* (DMA) channels, I/O port addresses, and memory addresses.

### RLE

Acronym for run-length encoding, a data-compression scheme.

### RLE compression

A data-compression technique in which successive bytes of identical data are converted to a 2-byte pair, consisting of the repeated data byte and the repeat count.

### ROM scan

(1) The process the system BIOS performs to detect any *option ROMs* on the PC. The system BIOS performs a read at addresses located on 2K boundaries between C0000h and EFFFFh. If an AA55h is detected at one of the addresses, a verification process determines whether an option ROM actually exists at that address.

(2) The process the operating system performs to determine whether the system BIOS supports *Plug and Play*. The operating system performs a read at addresses located on 16-byte boundaries between 0F0000h and 0FFFFFh. If a $PnP ASCII string is located, the system BIOS is Plug and Play compatible.

# S

### SCAM

See *SCSI Configured AutoMatically.*

### SCSI

See *small computer system interface.*

### Small computer system interface

An I/O bus designed as a method of connecting several classes of peripherals to a host system without requiring modifications to generic hardware and software.

### SCSI Configured AutoMatically

A protocol that defines a means of automatically setting the identifier assignment of any host adapters and SCSI *devices* connected to the bus.

### Soft ejection

A method of removing a *device* from the PC, or media from a PC peripheral, by using a software command.

### Soft power-down

The process by which the PC system can be powered down using a software command.

### SPI

Acronym for SCSI-3 Parallel Interfaces.

### Spin-down

A power management capability in which a hard drive shuts down its spindle motor to conserve power.

### Static resources

*Device* resources, such as IRQ signals, DMA channels, I/O port addresses, and memory addresses, that cannot be configured or relocated. See also *configurable resources*, *resources.*

### Surprise-style ejection mechanism

A simple mechanical button that physically disconnects a portable system from a *docking station* without any prior warning to the operating system or the system BIOS.

### System board

See *motherboard.*

# T

### Tree model

See *hardware tree.*

### Tuple

A data structure defined by the *PCMCIA* that describes a single, specific characteristic of a PC card. Tuples are chained together to form the PC card's card information structure (CIS), which describes to system software the PC card's *resource* requirements and other characteristics. Tuples consist of a tuple code, an offset to the next tuple, and a number of bytes specific to the tuple.

# V

### VBE/DDC

Acronym for *VESA BIOS Extensions/Display Data Channel.*

### VBE/PM

Acronym for *VESA BIOS Extensions/Power Management.*

### VCR-style ejection mechanism

A method for ejecting a portable system from a *docking station.* A VCR-style system provides a fail-safe (locking) mechanism for docking and undocking. Pressing the eject button signals the user's intent to the BIOS, which consults Windows 95, which in turn consults various hardware and software components of the system. Programs have a chance to save and close files they have open over the network, and potentially even to veto the undocking. Only when all processes approve the undocking event is the portable system ejected. A VCR-style mechanism is also useful during docking, because the docking station may reject a portable system that the user has attempted to insert in the wrong power state. At a minimum, a VCR-style system should have a locking mechanism. At most, a VCR-style system could have a fully motorized locking and unlocking mechanism.

### VESA

Acronym for Video Electronics Standards Association.

### VESA BIOS Extensions/Display Data Channel

A standard that defines a set of display BIOS extensions that provide a software interface for reading the identity of a DDC-compatible monitor.

### VESA BIOS Extensions/Power Management

A standard that defines a set of display BIOS extensions that provide a software interface for controlling the power management features of flat-panel displays and DPMS-compatible monitors.

### Virtual "anything" Driver

A *device* driver that runs at the privileged Ring 0 protect mode of the microprocessor. These drivers can extend the services of the Windows 95 kernel, or supervise hardware operations, or perform both functions. Such driver files are usually named according to the scheme V*xxxx* or V*xxxx*D, where *xxxx* refers to the device or service supported.

### VL-bus

Abridgment of VESA local bus. An *expansion bus* designed to provide a high-speed interface to microprocessors specifically based on the 386SX, 386DX, and 486 architectures.

### Voice view

Capability for a modem to dynamically switch between voice and data.

### VxD

See *Virtual "anything" Driver*.

## W

### Warm docking

A method of removing or installing a mobile system in a *docking station*, with which the computer can be docked or undocked while in a reduced power state, such as suspend.

APPENDIX D

# References

This appendix contains a list of works used in the preparation of this guide. Wherever possible, a source for the information has been included to make obtaining these documents easier.

# Bibliography

The following publications were used as sources of information for this guide:

ACCESS.bus Industry Group. *ACCESS.bus Specifications*, Version 2.2. 1994.

Adaptec, Inc., AT&T Global Information Solutions, Digital Equipment Corporation, Future Domain Corporation, Maxtor Corporation, and Microsoft Corporation. *Plug and Play SCSI Specification*, Version 1.0. March 30, 1994.

ANSI. *ATA (AT Attachment) 2 [X3T9.2 948D]*, Revision 2.0. January 1, 1994.

ANSI. *SCSI Configured AutoMatically [X3T9.2/93-109r5]*. September 30, 1993.

ANSI. *Small Computer System Interface (SCSI-2) [X3T9.2-375R]*, Revision 10K. April 28, 1993.

ANSI. *Small Computer System Interface (SCSI-3) Parallel Interface (SPI) [X3T9.2/91-10]*, Revision 3. March 30, 1992.

BCPR Services, Inc. *EISA Specification*, Version 3.12. BCPR Services, Inc., 1992.

Compaq Computer Corporation, Phoenix Technologies Ltd., and Intel Corporation. *Extended System Configuration Data Specification*, Version 1.0. October 5, 1993.

Compaq Computer Corporation, Phoenix Technologies Ltd., and Intel Corporation. *Plug and Play BIOS Specification*, Version 1.0A. May 3, 1994.

Hogan, Thom. *The Programmer's PC Sourcebook*, Second Edition. Redmond, WA: Microsoft Press, 1991.

IEEE, Inc. *Personal Computer Bus Standard P996*, Draft D2.01. Institute of Electrical and Electronic Engineers, Inc. May 14, 1990.

IEEE, Inc. *Standard Signaling Method for a Bi-directional Parallel Peripheral Interface for Personal Computers* (IEEE P1284 D2.00). August 13, 1993.

Intel Corporation. *PCI Local Bus Specification*, Revision 2.0. July 20, 1993.

Intel Corporation and Microsoft Corporation. *Advanced Power Management (APM) BIOS Interface Specification*, Revision 1.1. September 1993.

Intel Corporation and Microsoft Corporation. *Display Control Interface*, Version 1.3. May 17, 1994.

Intel Corporation and Microsoft Corporation. *Plug and Play ISA Specification*, Version 1.0a. May 5, 1994.

International Business Machines Corporation. *IBM Personal System/2 Hardware Interface Technical Reference - Architecture*. October 1990.

ISO. *Information Processing Systems - Small Computer System Interface (SCSI)*. July 15, 1989.

Micro Channel Developers Association. *Micro Channel Architecture Specification*, Version 2.1. September 1993.

Microsoft Corporation. *Chicago Docking System Design Guide*, Version 1.0. February 15, 1994.

Microsoft Corporation. *Microsoft Windows Sound System Developer's Assistance Kit: Hardware*, Revision 1.1. February 15, 1993.

Microsoft Corporation. *Plug and Play External COM Device Draft Specification*, Version 0.92. June 18, 1994.

Microsoft Corporation. *Plug and Play Parallel Port Devices*, Version 1.0. February 11, 1994.

Multimedia PC Marketing Council, Inc. *Multimedia PC Level 2 Specification*.

Phoenix Technologies Ltd. *Enhanced Disk Drive Specification*, Version 1.0. January 25, 1994.

Shanley, Tom. *EISA System Architecture*. MindShare Press, 1993.

Shanley, Tom, and Don Anderson. *ISA System Architecture*. MindShare Press, October 1993.

Shanley, Tom, and Don Anderson. *PCI System Architecture*. MindShare Press, 1993.

Small Form Factor Committee. *ATA Packet Interface for CD-ROMs, SFF-8020*, Revision 1.2. February 24, 1994.

Solari, Edward. *AT Bus Design, IEEE P966 Compatible*. San Diego: Annabooks, 1990.

Video Electronics Standards Association. *Display Power Management Signaling (DPMS) Standard*, Version 1.0. August 20, 1993.

Video Electronics Standards Association. *VESA BIOS Extensions/Display Data Channel, (VBE/DDC) Proposal*, Version 1.0, Revision 0.22p. June 10, 1994.

Video Electronics Standards Association. *VESA BIOS Extensions/Power Management (VBE/PM) Standard*, Version 1.0. February 4, 1994.

Video Electronics Standards Association. *VESA Display Data Channel Proposal*, Version 10.p, Revision 0.62p. June 2, 1994.

Video Electronics Standards Association. *VESA Display Information Format VDIF Standard*, Version 1.0. August 23, 1993.

Video Electronics Standards Association. *VESA Monitor Timing Standards for 640 x 480, 800 x 600, 1024 x 768, and 1280 x 1024 at 75Hz*, Version 1.0. October 4, 1993.

Video Electronics Standards Association. *VESA VL-Bus Plug and Play Addendum*, Version 0.1. March 9, 1994.

Video Electronics Standards Association. *VESA VL-Bus Proposal*, Version 2.0p. July 8, 1993.

Western Digital Corporation. *Enhanced IDE Implementation Guide*, Revision 5.0. November 10, 1993.

# Availability

The documents listed in this guide (or their more current revisions) can be obtained from the following sources:

*ACCESS.bus Specifications*

**ACCESS.bus Industry Group**
370 Altair Way, Suite 215
Sunnyvale, CA 94086

Telephone: 1-408-991-3517
Fax: 1-408-991-3773

*Advanced Power Management (APM) BIOS Interface Specification*, Revision 1.1

**Intel Corporation**
Literature Distribution Center

Telephone: 1-800-548-4725
Intel order number: 241704-001

The specification is also available in the CompuServe Plug and Play library.

*ATA (AT Attachment) [X3T9.2/90-143]*

**Global Engineering**
2805 McGaw Street
Irvine, CA 92714

Telephone: 1-800-854-7179
1-714-261-1455

You can obtain an electronic copy from the SCSI Bulletin Board:

Telephone: 1-316-636-8700

*Display Power Management Signaling (DPMS) Standard*
*VESA BIOS Extensions/Display Data Channel, (VBE/DDC) Proposal*
*VESA BIOS Extensions/Power Management (VBE/PM) Standard*
*VESA Display Data Channel (DDC) Proposal*
*VESA Display Information Format VDIF Standard*
*VESA Monitor Timing Standards for 640 x 480, 800 x 600, 1024 x 768, and 1280 x 1024 at 75Hz*
*VESA VL-Bus Plug and Play Addendum*
*VESA VL-Bus Proposal*

**Video Electronics Standards Association**
2150 North First Street, Suite 440
San Jose, CA 95131-2029

Telephone: 1-408-435-0333
Fax: 1-408-435-8225

*Multimedia PC Level 2 Specification*

**Multimedia PC Marketing Council**
1730 M Street NW, Suite 707
Washington, DC 20036

*EISA Specification*
EISA vendor device IDs

**BCPR Services, Inc.**
P.O. Box 11137
Spring, TX 77391-1137

Telephone: 1-713-251-4770
Fax: 1-713-251-4832

*Personal Computer Bus Standard P996*
*Standard Signaling Method for a Bi-directional Parallel Peripheral Interface for Personal Computers*

ASK*IEEE
P.O. Box 4327
Burlingame, CA 94011-4327

| | |
|---|---|
| Telephone: | 1-800-949-4333 |
| Fax: | 1-415-259-5045 |

*ATA (AT Attachment) 2 [X3T9.2 948D]*
*ATA Packet Interface for CD-ROMs, SFF-8020*
*Small Computer Interface (SCSI-2) [X3T9.2-375R]*
*Small Computer Interface (SCSI-3) Parallel Interface (SPI) [X3T9.2/91-10]*

**Global Engineering Documents**
15 Inverness Way East
Englewood, CO 80112-5704

| | |
|---|---|
| Telephone: | 1-800-854-7179 |
| | 1-303-792-2181 (outside the US and Canada) |
| Fax: | 1-303-792-2192 |

*SCSI Configured AutoMatically [X3T9.2/93-109r5]*

**SCSI BBS**

| | |
|---|---|
| Telephone: | 1-719-574-0424 |

*PCI Specification*

**PCI Special Interest Group**

| | |
|---|---|
| Telephone: | 1-800-433-5177 (US) |
| | 1-503-797-4207 (International) |
| Fax: | 1-503-234-6762 |

The following documents are available in the CompuServe Plug and Play library (log in, enter "go plugplay").

*Advanced Power Management (APM) BIOS Interface SpecificationPlug and Play*
*Plug and Play BIOS Specification*
*Plug and Play External COM Device Draft Specification*
*Plug and Play ISA Specification*
*Plug and Play Parallel Port Devices*
*Plug and Play SCSI Specification*

The following document is available in the CompuServe Windows Multimedia library (log in, enter "go winmm").

*Display Control Interface*

The CompuServe Plug and Play library also contains several diagnostic programs for testing Plug and Play hardware.

*Infrared Data Association Serial Infrared (SIR) Physical Layer Specification*

For general information about infrared technology, contact the Infrared Data Association (IrDA), an organization for defining infrared standards:

John LaRoche
Infrared Data Association Administrator
23 San Marino
Walnut Creek, CA 94598

Internet: jlaroche@netcom.com

A copy of the *Infrared Data Association Serial Infrared (SIR) Physical Layer Specification* is accessible by password account. You can access the FTP site by using anonymous ftp to hplose.hpl.hp.com (IP address 15.254.100.100). Use your email address as the password. Then issue the ftp user command to access the IrDA area:

```
user irda
password: t0phat
```

Note that the password includes a zero, not a capital O. Do not log into the FTP site as irda. Use the "user" command after you have logged in anonymously.

### Microsoft Compatibility Labs

Microsoft Corporation
One Microsoft Way
Redmond, WA 98052-6399

| | |
|---|---|
| Telephone: | 1-206-635-4949 |
| Fax: | 1-206-936-7329 |
| Internet: | mclinfo@microsoft.com |
| CompuServe: | 72350,2636 |

### Microsoft Developers Network (MSDN)

| | |
|---|---|
| Telephone: | 1-800-759-5474 |
| | 1-402-691-0173 (outside the US and Canada) |

### Microsoft Internet FTP server

| | |
|---|---|
| Internet: | ftp://ftp.microsoft.com/developr/pc95 |

APPENDIX E

# Docking System Scenarios

The docking station scenarios in this appendix describe the sequence of events that occur during various docking and undocking situations, including events occurring in the hardware, operating system, system BIOS, and device drivers. These scenarios are included to show, generally, how these events interact.

# Cold Booting

Microsoft® Windows 95™ keeps no record of the docking state a computer was in the last time it was started, so the cold-booting process is the same whether the user recently docked the computer or undocked it.

1. During the power-on self-test (POST) phase, the Plug and Play BIOS configures all motherboard devices and Plug and Play ISA cards necessary to boot the system. This involves serving as a resource arbitrator to make sure there are no conflicts in the IRQ signals, DMA channels, and I/O addresses allocated to these devices. After the POST process, control of the system configuration passes to the configuration manager in Windows 95.
2. Before processing CONFIG.SYS, Windows 95 determines the configuration the system is in, using the dock identifier and serial number. (If the user has multiple menu blocks set up while Windows 95 processes CONFIG.SYS, the system will process only the block mapped to the detected configuration.)
3. Windows 95 builds the hardware tree, a hierarchical data structure that tells what hardware is present in the system. Every nonleaf node in the tree is an enumerator. The children of the ROOT of the tree are all the static devices and the BIOS enumerator. The hardware tree is built as follows:

    a. The ROOT enumerator automatically enumerates all static devices listed in the registry.

    b. The configuration manager tells the BIOS enumerator to enumerate all of its children. The children of the BIOS enumerator are all the motherboard devices and all buses present in the system.

    c. The BIOS enumerator can enumerate all motherboard devices without doing any hardware detection, because it has the enumeration information in ROM.

    d. The configuration manager tells all other enumerators (such as the ISA enumerator) to enumerate their children.

    e. The ISA enumerator and all other bus drivers enumerate their children using standard Plug and Play device detection.

    f. As enumerators enumerate their devices, they call the configuration manager and ask it to create device nodes. The configuration manager checks the configuration flags (the bits set on a per-configuration basis for each device, which indicate whether to create a device node or not and whether to load the driver).

4. As the window manager part of Windows 95 is loading, the drivers for all Plug and Play devices in the hardware tree and for all static devices in the current hardware profile are loaded. Windows 95 does not attempt to load drivers for those device nodes marked as disabled for a specific configuration.
5. As drivers are loading and Windows 95 is configuring itself, applications call into the **HKEY_CURRENT_CONFIG** section of the registry (which has already been remapped for the new configuration) and read out their appropriate settings (for example, video resolution).

# Warm VCR-Style Undocking

Warm VCR-style undocking is a fail-safe way of disconnecting a portable PC from a computer while the computer is in a reduced power state (suspended or on standby). After the user presses the eject button or issues a command in the Windows 95 user interface to eject the portable, applications can first save and close any files they have open over the network. Only after all components signal approval of the undocking is the portable ejected.

## Initiated by Button on Dock

1. The user presses the eject button on the docking station. This generates a hardware interrupt or an SMI, which the Plug and Play BIOS traps.
2. The BIOS uses the event notification interface to communicate to BIOS.VXD that an undocking event has been initiated. This involves setting bit 0 of the Event flag to 1, to indicate that a message is waiting. For more information about the event notification interface, see the *Plug and Play BIOS Specification*.
3. BIOS.VXD polls this bit and notices that it is set, then calls the Plug and Play BIOS function Get Event to retrieve the ABOUT_TO_CHANGE_CONFIG message .
4. BIOS.VXD calls the configuration manager routine CHANGE_CONFIG. QUERY_CHANGE_CONFIG "query-removes" all device nodes for which the bits Don't Create or Disable have been set.
5. When a device node is query-removed, the configuration manager broadcasts a message to all event sinks (including the driver of the device itself) that the device is going to be removed. If there is no objection, it returns Success. If any application objects, it should query the user about what to do next.
6. If any of the query-removes fail, the QUERY_CHANGE_CONFIG returns Failure to BIOS.VXD.

7. If QUERY_CHANGE_CONFIG succeeds, the BIOS enumerator recursively warns all of its offspring of the undocking event. All of its immediate leaf-node children are motherboard devices, so the BIOS should have built-in knowledge about which of them are on the docking station and which are on the portable system. Only those devices not on the portable system are warned.
8. All of the BIOS enumerator's non–leaf-node children are other enumerators. Each will be marked as either on the docking station or on the portable system. For all enumerators marked as on the docking station, the BIOS enumerator sends the QUERY_REMOVE_SUBTREE message.
9. All enumerators that receive QUERY_REMOVE_SUBTREE should then warn all their device children. If they have enumerator children, they should pass on the QUERY_REMOVE_SUBTREE message.
10. Warning a device involves sending the DEVICE_QUERY_REMOVE message to the device driver, and broadcasting an event to all Windows 95 event sinks that the device is being removed.
11. If at any time an application rejects a query-remove, that rejection will filter back up to BIOS.VXD. If BIOS.VXD receives any rejections from device drivers, event sinks, or from the ROOT enumerator, it will cancel the undocking event by calling the Plug and Play BIOS function Send Message, with a message of ABORT.
12. If there are no "objections" to the undocking event, BIOS.VXD sends the OK message to the Plug and Play BIOS.
13. The BIOS then suspends the computer (if necessary) through the APM 1.1 interface and tells the VCR-style ejection mechanism to eject the portable system.
14. The computer remains suspended for some time.
15. The user "wakes up" the computer after the undocking event has taken place.
16. The Plug and Play BIOS sets the message bit. BIOS.VXD notices this, calls Get Message, and retrieves the DOCK_CHANGED message.
17. BIOS.VXD calls the configuration manager CM_RECOMPUTE_CONFIG service with the new dock serial identifier as a parameter (which it has retrieved from the Plug and Play BIOS using the **GetDockSerialID** function). The configuration manager recomputes the current hardware profile, updates the **CurrentConfig** key in the registry, and tells the ROOT enumerator to reenumerate the hardware tree.
18. The configuration manager broadcasts the message "configuration has changed" to all event sinks.
19. Any configuration-aware control-panel applications or other "interested" applications may receive the "configuration has changed" message and change their settings dynamically.

## Initiated by Windows 95

1. The user tells a Windows 95 user interface component to eject the portable system.
2. Windows 95 broadcasts an undocking event for which only BIOS.VXD is listening. This message says "please initiate an undocking sequence."
3. BIOS.VXD calls the Plug and Play BIOS service Send Message with the message UNDOCK_DEFAULT_ACTION. The purpose of this message is to tell the BIOS to behave exactly as if the user had pushed the button on the docking station.
4. The system then behaves exactly as in the previous scenario, starting at step 2.

# Warm VCR-Style Docking

A warm VCR-style docking mechanism is useful in rejecting improper docking—for example, attempting to dock a portable PC that is in the wrong power state.

1. The user inserts the portable system into the docking station.
2. If the portable is in a suspended state, the docking event should take place immediately.
3. If the portable is running and is incapable of hot-docking, the BIOS should suspend it before completing the docking event. If the suspension fails, the portable should be ejected; if it succeeds, the portable should then be docked.
4. In neither of these two cases is the ABOUT_TO_CHANGE_CONFIG Plug and Play BIOS message sent. This message is sent only during an undocking event; the message could lead to user interaction, which is not acceptable during a docking event because there may be no display.
5. The portable remains suspended for some time.
6. The user "wakes up" the portable after the docking event has taken place.
7. The Plug and Play BIOS sets the message bit. BIOS.VXD notices this, calls Get Message, and retrieves the DOCK_CHANGED message.
8. BIOS.VXD calls the configuration manager CM_RECOMPUTE_CONFIG service with the new dock serial identifier as a parameter (which it has retrieved from the Plug and Play BIOS using the **GetDockSerialID** function). The configuration manager recomputes the current hardware profile, updates the **CurrentConfig** key in the registry, and tells the ROOT enumerator to reenumerate the hardware tree.
9. BIOS.VXD also broadcasts a Windows 95 event that says "configuration has changed." Any configuration-aware applications can then change their settings accordingly.

# Index

# C

# D

# E

# J



# K



# L

# M

# N



# O

# Q



# R



# S

# T

## U



## V



## W

## Y

# INSIDE WINDOWS™ 95

*Adrian King*

***The Philosophy, Design, and Architecture of the Next Generation of Microsoft® Windows***

**512 pages**
**ISBN 1-55615-626-X**
**$24.95 ($33.95 Canada)**

INSIDE WINDOWS 95 goes behind the scenes to tell the story of the development of Microsoft's breakthrough technology. Author Adrian King is a former director of systems software products for Microsoft. And in this book he reveals the inner workings of Windows 95 with a unique, objective perspective on its design and implementation. You'll understand how Windows 95 will change the future of computing and why Windows 95 works the way it does.

After a tour of the goals, features, and the evolving architecture of Windows, the book delves into the major components of this innovative new operating system:

- The Base System—The high-performance features that make Windows 95 a full-fledged operating system: support for a native 32-bit API, preemptive scheduling, multiple privilege levels, and simultaneous network connections.
- The User Interface—The metamorphosis of the user interface design—the new shell, ease of use, support for long filenames, and shortcuts—with new guidelines for application developers.
- Applications and Devices—The Win32® API and tips on porting, multitasking, OLE, internationalization, color matching, DIBs, the printing subsystem, and more.
- Plug and Play—The new specification for hardware support that makes Windows—and hardware peripherals—easier to install, configure, and update.

If you're developing applications for Windows 95, making corporate-wide computing decisions for the future, or interested in what is coming to your desktop, you'll find INSIDE WINDOWS 95 essential reading.

**Microsoft**Press®